SOUL SAYS

SOUL SAYS

ON RECENT POETRY

Helen Vendler

The Belknap Press of
Harvard University Press
Cambridge, Massachusetts
London, England   1995

Library of Congress Cataloging-in-Publication Data

Vendler, Helen Hennessy.
  Soul says: On recent poetry / Helen Vendler.
    p.   cm.
  Includes index.
  ISBN 0–674–82146–7
  1. American poetry—20th century—History and criticism.
  I. Title.
  PS325.V47   1995
  811'.5409—dc20

94–42913
    CIP

For Xianchun Jiang Vendler

. . . Accept the certainty
That thou hast borne proportion in my bliss.
—G. M. Hopkins

Contents

(This is a form of matter of matter she sang)

(Where the hurry is stopped) (and held) (but not extinguished) (no)

—Jorie Graham, "Soul Says"

Introduction

The senses and the imagination together furnish rhythms for the poet. The rhythms of the poet translate themselves back, in the mind of the reader, into the senses and the imagination. What is it about the critic that cannot rest content with this silent transaction? Most of the time the critic is just another reader, and can put a book down, whether with appreciation or with irritation, without any wish to write something about that book. Yet certain books will not let the critic look away; they demand a fuller response, and they will not let go until another set of words, this time in the critic's own prose, renders again the given of the book. Something in the book—or in a single poem—is "a hatching that stared and demanded an answering look." That phrase is Wallace Stevens'; and though he used it about the poet's response to life (newborn every day), it is equally true of the critic's response to a significant piece of writing. Emily Dickinson called her response to life "my letter to the world / That never wrote to me." Criticism is also a letter to the world, more meditated than conversation, more widely aimed than scholarship.

The significant poem, for me, can be about anything, or almost anything. I have never been drawn in a positive way to subject matter: that is, I do not respond more enthusiastically to a poem about women than to a poem about men, a poem about nature than a poem about the city, a political poem than a metaphysical poem. Though I grew up in a city, my favorite poems, from Keats's "To Autumn" to Stevens' "The Auroras of Autumn," have often been ones using metaphors from nature; I have liked Protestant poets (from Milton to Clampitt) and Jewish poets (from Ginsberg to Goldbarth) as well as Catholic poets (from Hopkins to Péguy); though I can read only Romance languages, my two indispensable contemporary foreign poets are Paul Celan and Czesław Miłosz, whom I cannot read in the original. Though I am white, I could not do without the poetry of Langston Hughes and Rita Dove. I have written on both gay and "straight" writers. I bring up these questions of locale, religion, language, ethnicity, race, and sexuality because these days they appear so much in writing about literature, and because there is a jealous appropriation of literature into such socially marked categories.

At first I found it hard to understand, when such categories were ritually invoked, why people felt they could respond only to literature that replicated their own experience of race, class, or gender. I heard many tales beginning, "I never found literature meaningful to me till I read . . ." and there would follow, from a woman, a title like *Jane Eyre,* or, from a black, a title like *Invisible Man.* After a while, it dawned on me that these accounts mostly issued from readers of novels. The first time I heard Toni Morrison speak, she told of going from novel to novel "looking for me," and, for a long time, not finding herself, or her story, anywhere. Then, when she found representations of black women in fiction, they were being victimized, or killed, or exploited, a fact that filled her with anger. Since I was not a novel reader, I had never gone on that quest for a socially specified self resembling me. The last thing I wanted from literature was a mirror of my external circumstances. What I wanted was a mirror of my feelings, and that I found in poetry.

An adolescent reader of poetry finds herself in a world of the first-person pronoun: "My heart aches, and a drowsy numbness pains my sense"; "I awoke in the midsummer not-to-call night"; "How do I love thee? Let me count the ways." The all-purpose pronouns "I" and "you" are tracks along which any pair of eyes can go, male or female, black or white, Jewish or Catholic, urban or rural. Poetry answered so completely to my wish for a mirror of feelings that novels seemed by comparison overburdened, "loose and baggy monsters," and I cheerfully left them aside.

It now is clear to me how completely the traditional lyric desires a stripping-away of the details associated with a socially specified self in order to reach its desired all-purpose abstraction. "Oh, wert thou in the cauld blast, / I'd shelter thee, I'd shelter thee": yes, it was in Scots, but the feeling was easily transferable to me in America. "Thine eyen two will sley me sodenly": yes, it was said by a man to a woman, but it was equally sayable by a woman to a man. "Never seek to tell thy love / Love that never told can be": advice as sinister to a young woman as to a young man. I plunged on, untroubled by any sense of difference or apartness; and if a poet was a castaway, I too was a castaway; if a poet regretted Fern Hill, I too had a house I regretted and had lost; if Auden wrote about the shield of Achilles, Homer was mine as much as his. Perhaps my high school training in the antiphonal singing of Psalms lay behind my willing self-investiture in any poetic "I": "Out of the depths I have cried to thee, O Lord, Lord, hear my voice." We in the choir were to take such words as our own, as generations of Jews and Christians and atheists have done. And if it was not literally true when I said, "They have pierced my hands and my feet; they have numbered all my bones," I knew it was metaphorically true of all suffering, my own included. Metaphor, not mimesis, was my native realm. Everything said in a poem was a metaphor for something in my inner life, and I learned about future possibilities within my inner life from the poetry I read with such eagerness.

Lyric, from the Psalms to "The Waste Land," seemed, when I was seventeen, to be the voice of the soul itself. This, I take it, is what Jorie Graham means in calling one of her poems "Soul Says," which I have borrowed as the title for this collection of essays about lyric poetry. In lyric poetry, voice is made abstract. It may tell you one specific thing about itself—that it is black, or that it is old, or that it is female, or that it is celibate. But it will not usually tell you, if it is black, that it grew up in Atlanta rather than Boston; or, if it is old, how old it is; or, if it is female, whether it is married; or, if it is celibate, when it took its vows. That is, the range of things one would normally know about a voice in a novel one does not know about a voice in a lyric. What one does know, if it is socially specified at all, is severely circumscribed. (There are exceptions that prove the rule, but I am here concerned with the rule.)

What is the use of abstraction in lyric? And why are most lyrics abstract? And what of the somewhat socially specific lyric—one that ends, for instance, with the words "Black like me," as one of Hughes's poems does? Does it offer a track for my feet, or can only a black reader walk its path? And when the exception comes along, a poem full of novelistic detail like Ginsberg's "Kaddish," how is it that it keeps to its lyric intent? What is the human interest in shedding most, or all, of the detail in which one necessarily lives? What is gained, and what is lost, when a poet—one now nameless and sourceless and vanished—writes,

> Western wind, when wilt thou blow,
> The small rain down can rain?
> Christ, that my love were in my arms,
> And I in my bed again!

When we look for analogies to such work in the other arts, we might speak of the sketch, the *Lied,* the solo dance. What are they to the oil painting, the opera, the corps de ballet? Their first appeal is the appearance of spontaneity; no one can pretend that the *Mona Lisa* has been dashed off, or that *Aida* has been artlessly uttered. The lyric, though, has the look of casual utterance, of immediate outspokenness: "When I see birches bend to left and right, / I like to think some boy's been swinging them." And it has the look of encounter, of naked circumstance: "Since there's no help, come, let us kiss and part." And it can happen, or seem to happen, even prematurely, as the poet, stunned by a death, must, as he says to the laurels, "shatter your leaves before the mellowing year." While the rhythm of fiction is long-breathed and deliberate in pursuit, the rhythm of lyric is wayward, even hesitant, but always intense, and surprising:

> Let us go, then, you and I,
> While the evening is spread out upon the sky,
> Like a patient etherised upon a table.

Spontaneity, intensity, circumstantiality; a sudden freeze-frame of disturbance, awakening, pang; an urgent and inviting rhythm; these are among the characteristics of lyric, but there is one other that is even more characteristic, and that is compression. In view of the length of certain lyrics (from "The Epithalamion" on), this claim can seem dubious; but as soon as one recognizes that the single day Spenser covers in his wedding poem is the equivalent of the one day Joyce covers in *Ulysses,* the compression of the lyric (especially from a poet so given to digressive expansion as Spenser) is positively striking.

What does compression have to do with the abstraction to which Jorie Graham gives the name "soul," by contrast to the more socially specified human unit we normally call, these days, the "self?" If the normal home of selfhood is the novel, which ideally allows many aspects of the self, under several forms, to expatiate and take on substance, then the normal home of "soul" is the lyric, where the human being becomes a set of warring passions independent of time and space. It is generally thought that the lyric is the genre of "here" and "now," and it is true that these index words govern the lyric moment. But insofar as the typical lyric exists only in the here and now, it exists nowhere, since life as it is lived is always bracketed with a there and a then. Selves come with a history: souls are independent of time and space. "I tried each thing," says Ashbery; "only some were immortal and free." The lyric is the gesture of immortality and freedom; the novel is the gesture of the historical and of the spatial.

Readers read with design. The historically minded read socially mimetic literature as a source for information retrieval: What can we learn from the novels of Dickens about notions of criminality in nineteenth-century England? How did working women describe themselves in their journals? For such readers, no lyric source can seem as rich as a novel. The psychologically minded read literature as a source of culturally coded discourse on the passions; for such readers, the novel offers a multitude of characters interacting in highly motivated ways, impelled by a variety of interests and feelings. The lyric might seem, by contrast, impoverished, existing as it does without much of a plot, and without any significant number of dramatis personae.

In fact, the lyric has come in for a good deal of criticism on this account. The sonneteers are reproved for not allowing a voice to the female object of their desire; and if Elizabeth Barrett Browning is no more disposed than Petrarch to allow her beloved to get a word in edgewise, her "suppression of the other" is to be blamed, it is suggested, on the bad male example of her predecessors. Even Bakhtin, with his subtle and comprehensive mind, thought the lyric to be monologic and therefore (given his taste for the dialogic and the heteroglossic) a disappointing genre. Such judgments stem from a fundamental misunderstanding of the lyric. When soul speaks, it speaks with a number of voices (as the writers of psychomachia knew). But the voices in lyric are represented not by characters, as in a novel or drama, but by changing registers of diction, contrastive rhythms, and varieties of tone. There is no complex lyric that does not contain within itself a congeries of forces, just as there is no sonata of Mozart's that—voiced though it is by a single instrument—does not contain forms of call and response in many emotional tonalities. The "plot" of a lyric resembles that of a sonata: "As if a magic lantern threw the nerves in patterns on a screen" (Prufrock). And since almost every word in lyric language has a long history, each word appears as a "character" heavy with motivation, desire, and import. When these "characters" undergo the binding force of syntax, sound, and rhythm, they are being subjected to what, in a novel or play, we would call "fate." The "destiny" of the words in a lyric must be as complex as the destinies of human beings in life, or the lyric would not be, in its way, adequate to the portion of life it undertakes to represent, the life that the soul lives when it is present to itself and alone with its own passions.

Rhythms have historical meaning, and so do stanza forms; genres have historical meaning, and so do personae. The satisfactions of lyric, for those attached to this form revealing the inner life, are as rich as the satisfactions of novels and plays for those attached to the forms revealing life in society. The interaction of the "soul" and the "self" within a single person is one of the great themes of lyric when it decides to face outward rather than inward: this is the undertaking of poets like Yeats and Ginsberg. They solve the problem differently: Yeats coerces his occult historical systems into a concern with the fate of a single soul; Ginsberg alternates painful social detail and exalted meditation. Yet even such "social" poets remain within the rule of abstraction, so that Ginsberg can ask himself, knowing that he is not writing a novel about his mother's life, "O mother what have I left out / O mother what have I forgotten." Lyric is indexical, not exhaustive; it mentions, and the reader is to expand the mention to the whole arc of experience of which the mention is the sign.

The virtues of lyric—extreme compression, the appearance of spontaneity, an intense and expressive rhythm, a binding of sense by sound, a structure which enacts the experience represented, an abstraction from the heterogeneity of life, a dynamic play of semiotic and rhythmic "destiny"—are all summoned to give a voice to the "soul"—the self when it is alone with itself, when its socially constructed characteristics (race, class, color, gender, sexuality) are felt to be in abeyance. The biological characteristics ("black like me") are of course present, but in the lyric they can be reconstructed in opposition to their socially constructed form, occasioning one of lyric's most joyous self-proclaimings: "I am I, am I; / All creation shivers / With that sweet cry" (Yeats).

The poets about whom I have written in the essays in this book are poets whom I admire. There is really nothing to say about an inept poem except to enumerate its absences—"This poem has no energy; this poem relies on clichés and has no original diction; this poem has no compelling occasion; this poem has no tensile strength or compression; this poem has no enabling structure." It is not interesting for a critic to compile a list of lacks. In all the poets here, there is presence rather than absence, force rather than feebleness, originality rather than derivativeness, strenuousness rather than slackness, daring rather than timidity, idiosyncrasy rather than typicality. In almost all of these cases, one can say, "That's Bidart," or "Gary Snyder, of course," or "Graham, unmistakably," or "Heaney, yes." That is, one could not mistake Snyder for Dove, or Clampitt for Heaney, or Glück for Graham, or Goldbarth for Ginsberg. Each has left a mark on language, has found a style. And it is that style— the compelling aesthetic signature of each—that I respond to as I read, and want to understand and describe.

When I was asked to write, for *Antaeus,* a self-portrait under the rubric "The I of Writing," I had to think about myself in the act of undertaking the sort of writing I do—a writing that takes its origin from an earlier piece of writing, one which I feel at first blindly and dumbly, and then gradually come to know with some degree of accurate understanding. This is what I said in as my self-portrait as a writer:

"Not I, not I, but the wind that blows through me." Writing, I am deaf and blind; then suddenly I wake to the radio, and to ground covered with snow. Not asleep in body, not asleep in mind, but asleep in the senses and awake in an away, an otherness. The otherness is felt by my hand as it rewrites words—*the bronze decor, a shadow of a magnitude, so strength first found a way.* The hand is not female, the hand is not male; its *celestial stir* moves in a hyperspace neither here nor there, neither once nor now. The timeless hand moves in a place where memory cannot be remembered because it is part of a manifold undivided in time. The hand has no biography and no ideas; it traces a contour pliable under its touch. The braille of the poet's words brushes my fingers and moves through them into my different calligraphy. The calligraphy tells less than the fingers feel; *sumptuous despair* loses its dark glamour as the hand falters after it. But the hand loves the contour, tracing obscure lineaments, translating them into language. Is the language signed? Only namelessly by its century and its country of origin, influencing invisibly the contour it has felt. The hand is anonymous, mine and not mine, even if my name signs what it has written.

This passage is, I now see, written within the sphere of lyric, where I am as anonymous as the poet of "Western wind," though as much within my century as he within his. To me, what soul says seems convincing, and self seems a contingent adventitiousness always in tension with it. Yeats reversed the terms, and made "self" mean the abstraction of carnal voice, while "soul" was the abstraction of discarnate voice. These are terms that can be defined at will; the Yeatsian "self" is what Jorie Graham calls "soul." Each is the abstracted voice of the whole person, body and mind, riven by the feelings always coursing from the senses to the passions, struggling to say what words, when formally arranged, can say as the experience of the inner life makes itself articulate and available to others. It is through poets such as those I reflect on here that the coming centuries will be able to know, as Stevens put it, "what we felt at what we saw."

1

The Reversed Pietà

Allen Ginsberg's "Kaddish"

The poem "Kaddish," now thirty years old, appeared in 1961 with two manifestos by Ginsberg bracketing it. The first, on the copyright page of the volume *Kaddish,* announced that "the established literary quarterlies of my day are bankrupt poetically thru their own hatred, dull ambition or loudmouthed obtuseness," and, in acknowledging previous appearances of the poems in journals, remarked that two of those publications were begun by "youths who quit editing university magazines to avoid hysterical academic censorship." This Ginsberg manifesto is one of irritated satiric energy; the other, appearing on the back cover of the volume, abounds in passionate phrases like "broken consciousness," "suffering anguish of separation," "blissful union," "desolate . . . homeless . . . at war," "original trembling of bliss in breast and belly," "fear," "defenseless living hurt self," and "hymn completed in tears." Things that are separate in the manifestos—satire and pathos—come together in Ginsberg's great elegy for his mother. Though "Kaddish" will always remain a son's poem, a poem which we enunciate in the position of a mourning child, it is now more than ever Naomi Ginsberg's poem, too—a poem bringing into representation, with both tragic and comic energy, a woman's hideously afflicted life. In this reversal of the cultural icon we call the pietà, we see not the mother holding the broken body of the son, but the son holding the broken body of the mother. "I saw my self my own mother and my very nation trapped desolate," says Ginsberg in his manifesto; but it is his mother that is the chief icon of the trappedness.

"Kaddish" declares its descent from classical elegy in its epigraph from Shelley's Hellenizing "Adonais"—"Die, / If thou wouldst be with that which thou dost seek!" Personal extinction becomes real at the death of the sheltering parent; and Ginsberg, through his own resistance to death, has to find a way to the identity of idealization and dissolution understood by Shelley.

"Kaddish" is chiefly an elegy of the body—the physical body and the historically conditioned body of Naomi Ginsberg. Is it the first such elegy of the body (rather than the transcendent self) of another? *Leaves of Grass* was the first American book to expose at length the physical and historical body, but that body was Whitman's own; in "Kaddish" it is Naomi's body that is born, grows, gives birth, is scarred in flesh and brain, rots in a living death, dies, and is buried. The absence of a developed Jewish doctrine of the afterlife may in part explain why this poem—named so defiantly with a title foreign to non-Jews—is a poem of the body. The biblical history internalized as the history of the Jewish people may explain why it is also so much a poem of history. Finally, besides being a poem of the body and a poem of history, it is a poem of balked prayer. The prayer of the Kaddish, quoted in the second part of the poem, forms, as Ginsberg has said, "the rhythmic substrate" of the poem: "Yisborach, v'yistabach, v'yispoar, v'yisroman, v'yisnaseh, v'yishador, v'yishalleh, v'yishallol. . . ." Ginsberg, in California when his mother died, missed her funeral, where (as Ginsberg's brother wrote him) there were not enough people present to form a minyan, so Kaddish could not be said for her. Several years later, Ginsberg wrote his own "Kaddish" to repair the lack. The rhythm of the Hebrew Kaddish shows itself chiefly at the end of the first part of the poem, the elegy proper: "Magnificent, mourned no more, marred of heart, mind behind, married dreamed, mortal changed . . . / almed in Earth, balmed in Lone"; and, a moment later, "This is the end, the redemption from Wilderness, way for the Wonderer, House sought for All . . . Death stay thy phantoms!"

A poem of the body, then; and a poem of history; and a balked rhythmic prayer or hymn. "Kaddish" has five numbered parts, and one extra-numeric "Hymmnn" between Parts II and III. Part I is a lyrical overture addressed to Naomi, sounding the themes that will follow. Part II is a history—a recapitulation of Naomi's life intertwined with that of her son; in it, Naomi is alternately addressed in the second person and described in the third person, so that this part of the poem is both a colloquy with her and a history of her life. This is the part that is savagely comic—stucco'd (as Whitman might say) with birds and quadrupeds all over. In the "Hymmnn" of chanted blessings (imitating the recital of blessings in the Kaddish) that follows Part II, Naomi is both a living "you" and a dead "Thee." Part III is a prayer against forgetting—"Only not to have forgotten"—followed by a summary historical list of the insults to Naomi's body. Part IV is a litany with the refrain "Farewell." And Part V is a fugue in which the idealizing voice of prayer is repeatedly mocked with the crow's voice of mortal dissolution—"Lord Lord Lord caw caw caw."

In the Part I overture, the poet calls himself hymnless and Heavenless. How then does he arrive, many pages later, at his heavenly "Hymmnn" of blessings? It is Part II that lies between, the unbearably graphic, scandalous, farcical, and horrifying narrative of events in Naomi's life. "How can he write such things about his mother?" I was asked by one shaken student. Ginsberg spares us nothing of the maternal body: "Convulsions and red vomit coming out of her mouth—diarrhea water exploding from her behind—on all fours in front of the toilet—urine running between her legs—left retching on the tile floor smeared with her black feces—unfainted." In Ginsberg the Jewish immigrant novel meets lyric existentialist farce: "We're all alive at once then—even me & Gene & Naomi in one mythological Cousinesque room—screaming at each other in the Forever." The son, in the moment in which the poem looks satirically at its own parallel doings in life, tries to hold back madness with words: "I pushed her against the door and shouted 'DON'T KICK ELANOR!'" And at the moment in which the poem looks most tragically at its own doings, the mother does not recognize the son: "You're not Allen—." Can a poet elegize someone who no longer recognizes him? Can words, futile against madness in life, conquer madness after death?

In expanding elegy to take in such "un-English" details as Camp Nicht-Gedeiget, quotations from the Hebrew Kaddish, scenes in the Bronx and Newark, and Naomi's half-delusional list of enemies including "Hitler, Grandma, the Capitalists, Franco, Mussolini," Ginsberg wrenched the form away from its classical gravity and taught his contemporaries a lesson in American colloquiality (as Robert Lowell later acknowledged while loosening his own style). The poem is Ginsberg's own story as well as his mother's story, and it inserts into American lyric the self-conscious and alienated Jewishness of at least one of its poets, a Jewishness that Ginsberg's father, Louis, in his more innocuous "assimilated" poetry, had been unable to voice. The androgynous nature of "Kaddish," as the son-poet becomes stronger than his father by defining his own life as half Naomi's life, recalls the way the poet John Berryman eventually found his own voice through appropriating the sensibility of Anne Bradstreet as he imagined it. Ginsberg's "Kaddish" is not so much an incorporation of woman as a capitulation to her: she is "Naomi, from whose pained head I first took Vision." The Muse, so helpless in "Lycidas"—"Nor could the Muse herself defend her son"—has moved into a position of power here, appearing as a "Communist beauty, Russian-faced" (in defiance of American fears in the fifties of both Russia and Communism). But Naomi's eventual collapse into madness makes the Orphic son-poet wonder whether he can defend his mother.

The dignity of "Kaddish" is not compromised by, but is rather constituted by, its shameful and embarrassing disclosures, as well as by its hysteria, argot, and theatricality—all "Jewish" qualities by conventional English and American Protestant standards, qualities largely suppressed in earlier immigrant Jewish poetry in deference to those standards. The madness of Naomi—and the consequent diction of the poem, which has to match her weird sublimity and hyperbole with its own—are clearly shown to be overdetermined phenomena; there are so many cultural and historical causes erupting into madness and poetry that it is impossible to list them all, though the extraordinary litany of Part IV makes the attempt.

This litany requires some explanation. It seems to resume much that the first three parts—the overture, the life history with its hymn, and the memorial recapitulation "Only not to have forgotten"—have already described. And at first the litany seems merely an extension of the Part III memorial that preceded it ("Only not to have forgotten") in its opening, "O mother / what have I forgotten." But it then modulates from a farewell into an undaunted physical inventory of Naomi's body—its appearance and its history. We can, perhaps, see the first half of this section as the elegiacally conventional, but always shocking, ritual viewing of the corpse before burial. The poet's steady gaze passes without flinching to each body part in turn, in a posthumous blazon disarticulating the once unified parts from each other. But then this section of the poem comes to a halt on, and remains fixated on, the least physical of body parts, Naomi's eyes. It dwells on them for twenty-eight lines, while they painfully fill to overbrimming with the physical, mental, familial, and political sufferings of Naomi's history—Russia, no money, false China, Aunt Elanor, starving India, pissing in the park, America taking a fall, failure at the piano, Czechoslovakia attacked by robots, killer Grandma—all the way down to the surgical attacks on the body itself—pancreas removed, appendix operation, abortion, ovaries removed, shock treatment, lobotomy—and the last crippling blows (one inner, one outer), divorce and stroke. It is an extraordinary passage, acting out to extremes and beyond Keats's words, "Do you not see how necessary a World of Pains and troubles is to school an Intelligence and make it a soul?" The blank eyes of the Russian child Naomi, arriving as an immigrant in the New World, gradually fill with consciousness through pain, and then move from consciousness to Vision—till they decline from Vision to madness. As they fill with experience, they become repositories of all sorrowful human awareness. They finally stand alone as spiritual wells of knowing:

> with your eyes alone
> with your eyes
> with your eyes
> with your Death full of Flowers

The flowers recall Ginsberg's Blakean talisman the Sunflower, which, whatever the cost, follows the light of reality, which Ginsberg here calls "Sun of all Sunflowers"; and they recall the apotheosized Naomi before madness, her "long black hair . . . crowned with flowers."

The ascent to the eyes crowned with flowers counters, while not eradicating, the horror of Naomi Ginsberg's end in the lunatic asylum, and reasserts Ginsberg's belief—or hope—that somewhere behind schizophrenia and lobotomy lingered Naomi's early saner self, a belief vindicated by the consoling letter he receives after her death, in which Naomi once again knows him: "Get married Allen don't take drugs." The letter releases the son, too, from his last visual image of his mother in the locked ward of the state asylum, as it says, "The key is in the sunlight at the window—I have the key."

What would "Kaddish" be without the miraculous posthumous letter, the reprieve from despair? The letter stands as the crowning spiritual apotheosis of Naomi as mother and visionary, and is paired, thematically, with her physical apotheosis as a young Communist Muse with a mandolin. A traditional Western elegy would end with the double apotheosis. But Ginsberg goes beyond the consoling letter and gives his elegy a less transcendent Buddhist end, in which human experience, however full, is finally both spiritually and physically obliterated: "Naomi underneath this grass my halflife and my own as hers . . . / my eye be buried in the same Ground where I stand in Angel." Naomi's tear-suffused eyes and the poet's eye will both be buried in her grave. The only eye that remains at the close is that of the Universe: "Lord Lord great Eye that stares on All and moves in a black cloud." Against the impersonal, dark, and staring Eye of Necessity, Ginsberg sets the brief claim of lyric voice, "my voice . . . / the call of Time . . . an instant in the universe . . . / an echo in the sky the wind." He is remembering Hart Crane's "The Broken Tower":

> And so it was I entered the broken world
> To trace the visionary company of love, its voice
> An instant in the wind (I know not whither hurled)
> But not for long to hold each desperate choice.

The end of "Kaddish" is almost a standoff, as the ravens of unresting thought (Yeats's phrase) beat back the son's prayer in the desolate cemetery on Long Island. As Part V begins, the crows' "Caw caw caw" antiphonally counters the son's "Lord Lord Lord," and at first the competing chants are held to a single anaphoric position at the beginning of each line. In the penultimate line, the standoff breaks down, and the crows begin to shriek after every halting broken phrase, phrases that summon up the poet's life or his mother's or father's—

> caw caw all years my birth a dream caw caw New York the bus
> the broken shoe the vast highschool caw caw

At this point, the poet summons up all his Blakean force and cries out
to the crows that these horrors are nonetheless "all Visions of the Lord."
With that, the crows, though persisting, are balked of ultimate victory;
the last line begins and ends with "Lord":

> all Visions of the Lord
> Lord Lord Lord caw caw caw Lord Lord Lord caw caw caw
> Lord

The necessitarian Lord here invoked is the Eye in the black cloud, the
Eye that only "stares" (a Yeatsian stare remembered perhaps from "Lapis
Lazuli"—"On all the tragic scene they stare"). This Eye does not mark
the fall of the sparrow. It is observational, not providential. The tender-
ness of "Kaddish," which creates in some of its moments a "death full of
Flowers," is not allowed finally to govern the poem. And of those two
manifestos bracketing the *Kaddish* volume with which I began, the one
on the back cover summing up the "broken consciousness of mid twenti-
eth century suffering anguish of separation from my own body" is the
one that relates most truly to the title poem. The irritable front-cover
manifesto recalling the literary wars of the fifties between the university
quarterlies and the Beat poets tends to fade in memory, while the back-
cover testimony lasts. Though the topical quarrel is true, and lively, and
worth remembering in literary history, the poem recalls itself to us now
chiefly as memorable rhythmic speech. The monumental quality of
"Kaddish" makes it one of those poems that, as Wallace Stevens said, take
the place of a mountain. The eventual power of poetry always exists on
an "exquisite plane," as Stevens said, beside which reality—even a reality
as transfixing as the life of Naomi Ginsberg—is only, as Stevens con-
cluded, "the base." "Reality is only the base," he wrote. "But," he added,
"it is the base." In terms of literary history, we might say the same about
the conventional elegy as we knew it in the past—with its Muse, its
singer, its flowers, its eulogy, its dirge, its apotheosis. It is only the base
of "Kaddish," but it is the base. And on that classical base Ginsberg cre-
ated the most nonclassical poem in the American elegiac canon, the im-
migrant elegy that seemed waiting in the air to be written, as we found
to our astonishment when we first read it thirty years ago.

2

Flower Power

Louise Glück's
The Wild Iris

Louise Glück is a poet of strong and haunting presence. Her poems, published in a series of memorable books over the last twenty years, have achieved the unusual distinction of being neither "confessional" nor "intellectual" in the usual senses of those words, which are often thought to represent two camps in the life of poetry. For a long time, Glück refused both the autobiographical and the discursive, in favor of a presentation that some called mythical, some mystical.

The voice in the poems was entirely self-possessed, but it was not possessed by self in a journalistic way. It told tales, rather, of an archetypal man and woman in a garden, of Daphne and Apollo, of mysteriously significant animal visitations. Yet behind those stories there hovered a psychology of the author that lingered, half-seen, in the poems. Glück's language revived the possibilities of high assertion, assertion as from the Delphic tripod. The words of the assertions, though, were often humble, plain, usual; it was their hierarchic and unearthly tone that distinguished them. It was not a voice of social prophecy, but of spiritual prophecy— a tone that not many women had the courage to claim.

It was something of a shock, therefore, when Glück's recent book *Ararat* turned away from symbol to "real life," which she described with a ruthless flatness as though honesty demanded a rock-bottom truth distilled out of years of reflection. In that book Glück restrained her piercing drama of consciousness, and reined in her gift for poetic elaboration. It was clear that some sort of self-chastisement was under way.

Now, reversing course, she has written a very opulent, symbolic book, full—of all things—of talking flowers. The book is really one long poem, framed as a sequence of liturgical rites: the flowers talk to their gardener-poet; the poet, who is mourning the loss of youth, passion, and the erotic life, prays to a nameless god (in Matins and Vespers, many times repeated); and the god, in a very tart voice, addresses the poet. As the flowers are to their gardener-poet, so is she to her gardener-god; the flowers, in their stoic biological collectivity, and their pathos, speak to her, sometimes reproachfully, as she speaks, imploringly, to her god. The god has a viewpoint both lofty and ironic, and repeatedly attacks the self-pity or self-centeredness of the poet. These are dangerous risks for a late twentieth-century poem to take, but Glück wins the wager of her premises. The human reader, too, is placed in "this isthmus of a middle state" (Pope) between the vegetatively animate world and the severe spiritual world, and shares the poet's predicament.

Glück is here returning to an earlier sequence of hers called "The Garden," which rewrote the myth of Eden. As *The Wild Iris* progresses, we see that Eden has collapsed. The opening mood of the book reflects the absolute pointlessness of living when one can think of nothing to hope for. Despair prompts the liturgical addresses to the god (seven Matins by day in the first half of the sequence, ten Vespers by night in the second half). Most of the other titles in the sequence are names of flowers, beginning with the wild iris and ending with the silver lily, the gold lily, and the white lilies.

Glück links herself in these flower poems to her two chief predecessors in the use of flowers as images of the soul, George Herbert and Emily Dickinson. In spiritual deprivation, the soul is like a bulb hidden underground. In spring, it finds its season of flowering and renewal. Here is Herbert:

> Who would have thought my shriveled heart
> Could have recovered greenness? It was gone
>   Quite underground, as flowers depart
> To see their mother root, when they have blown;
>   Where they together,

> All the hard weather,
> Dead to the world, keep house unknown. . . .
>
> And now in age I bud again,
> After so many deaths, I live and write;
> I once more smell the dew and rain,
> And relish versing; O my only light,
> It cannot be
> That I am he
> On whom thy tempests fell all night.

And here, to bridge the gap of time between Herbert and Glück, is Dickinson:

> Through the dark Sod – as Education –
> The Lily passes sure –
> Feels her white foot – no trepidation –
> Her faith – no fear –
>
> Afterward – in the Meadow
> Swinging her Beryl Bell –
> The Mold-life – all forgotten – now –
> In Ecstasy – and Dell –

In a more effortful moment, closer to the more despairing Glück poems, Dickinson wrote about the helpless religious pleading of the seed "That wrestles in the Ground, / Believing if it intercede / It shall at length be found."

But the lessons that the soul was taught in the seventeenth century and the nineteenth century have to be rescripted for the late twentieth century. No longer convinced of the preciousness of each individual soul, are we to grieve over our individual losses? In one of Glück's poems, the bed of scilla reproaches the poet for her focus on the erotic self, and urges her to abandon herself to collective biological being, to be one of an undifferentiated bed of human flowers. The collective wisdom of the scilla bed is one way of looking at one's fate: to say of oneself and others, "We go where we are sent by the wind of Fate, take root by water, and hear the mingled musics of life's current and its songs." Here is "Scilla," as the flowers reprove the poet:

> Not I, you idiot, not self, but we, we—waves
> of sky blue like
> a critique of heaven: why
> do you treasure your voice
> when to be one thing
> is to be next to nothing?
> Why do you look up? To hear
> an echo like the voice
> of god? You are all the same to us,
> solitary, standing above us, planning
> your silly lives: you go
> where you are sent, like all things,
> where the wind plants you,
> one or another of you forever
> looking down and seeing some image
> of water, and hearing what? Waves,
> and over waves, birds singing.

The poem "Scilla" is arranged on a few strings: one is the necklace of -*ings* (thing, nothing, standing, planning, things, looking, seeing, hearing, singing)—nine of them in seventeen short lines. The four successive questions comprise another string, and yet another is linked by water: "waves of sky blue," "some image of water," "waves," "waves." Even the word "echo" brings up the myth of Narcissus bending over water; we "look up" to hear the echo, and "look . . . down" to see an image. The sharp reproof of "Scilla" asks whether it should not be enough for us to see waves and hear birdsong. What, after all, do we need the post-reproductive erotic life for? And why should we lament its absence so bitterly?

Just when we might begin to believe in the scilla-solution and try to live like plants, Glück's god enters with *his* correction of the scilla's point of view:

> Whatever you hoped,
> you will not find yourselves in the garden,
> among the growing plants.
> Your lives are not circular like theirs:
>
> your lives are the bird's flight
> which begins and ends in stillness—
> which *begins* and *ends,* in form echoing
> this arc from the white birch
> to the apple tree.

And would the poet want, in any case, to relive the erotic life? Glück answers with a picture of the archetypal young couple in the Garden:

> I couldn't do it again,
> I can hardly bear to look at it—
>
> in the garden, in light rain
> the young couple planting
> a row of peas, as though
> no one has ever done this before,
> the great difficulties have never as yet
> been faced and solved.

By the next poem, the garden is being called "the poisonous field," and the couple, fallen into mutual recrimination, are sharply chided by the god, who reminds them that they suffer equally and should rise in spiritual stature through grief. As the man and the woman sink in self-pity, each saying, *"No one's despair is like my despair,"* the god retorts,

> Do you suppose I care
> if you speak to one another?
> But I mean you to know
> I expected better of two creatures
> who were given minds: if not
> that you would actually care for each other
> at least that you would understand

> grief is distributed
> between you, among all your kind, for me
> to know you, as deep blue
> marks the wild scilla, white
> the wood violet.

Glück's god is here voicing the Keatsian belief that individual grief creates personal identity, the "colors" of character. The ravishing musicality of Glück's ending emphasizes the surprisingly consonant nature of various identities: the *violet* is *white*, the scilla is *wild*, and *wild* and *white* and *violet* in the *woods* make for a phonetic beauty that stands for natural and moral beauty.

I have gone through this much of Glück's narrative simply to show its didactic and dialectical nature, its dimensions, its mythical means. The sequence is constantly surprising as it moves along, since we have no idea who will speak next, in what tone, with what spiritual argument. There is an exquisite defense, for instance, in "Love in Moonlight," of all that the erotic life has meant, could mean, did mean. Outside, we see a summer evening, "a whole world thrown away on the moon":

> and in the dark, the gold dome of the capitol
> converted to an alloy of moonlight, shape
> without detail, the myth, the archetype, the soul
> filled with fire that is moonlight really, taken
> from another source, and briefly
> shining as the moon shines: stone or not,
> the moon is still that much of a living thing.

Surely this fifteen-line "sonnet" in elegiac memory of the borrowed light of passionate love will hold its own against the strictures of scilla or the scilla's god.

And how does the story end? It has several endings. One is the poet's; she blossoms in spite of herself (the last Vespers). Three are the god's: the tender "Sunset," the stern "Lullaby" and the pitiless "September Twilight," as the god erases his work. Two are poems spoken by a single flower: "The Silver Lily" reassures the poet about the end, while "The Gold Lily" is full of terror and abandonment. Finally "The White Lilies" offers a colloquy between two lovers, as one calms the fear of the other with the old paradox that temporal burial is the avenue to imaginative eternity:

> Hush, beloved. It doesn't matter to me
> how many summers I live to return:
> this one summer we have entered eternity.
> I felt your two hands
> bury me to release its splendor.

These old reciprocals—burial and permanence, mortality and eternity—are lyric standbys. But Glück's white lily, unlike Dickinson's and Herbert's flowers, will not rise from its "mold-life" except on the page.

What a strange book *The Wild Iris* is, appearing in this fin-de-siècle, written in the language of flowers. It is a *Lieder* cycle, with all the mournful cadences of that form. It wagers everything on the poetic energy remaining in the old troubadour image of the spring, the biblical lilies of the field, natural resurrection. It depends, too, on old religious notions of spiritual discipline. It is pre-Raphaelite, theatrical, staged and posed. It is even affected. But then, poetry has a right to these postures. When someone asked Wallace Stevens' wife whether she liked his poems, she answered, "I like Mr. Stevens' poems when they are not affected. But they are so often affected." And so they were. The trouble lay, rather, in Elsie Stevens' mistrust of affectation. It is one of the indispensable gestures in the poet's repertory.

3

Veracity Unshaken

A. R. Ammons' *Sumerian Vistas*

At a sixtieth-birthday convocation in 1986, the poet A. R. Ammons was asked, "Do poets have a public responsibility?" He replied, without hesitation, "No." But another question—"Is poetry subversive?"—elicited a longer statement: "Yes, you have no idea *how* subversive—deeply subversive. Consciousness often reaches a deeply intense level at the edges of things, questioning and undermining accepted ways of doing things. The audience resists change to the last moment, and then is grateful for it." A moment later, he corrected himself: "It may not be in the long range subversive. We love our conventions, but are afraid of being locked in by them."

It is clear that Ammons believes both that poetry has a public effect and that the effect does not depend on whether poets consciously assume "public responsibility." His wish to draw a distinction between public responsibility (writing with one eye on the topical) and public effect (in the short run, subversion; in the longer run, perhaps, conversation) is only one proof of his careful and anxious intelligence.

Like Ashbery and Merrill, Ammons is a nonideological writer who takes long views. All three have assumed the thankless cultural task of defining how an adult American mind not committed to any single ideological agenda might exist in a self-respecting and veracious way in the later twentieth century. Ammons differs from Ashbery and Merrill in being trained in the sciences. (He graduated from Wake Forest with a B.S.) Perhaps in consequence, he is not afraid to represent the human presence as it has actually occurred in the universe: not at the center but at the edge of its galaxy, which itself is one temporary and random point in a very long historical continuum. He not only sees our existence in that light; he *feels* it to be so. At the same time, he respects the way in which consciousness must be a center unto itself, no matter what its position in the universe.

The title of Ammons' recent book, *Sumerian Vistas,* emphasizes his long view of human existence. In his youth, he first turned to Sumer (where writing was invented) as a vantage point. At twenty-nine, he published in his first book, *Ommateum,* several lyrics in which he adopted, as a refuge from acute temporal anxiety, the persona of a prophet who had come to ancient Sumer and had perceived the immense distance between besieged life and calm necessity:

> I have grown a marsh dweller
> subject to floods and high winds . . .
>
> rising with a handful of broken shells
> from sifted underwater mud
> I have come to know how high
> the platform is, beyond approach,
> of serenity and blue temple tiles.

The "Sumerian" dweller in catastrophe of that early poem now writes *Sumerian Vistas.* Though Ammons' vistas do not deny age (the grave is mentioned fairly often, and a sequence on inscription is entitled "Tombstones"), his tone has not changed: it still has all the spring and backlash and curiosity of his young voice. His titles still show punning casualness ("Working Out," "Abstinence Makes the Heart Grow Fonder") as well as epigrammatic brevity ("Dominant Margins," "Scaling Desire"). As usual, his borrowings from scientific diction—"Information Density," "Negative Symbiosis," "Red Shift"—are used with high freedom; "Red Shift," for instance, is not about stars but about a winter-pale begonia (and its owner) receiving a new infusion of "bright blood" from the spring sun.

Ammons is a poet of determined factual exactness. In poems as neat as laboratory drawings, he tells the truth about biological life—for example, that everything eats something else in order to live. If a jay stops the song of a cicada, and attacks its eyes as if they were just another set of seeds to crack open for food, that is the nature of existence—a matter for even-toned recognition rather than lament, terror, or indignation. Lament, terror, and indignation nonetheless have their place, as flashes of feeling, in Ammons' poems; but they are components, not determinants, of cognition. Here is "Sight Seed":

> When the jay caught
> the cicada midair, a fluffy,
> rustling beakful, the
> burr-song flooded dull but
> held low: the jay perched and
> holding the prey to the branch
> as if to halt
> indecorous song pecked
> once, a plink that did it,
> but in the noticeable silence
> proceeded at ease
> and expertly to
> take this, then that eye.

When an eye ("i") is consumed, it becomes part of what follows "i," perhaps a "j." It would not be unlike Ammons to intend the pun.

Ammons is so expert in thinking of himself as a corpse, already dissolved into dust and air, that his own dissolution provides an airy poetics of dispersion, reflecting "genetic material's / extravagant loss along the / edging peripheries of accident." The fact of eventual disappearance also suggests an ethics. Given one's end, how should one live? "Backcasting" answers this way:

> I can tell by
> the way
> gravel will spill
> through me some

day it's
all right to
mess around: I can
tell by the way

light will
find me transparent I
can't be gross:
I drift,

slouch about, spoof:
I true the
coming-before
to the consequence.

One can imagine the demands put by Ammons' muse: "Write a poem on dying that will be as light as the dust and transparency you will become. Then deduce from those motes and air a way of living suitable to that ending. From the consequence of eventual dissolution deduce a premise for existence: true the coming-before to the consequence." The deduced premise, for Ammons, is to lessen ponderousness: the poet can mess around, be airy, drift, slouch, spoof. The poem itself must be full of air spaces, loose siftings, casual rhythms, or it will not be the believable messenger of its entropic message.

Ammons was brought up on the Bible (it was the only book in the house, he has said, in his rural North Carolina boyhood), and the earnestness of a biblical tone has always been part of his repertoire. In the light of that early biblical impress, his post-Christian (though reverent) position is all the more original. It is still rare to find poetry of serious intellectual premises that can get along without disabling religious or ideological nostalgia.

Ammons shows us what it's like to live with a natural, internalized sense of biological evolution. His imagination takes it for granted. The haphazard evolutionary process—by which the primal soup produced protoplasm, vegetation, vertebrates, amphibians, and, finally, us—is undone, he recognizes, by the equally dubious process by which in return we grind the greenness out of nature. Ammons sums up both in his twenty-two-line poem "Questionable Procedures":

A bit of the universe's
business slopped
over and, strung
out of the way,
cooled and lode-slow
gave rise
here and there to
a quickness like
shade, protoplasm,
a see-through
coming and going of
dots and pulsing veils
that soon enough filled
the bit seas:
the veils and cauls
toughened, curled
into rolls, centralized
backbone: taking to
the land and coming up
into us, our agency,
they milled the
green continents white.

Why would anyone *want* to sum up all of evolutionary and human history in seventy-odd words? One answer is that lyric poets have always resented the lay notion that their gamut is smaller than that of epic poets, putting certain grand subjects beyond their reach. A second answer is that if evolutionary history lies in the modern secular mind as a myth of becoming, it must have attracted constellations of feeling to itself, and these must be articulated by contemporary poetry. A third answer is that for the appalled observer an evolutionary history that turns destructively on itself deserves comment, the more epigrammatic and memorable the better. "Such a result so soon—and from such a beginning!" said Whitman, stricken by the appearance of his adult face in a hand mirror; but whereas Whitman supposes an original moral innocence, and glances only at the span of a single life, Ammons supposes an original moral neutrality and deplores human destruction over the whole span of spe-

cies life. The power of lyric form to clasp even the aeons of the modern
evolutionary imagination is as firmly asserted here as in Lowell's son-
net "History."

Ammons' work is post-Christian not only in its marginal positioning
of man, and in its acceptance of evolution rather than special creation,
but also in the way it emphasizes the inevitably aspectual nature of per-
ception and cognition. Like his predecessor Stevens, he denies the univo-
cal positing of a single attainable truth (of the sort conventionally pro-
posed by Christian theology). The title of Ammons' first book,
Ommateum, refers to the compound eye of an insect, and his prose pref-
ace to that collection says, "The poems suggest a many-sided view of
reality; an adoption of tentative, provisional attitudes, replacing the par-
tial, unified, prejudicial, and rigid."

Tentative and provisional thoughts require discretion and grace in ex-
pression. In an interview published in *Pembroke* in 1986 Ammons said,
"To me, the really great poet feels as deeply as anyone these matters, but
touches only and controls them lightly with delicate gestures that just
merely register they are there. To me, the second- or third-rate poet . . .
begins to bushwhack and hack and cut and try to create an artificial fury
because he thinks that will give him the gestures of great poetry, but it
gives him just the opposite." Readers unaccustomed to discretion in ges-
ture prefer loud noises. For them, poetry is a matter of violent statement.
But for Ammons a poem is a "disposition . . . rather than an exposition."
He has said, "It may be made out of words but it's no longer saying
anything. It's just complete." The poem has found a system of relational
completeness within itself, and a relational completeness in the company
of its fellow-poems; both of these are something silent, and they are
more complex than statement, though statement is one of the means
to them.

Like most of Ammons' other volumes, *Sumerian Vistas* contains long
poems as well as short. ("In short poems, I'm on a tightwire, and in long
poems, the plain is wide and the direction uncertain," he has said.) Short
poems become riddles in which he often deliberately exploits the ambig-
uous power of words that can serve as several different parts of speech.
In the opening of "Earliest Recollection," for instance, the words "thaws,"
"snow," "clear," "leaves," "touched," "last," "fall," and "gathering" can
each act more than one part in the game of syntax: "thaws" could be a

verb or a plural noun; "clear" could be a verb or an adjective. We hesitate, placing them, as we read the lines:

> Thaws snow-clear the fields
> and woods, and leaves
> snow's small weight
>
> touched down last fall
> crinkle to the breezes
> and rise gathering dry.

Ammons' suspension of ambiguous parts of speech in an open field mimics the hovering act of perception itself.

Ammons' shorter poems, like "Earliest Recollection," often recount the vicissitudes of accident or chance, but the longest poem in the new volume, "The Ridge Farm," exemplifies his sense of the sacredness of necessity—that interaction of all universal motions:

> sap, brook, glacier, spirit
> flowing, these are sacred but
> in a more majestic aloofness
> than we can know or reason with.

Ammons acknowledges the deep human wish for the "easy sacredness" of a personal divine providence ("some band or / quality of concern to / recognize us here"), but he calls us to recognize what he sees as a loftier sacredness—"something / high to realize, recalcitrant, / unyielding to makeshift in / its quality." As Ammons, with sternness and accuracy, makes his reports on high impersonal necessity, his country goes on funding television evangelists and papal visits. This standoff would make one despair of the gulf between a poet and his culture were it not that cultures eventually catch up to their poets.

"The Ridge Farm," like Ammons' other long poems, offers us a gift we may be reluctant to receive, the privilege of living for a while inside an original and querying adult intelligence. This intelligence has three chief registers: it notices with joyful precision the Thoreauvian world of natural fact; it spins fine-grained meditations on the mind's ways of being;

and it urges an ethics founded on the possibility of cultural illumination and human concern.

It is Ammons' entrancing southern storytelling voice that carries us along in his narratives of natural fact. Intent, for instance, on watering a dried-up plant in a jar, Ammons picks up a watering can neglected all winter, and the story begins:

> I noticed last fall's leaves in the
> can and thought well that will improve
> the juice but I thought it did smell
> funny: I poured water into the jar-top
> and most of it, drought-refused, ran over or
> out: so I waited for the soak to take and
> began to think something really
> smelled: I poured some more rich brown
> juice into the jar and then upended
> the can to let the leaves fall out and
> out plunked this animal clothed in
> leaves so I couldn't tell what he was
> except his thick tail looked thicker
> than a rat's: mercy: I'd just had
> lunch: squooshy ice cream: I nearly
> unhad it: I expect the crows will come
> and peck it up, up, and away, the way
> they do squirrels killed on the
> streets: pulling at the long, small
> intestines and getting a toehold on
> small limbs to tear off the big flesh
>
> the rat was a mole: the arctic air
> yesterday afternoon dried him out and
> the freeze last night stiffened him much
> reduced in size and scent: so
> I broke out the shovel, dug up a
> spade, dumped in the mole: there let
> him rot, the rat: I can see how
> something blind could get into my

wateringcan: but with those feet!
I can hear him scratching up the side:
to get in, or out: but also I can hear him
sloshing, the blind water darkened by
night, till nobody came.

There has been nothing like this in American poetry before Ammons—nothing with this liquidity of folk voice. And this down-to-earth narration sits at home in Ammons' mind next to his riddling intellectual speculativeness, which ranges from creative rummaging ("home is / where the doodle is") to moments of cultural despair:

culture, hardened to shellac's empty
usage, defines in definitions
hoaxdoms of remove from the true life
which
is smaller, leaner than a brook, no
louder, variable as, to the true rain.

Into the hardened hoaxdoms of culture come particles of human veracity and concern, lighting up one partial space. Though he rejects religious superstition, Ammons is still the poet of our Protestant past in his trust in the inner light. That ethical light is intermittent but, he believes, immortal in its recurrence:

a light catches somewhere, finds human
spirit to burn on, shows its magic's
glint lines, attracts, grows, rolls
back space and dark. . . .
                      it dwells:
it dwells and dwells: slowly the light,
its veracity unshaken, dies but moves
to find a place to break out elsewhere:
this light, tendance, neglect
is human concern working with
what is: one thing is hardly better
or worse than another: the

split hair of possible betterment makes
dedication reasonable and heroic:
the frail butterfly, a slightly
guided piece of trash, the wind takes
ten thousand miles.

The strictly limited extent of light and concern is not lost on Ammons.
"All is in an enormous dark," as Hopkins said:

Flesh fade, and mortal trash
Fall to the residuary worm; / world's wildfire, leave but ash.

Nonetheless, the Psyche-butterfly ("mortal trash" to Hopkins, a
"slightly / guided piece of trash" to Ammons) will travel far in space and
time. Properly, Ammons' understated ending has the delicacy of haiku;
in fact, it almost rewrites itself into haiku:

A frail butterfly,
slightly guided piece of trash,
wind-borne thousand miles.

Ammons' Oriental quietism and Quaker light stand in deliberate, if
mild, opposition to the murderous ideological intentions of mankind:

I can in beds of flowers hold
my head up, too: whereas,
the forms of intention, the
faces swept chill-firm with conviction

can assemble and roll down
streets and declare divisions
that save or kill: I go to
nature because man is scary.

By now, Ammons has amassed a lifetime's worth of wayward, experi-
mental, cursive, volatile verses, ranging from the briefness of *Briefings*
(1971) to the long unwinding of *Tape for the Turn of the Year* (1965)—to

name two characteristic extremes in his practice. His definitive *Collected Poems*, when it appears, will be one of the influential American books of this century, notable for its forgoing of dogmatism in a dogmatic time and for its tender, shrewd, and nonchalant charting of a way to live responsibly within natural fact, scientific imagination, and ethical discovery.

4

Recomposed and Clarified

James Merrill's *The Inner Room*

When James Merrill was awarded the Bollingen Prize by the Yale University Library, the *New York Times* huffily editorialized that there was "A World West of Yale." It reproved the library for once again rewarding "poetry that is literary [*sic*], private, traditional," and for insisting, through its awards, that "poetry is a hermetic cultivation of one's sensibility and a fastidious manipulation of received forms." "The academic grip on the Bollingen," the *Times* added darkly, "ought to be loosened." The myth of American Redskins and Anglophile Palefaces (Philip Rahv's terms) dies hard.

The poetry of the illiterate is as literary, of course, as the poetry of the literate, only more unconsciously so; it recites its pieties quite unaware that it has inherited them, through generations of magazine verse, from its predecessors. Only a poet who knows his forms is free to be free within them, just as only one who has cultivated his sensibility is not a victim to it. The editorial writer of the *Times* may have disliked poetry in general, or Merrill in particular. But behind the editorial lies the subliterate wish, immortalized by Marianne Moore, for a poetry "written in plain American that cats and dogs can read."

Who knows, Merrill himself may wish he had been born Walt Whitman. It may be every poet's dream to sing, in Yeats's words, the "song of the noble and the beggarman." But Merrill's gifts make him belong to the line of Herbert, Pope, James, and Mallarmé—the line of writers interested in intricacy of form, and teasing obliqueness of content. The other line of writers—Bunyan, Wordsworth, Frost—use what we call the plain style, or ordinary language, or the words of "a man speaking to men." These latter phrases have always been one rallying point for poetry; but against them there are other rallying cries: "Sweet phrases, lovely metaphors, honey of language" (to use Herbert's caressing words).

Merrill is entirely conscious that he belongs among the "Parnassians" of poetry, for whom consonants are as important as sense. Is he, are they, the aristocrats of a perpetual operatic *ancien régime*, forever suspiciously regarded by the solid groundlings of language, the repository of common meaning? Here is "The Parnassians," Merrill's ironic sonnet on his own refined poetic practice, uttered, one might almost say, in the resentful voice of the *Times:*

> Theirs was a language within ours, a loge
> Hidden by bee-stitched hangings from the herd.
> The mere exchanged glance between word and word
> Took easily the place, the privilege
> Of utterance. Here therefore all was tact.
> Pairs at first blush ill-matched, like *turd* and *monstrance,*
> Tracing their cousinage through consonants,
> Communed, ecstatic, through the long entr'acte.
>
> Without our common meanings, though, that world
> Would have slid headlong to apocalypse.
> We'd built the Opera, changed the scenery, trod
> Grapes for the bubbling flutes mild fingers twirled;
> As footmen, by no eyelid's twitch betrayed
> Our scorn and sound investment of their tips.

If it is true that to a Parnassian the gestures of populist poetry seem gross, heavy-footed, ugly—or lax, vacant, repetitive—it is equally true that to those who like broad explicit moral strokes or solid romance, "Parnassian" writing will seem precious, arch, "knowing," decadent. And since every style has the defects of its qualities, the Parnassian style, when it doesn't come off, *is* overrefined and self-conscious. (The populist style, when *it* doesn't come off, is bathetic, sensationalist, sentimental.)

Artists know the pitfalls of their chosen style at least as well as their critics do, and Merrill is no exception. His footman-speaker articulates every criticism that has been aimed at his maker's style: it is, he says, always in danger of a willed seclusion, tempted to adopt a privileged etiquette almost Japanese in its elaboration, refining its form into its smallest harmonies (the conjunction, for example, of *t* and *r*), no matter how bizarre the consequent content (a turd-monstrance). It is in danger, always, of forgetting where the ladders to its champagne-loges start: in the "common meanings" of earth and action. Would there ever be the double-meaning "tips" for the footmen, on the other hand, were it not for the Parnassian's insights?

Merrill must find it depressing to see how quickly the external features of his Parnassian style have been copied—to behold, in the poems of his imitators, clever rhymes, quirky stanzas, winsome asides, deflected syntax, jeweled effects—without anyone at home inside, so to speak, without a ghost in the machine. These repellent displays are now everywhere in the poetry journals. Merrill's intimacy of address, his conversational narrations, are reproduced by poets with no sense of intimacy and no stories to tell. And so, to describe Merrill, it is no longer enough (as it might once have been) to point out the features of his original and beautiful style. It is necessary to go further, to inquire into the inner motives that engender such a style, those very motives missing from the lifeless copyists of manner.

In trying to approach these motives, I will pass over the less steady poems in this volume, those where some tonal strain suggests a less than successful agreement between motive and manner. Some of these poems are attempts to find adequate art forms for an AIDS elegy. In one of them the poet says, "I need a form of conscious evasion," and perhaps both the consciousness and the evasion are in these instances enemies of aesthetic success.

I would rather look at poems where Merrill is at home in his motives, and where nothing is too conscious or too evasive. I return to my original question: If we imagine poetic authenticity to be proved by a style that, by its surface, creates a convincing interior, then what is the inferred interior in Merrill, and how does it match, or generate, the style? My

example for this purpose is Merrill's exquisite poem (from his title se-
quence) about adult erotic experience (the implied contrast is with that
youthful form of sex that never opens its rapturously closed eyes or puts
its dazzled experience into words). The young initiate is only a lover; but
the adult writer, yielding his senses one by one to sex, is both "actor
and lover":

> Actor and lover contemplate the act
> So-called of darkness: touch that wrestles tact,
>
> Bedsprings whose babble drowns the hearing, sight
> That lids itself, gone underground. Torchlight
>
> Gliding down narrow redly glimmering veins,
> Cell by cell the celebrant attains
>
> A chamber where arcane translucences
> Of god-as-mortal bring him to his knees.
>
> Words, words. Yet these and others (to be "tarred"
> And "set alight" crosswise by "Nero's guard")
>
> Choreograph the passage from complex
> Clairvoyance to some ultimate blind x,
>
> Raw luster, rendering its human guise.
> The lover shuts, the actor lifts his eyes.

An analysis of motive here will initially find a thronging set of "causes"
of Merrill's language: literary allusion (the act of darkness); etymological
pun (touch, [tactile], tact); synesthesia (babble drowns hearing); and
narrative (sight that goes underground). Then begins a cinematic fantasy
of an anatomical journey, in which sensuality (redly glimmering veins),
religion (the cells of a celebrant worshiping a god), science (a descent
cell by cell), and inquiry (attaining a chamber, finding something arcane)
are conjoined.

I stop here to say that gradually this style is sketching a person—one
who remembers Christian injunctions against sex (the act of darkness)
even as he also recalls pagan worship of Eros (the god as mortal), one
who sees himself both as the celebrant of a mystery and as the investiga-

tor of a labyrinth, one who has not forgotten biology in his theology of love. He is someone capable of self-obliteration, almost, falling to his knees. At the same time, he is impatient with his own description of sexual exploration ("Words, words"). Hating his own compulsion to choreograph sex in words, he reenacts the pagan/Christian antithesis by turning his self-censor into Nero's guard crucifying troublesome Christian presences.

Believable motives in poetry are more believable if we see the constructed self do over again what we have just seen him doing. And that is what happens here: the "actor" part of the personality, conscious and open-eyed, trying to understand and track experience, has been gradually undermined by the sexual journey, and has fallen on his knees, overcome. He has reacted to this with an abrupt awakening—"Words, words"—and some brisk executions. But even in retrospect, even admitting his wish to annotate feeling through words, he is once again overpowered by blind sexual immersion, as the words trace a second time the passage "from complex clairvoyance to some ultimate blind x"— where x ("raw luster") stands for the moment when he falls to his knees, all lover. The last line sums up, in a third phrasing, the twice-enacted narrative of this constructed self: "The lover shuts, the actor lifts his eyes."

An illusionistic poem would want simply to reproduce, once, the journey to the blind x. It would take its reader along, and reader and writer would fall to their knees in the chamber, and that would be that. In refusing such an illusionistic "inside" effect, Merrill's poem suggests that one is always, in adulthood, in one's prostrations to Eros, an ironizing spectator of oneself-as-actor. The lady sawed in half by the magician and miraculously restored, in Merrill's earlier "Yánnina," stands for the same "scissoring and mending" by which we are at once enthusiasts and ironists. It is hard to say whether the enthusiast is the ironizer of the ironist, or vice versa. It is certain that a separation of irony from enthusiasm would vitiate any poem that wanted to claim an adult stance for itself.

The coherence of the behavior tracked in the first part, repeated in the second part, and summarized in the closing part of this poem is the guarantee that a single imagined subjectivity inhabits the poem. Merrill's imitators strew their stanzas with allusions and puns, with an alternation of the sensual and the social, the "raw" words and the "clairvoyant" words, in an utterly arbitrary way. No inner coherence, no plausibly implied narrative generates the ornamental gingerbread of their lines. Merrill, by contrast, builds up from small cross-hatchings, as an etcher might, creating regions of lights and darks that ultimately cohere into a personal visual field.

These days Merrill's poems tend to bear death within them. At the same time, his sexual intensity—often diffused into some symbol of burgeoning life, here most strikingly a morning glory—is heightened. In childhood, says the morning glory poem (dedicated to Howard Moss), we were like flowers wholly tuned to primal energy, aspiring (as Merrill's prolonged syntax suggests) to reciprocity with the cosmos: we experienced

> The single day, at six or seven,
> When each was little but a wide-ribbed heaven
> Turned wholly to the cosmic one
> Of pulsing depths, blue deepest overhead,
> And where, though busy Eros visited,
> All we knew, all we lived for, was the Sun.

Inside the morning glory poem lies a narrative of the murder, in Greece, of a homosexual acquaintance. Merrill's willingness to encapsulate savagery in the midst of his idylls is another trait that distinguishes him from his cautious imitators. He is more disabused than they are, and his hawklike eye watches and grasps the flaws in the world. Even in Rome, passing the Castel Sant'Angelo, he sees "an Angel's / Bird-of-prey shadow rippling / Down from his ramparts."

And if he is unwilling to relinquish the blind passion proper to youth, he is not about to hide the humiliating losses proper to age. One of the most intricately "plotted" poems here is "Losing the Marbles": it is about forgetfulness as a fact of life as one turns the corner from middle age into age *tout court*. The poem opens with pleasantries, not so pleasant, about a calendar mislaid and names forgotten; and then we come to Merrill's central symbol of the loss of cortical cells. A poem-manuscript has been rained on, and some of its words obliterated. On its half-unreadable "papyrus," the poem looks like one of Sappho's enigmatic fragments:

> body, favorite
>   gleaned,   at the
>   vital
>   frenzy—

And so on, for seven stanzas. The game is to deduce what the poem's lost cells may have been holding; and we instinctively reach to close the gap, not even knowing the meter. Might it be,

> O body, favorite of the Muses,
> Field once gleaned, what theft has borne
> Your ripeness off? My vital lyre
> Has lost its frenzy—what can adorn . . .

We become, with Merrill, scholars of the papyrus, hunters for lost words—and find ourselves (in a mockery of classical scholarly reconstructions) wholly mistaken. With the aid of his unreliable memory, Merrill reconstructs his destroyed poem, and it turns out to be an ode in sapphics, of which the first stanza, reclaimed, reads:

> The body, favorite trope of our youthful poets . . .
> With it they gleaned, as at the sibyl's tripod.
>   insight too prompt and vital for words.
>   Her sleepless frenzy—

Later in the poem, Merrill suggests that one who interprets for an aphasic friend, thereby sustaining the possibility of community, is engaging in a creative act comparable to deducing from a single dactyl the potential for the ode:

> Who gazed into the wrack till
> Inspiration glowed,
> Deducing from one dactyl
> The handmaiden, the ode?

Or when aphasia skewered
The world upon a word,
Who was the friend, the steward,
Who bent his head, inferred

Then filled the sorry spaces
With pattern and intent,
A syntax of lit faces
From the impediment?

"Losing the Marbles" concludes with a regretful Keatsian sweetness. As a present on his birthday, Merrill tells us, he received from "the friend whose kiss that morning woke me" a pouch of marbles that he has "embedded at random in the deck-slats / Around the pool," that "oubliette." At night they sparkle "tinily underfoot,"

As though the very
Here and now were becoming a kind of heaven
To sit in, talking, largely mindless of
The risen, cloudy brilliances above.

Because Merrill has found a way to put everything from murder to mindlessness into a style that could have been purely decorative, the style itself has stretched its possibilities with each successive volume. Just as the flat motifs that Matisse found in Islamic decorative art became ingredients, on his canvases, of striking atmospheres of sensation, so puns, ambiguities, and the stanzaic shapes of English expand and grow when they are incorporated into Merrill's handsomest and most ambitious poems.

It is no accident that the verse play included in this volume, *The Image Maker*, gives us a portrait of the poet as *santero*, a Caribbean fashioner of *santos*, domestic saint figures who combine Yoruba lore and Roman Catholicism. To intuit the explicit obverse and hidden reverse of community belief, and carve these into images identified by their style as coming from one man's hand—this is what Merrill offers as an implicit definition of his aim. The "mortal weariness" of this task—the reconstitution of life in art—shows through in an excellent poem called (after the meal described within it) "Ginger Beef." In it, Merrill finds an ironic symbol for his art—the titular culinary *pièce de résistance*, ready to be served:

> Lift from the crock, let stand;
> Then chill, trim, slice and recompose
> Within its essence, clarified topaz.

Not, perhaps, to everyone's taste. But a feat—trimmed, sliced, recomposed, clarified. Especially clarified.

5

Southern Weather

Dave Smith

Dave Smith is a poet descended less from the modernists than from a strange, violent, masculine line of poetry that begins with *Beowulf*, continues in the Milton of *Paradise Lost,* and finds its American home in authors ranging from Poe to Richard Hugo and Robert Penn Warren. For these writers, and for Smith, the page becomes something wrestled into submission, its repudiatory blankness overcome by a broad and strong calligraphy laid against it. The amount of sheer gothic weight mustered against the page can frighten the reader who has less of an investment than these writers have in the combats of language and in the wish to tell some brutal truths.

In his first important book, *The Fisherman's Whore* (1974), Smith exposed, in both lyrical and documentary fashion, the rhythmic and grinding work of the watermen in Chesapeake Bay. (Smith is a native Virginian.) *Cumberland Station* (1976), with poems of home and ancestors, continued to exhibit an apparently realistic surface, but interesting things were happening inside the poems: narratives were crosscut into fragments, details were sometimes left unexplained, and tonal effect was favored over expository clarity. Lyric poets who want to tell stories soon discover that Dreiserian leisure is not a lyric option, and have to find ways to sketch a narrative both economically and truthfully. Reading *Cumberland Station,* one might have guessed that a species of expressionism was waiting in the wings. In *Goshawk, Antelope* (1979), that expressionism displayed itself in anguished narratives that were not self-explanatory but had the urgency and desperateness of dream. At the same time, Smith continued to write realistic nature poems, which took as their subject the landscape of Wyoming (where Smith has never lived). Later, these were succeeded by poems of Utah (where Smith *has* lived). Smith's more macabre poems acknowledged at least one aspect of their parentage in the title of his 1981 volume, *Homage to Edgar Allan Poe*. Smith lived in Poe's Richmond before moving to Baton Rouge, where he edits *The Southern Review*.

Cuba Night, Smith's most recent volume, follows his selected poems, *The Roundhouse Voices* (1985), a book too austerely thinned to give an adequate overview of his twenty years of poetic production. *Cuba Night* itself is both representative and rebellious. The southern-gothic themes—family, memory, fear, fate, sex, violence—remain, but the hope of forming them into structures of either historical intelligibility or philosophical consolation is becoming ever more precarious. Smith bursts out in the midst of poems with questions that polite company has long since disallowed: "Why are we here?" "What should we see in this artifact?" "What could he do, or me, or you?" "Why am I me?" "What matters to anyone, I thought, in a deer / I may or may not have seen?"

The fear that the pursuit of writing may not be a justifiable way of spending one's life, that art may not be an accurate way of representing the lives of others, seeps like a destructive acid through all twentieth-century writing, and is not absent from Smith's work. The problem is not resolved (as it hardly can be in a culture that does not notice whether poems are being written about it or not). The inherited confidence of the modernists that art counted for something in the long run, even if in the short run it made nothing happen, was European in origin, and was derived from the patronage of art by courts and by churches. Smith, like many postmodernists, is impatient of the long run and its equable telescopic views. He rages against a quilt displayed in the Bennington College library:

> Pretty is
> as pretty does, this tidy architecture says,
> its squares like houses stitched in firm.
> A village of cloth American as a Currier & Ives.

But this too-perfect Puritan fantasy rankles,
moves us back, forward to focus, find the room
with that girl ended in some posture of abandon
near the piss-pot toppled to a reeking stain.

This is an anti-Whitman poem, repudiating the pastoral domestica-
tion of the American peasant stylized in poems like "Come Up from the
Fields Father." The art of the Puritan quilt—America's Mondrian
effect—belies the life of pain and death from which it issued:

Hung here, the quilt's a shapeless play-pretty,
American abstract, survivor of no one's evil.
They've nailed it up in the air, out of reach
of the sun that remembers the bed, the woman
groaning and bleeding until she was colorless,
a dark space no one looked at or questioned.

It is of no use to protest that the user of the quilt may not have been
the hemorrhaging girl of Smith's imagination—that she may have died
quietly in her bed, full of years and pleasures. Smith's overriding con-
viction is that somewhere there is a gap between suffering and art. When
he sees something culturally defined as "art," he will hurl a "reeking
stain" at it.

It may be that the dice are loaded here, and that Smith would not be
moved to such fury by foreign art—by, say, a tapestry. Perhaps the quilt
stands less for art than for our idea of America, which effectively hides
our dislocated and deprived citizens under a façade of Currier & Ives
"tidiness." The shame of slavery hiding under the "civilization" of the
South may have obliquely prompted Smith's fury at the quilt. There are
poems in *Cuba Night* that make this connection. In the long opening
poem, "To Isle of Wight," Smith drives out of Richmond to the county
named Isle of Wight, and his initial narrative of the ride becomes a sym-
bol of the Southerner's mental world, populated by an irreconcilable
group of inmates: Lee and Patrick Henry, the dead gentry, domesticated
blacks, tobacco sellers and slaves, Poe, the modern inhabitants of the city,
the black churches, Nat Turner, and the Indians, long dead, who saw the
British come ashore:

> I ride through Richmond over gray
> cobblestones, passing porticoed houses,
> locked iron fences of gentried shadows, pale
> as their Anglican ancestors, then private
> clubs where the only blacks are still waiting
> tables, their faces smooth and innocent
> as the dead gaze of Lee's looming statue. . . .
>
> [I ride] through Shockoe Bottom
> where the state began: slaves, produce markets,
> centuries of tobacco. Now boutiques, bars,
> condos, all-night joints for lawyers cruising
> after coke in Volvos. Here you pick up
> Church Hill, passing under Patrick Henry's
> impeccable shrine, street filth everywhere,
> brick hulks the home of whores, winos, poor blacks
> increasingly thumbed out, casualties
>
> of developers in restoration.

"To Isle of Wight" is written in ten-line stanzas of mostly decasyllabic lines, the syllable count and stanza shape serving as checks on Smith's documentary fervor. The block-shaped stanzas act as verse paragraphs, breaking the ride into manageable units.

In other poems, Smith's shorter stanzas often run unhesitatingly one into the next, and his stanza breaks seem arbitrary. For Smith, form doesn't really have to do with stanzas or line lengths so much as it has to do with a structure of images that for him compose a gestalt. When the structure is finished, so is the poem. This is the case in the title poem, which recalls the night of the Cuban missile crisis. It is written in two stanzas of ten lines, and three of nine. Could the ten-line stanzas have been reduced to nine lines? Or the nine-line stanzas expanded to ten lines? And if not, why not? And why stanzas at all, since they are not separated at stanzaic or imagistic points of closure? These are not really the questions, perhaps, to ask of this electric poem—a montage of death warnings, family fears, tragic accident, undone love, and political threat. But by writing with stanza breaks and near-equal stanza lengths Smith invites us to consider whether these formal features have any important structural function. In *Cuba Night* and other poems here, they seem to exist chiefly to give the reader a breathing space, so that the lines do not form an impenetrable and intimidating wall of words.

Smith works his raw material—raw in its crudeness, its flatness, its indubitableness—hard, insisting often, sometimes mistakenly, on the crude formulation as well as the crude fact: the dead are "meat," the layers of paint on a wooden gargoyle become "a whore's makeup," an accident victim is "drooling blood on a stranger's ditch." Smith walks a difficult line between the indignant and the overripe; since his subject is the drastic and the destructive, his language perhaps needs to risk over-kill. When he manages a balance between the natural wrongness of life and the genuine rightness of art, the poem can radiate a fierce splendor. In "Camellias," for instance, the poet, wakened at night by an animal scream, flicks on the light and sees a predator at the kill. The naked color of unmasked appetite is compared with the pink of garden camellias:

> Instantly something clenches
> the earth, digs in, doesn't
> bolt, lifts itself to see, mouth partly open,
> the tiny tongue in throat-black,
> and throat as well, disguised but pink
> as the unfolded, dewy crenellations
> of camellias uncountably opening
> themselves in seasons
> pure as Florida. It is all framed
> by the flawless black meat and fur coiled
> upon itself like night-after-night.

In this late, revengeful version of "death is the mother of beauty," death is no longer a dying fall but, rather, a trap sprung. Within the light of psychological revelation are clasped together the open throat and its broken victim. Things are not beautiful to Smith unless they disclose a rending within:

> In beauty something is jerking a small other
> apart, breaking the slight bones,
> the cross-stitched sinews.

This is a specialized taste, one that Smith forces on those who may not share it. His tableaux of fatal auto crashes, ravaged girls, stillbirths, shot ducks, suicides, and fights dare us to deny their verisimilitude. His definition of beauty that I have just quoted suggests that he is beginning to explore his own complicity in his chambers of horrors. When he relents, as he has often done in poems about his wife and children, there can be a slackening of tension which seems almost forgetful, as though in Smith violence and tenderness have as yet found no sure means of coexistence.

Smith has always shown an uncanny talent for catching the adolescent feelings of young men. A representative poem, "Careless Love," shows a man remembering his younger self as a boy at the beach, teetering on the edge of marriage; characteristically, his girl is calmer and bolder than he is. The man says to her now:

> I remember
> not why but how you chose me. . . .
> From your hair came
> the smell of flesh, of salt tides
> flooding back giddy
> minutes of happiness. I saw
> the bloody spot
> of dawn the ocean dragged behind.
> "We'll get married,"
> you said, peeling your suit off.
> "Don't be afraid."

"The bloody spot"—never long absent from Smith's mind—is here domesticated to a subordinate glare, threatening but not destroying happiness.

At moments, Smith thrashes against his own violence, and those moments result in what are for me his most interesting, if not always his most accomplished, lines. He tells a weird and compelling story from his childhood, of a neighbor who, against all advice, built a house on land with a high water table. Of course, the cellar was soon half filled with thick swamp water. The neighbor's response was to moor a canoe in the basement. The child-poet and the neighbor's son dream that the canoe might one day rise through the cellar ceiling and float out through the house, "but day by day / the walls closed in, and nothing changed." The grown poet reflects on the neighbor's claustrophobic sojourns in the cellar, paddling his canoe from one wall to the other:

> No eye could see much in your life's
> horizon, spiders, cocoons,
> shiny killers in hard black shields,
> but in this room-sized lagoon
> I came to imagine the strange selves
> I keep writing down.

And the posture of the man in the canoe becomes that of the poet in his chair:

> When I go down
> in my chair to write, I see you
> begin to conceive it, the outrageous
> boat proud upon the earth's
> scummy upwelling, its carriage a soul's
> indifferent to despair as to joy.

This proud bearing, surmounting joy and despair with stoicism, is not yet Smith's: he cries out, he protests, he sulks, he hates, he revenges himself. But the fact that he envisages a less personal set of responses, and in some way distrusts his own delectation in the tragedies of the insulted and the injured, gives this poem, "The Canoe in the Basement," a theoretical pride of place in *Cuba Night;* it measures the temperature of various enigmatic but not violent phrases scattered through the volume. These are phrases that have the savor of corpses: "silence, ignorance, season's passage"; "Disinterred, the past grins. Mute. Past"; "grateful for the rain washing his steps from earth"; "A cold enigma"; "faces . . . moonstones, blank mirrors." These phrases are the chilly late flowers of a coming season pushing up through Smith's steaming earth.

To these phrases belongs the cool, eloquent poem called "Writing Spider." The poet as a child watches the spider at work, preparing her web for the corpses she will install in it:

Electric against the black law of the trees,
huge yellow zigzags around her
like lightning. A mystery, I think.

There's not yet the evidence we expect, swaddled
stingers, fuzzy cocoons well prepared—
but for whom? The web glistens. . . .

How old am I when I lift the stick,
prod this and that corner of her concentration?
It requires her to type back and forth
her swaying, signing possession.

I want to touch her now but instead
blow casual, ordinary breath
over the moment of her beautiful resting.

The emblem of the spider seen in her aesthetic (rather than her destructive) motion is an old one in poetry. Dickinson, looking at a male spider, claimed him as her own: "Neglected son of genius / I take thee by the hand." In Smith's poem, the momentary refraining of the spider from inflicting suffering, and the arrest of the poet's hand as he breathes rather than touches, cannot be said as yet to represent the poet's usual manner. For now, he hurls himself, blindly, against his potential death (in one poem he mentions that he has diabetes) and, at his most extreme, makes it happen. "To Isle of Wight" ends in a fatal accident as the half-asleep, half-drunk speaker crashes into a hearse coming from the funeral of a black man. He hears voices above him:

A man says "Gon' die." . . .
He says "Don't ask,"
when one wants my name, Then, "He Isle of Wight,"
and I hear them shuffle as if to leave.

No! I gasp against hands on me. *I'm kin!*

The desperate claim of the southern white on the southern black seeps away, unheard or unheeded, as another southern-gothic tale ends in a Faulknerian debacle. A southern weather—sultry, sullen, and unforgiving—permeates this book. To Northerners that weather always has a slightly foreign and melodramatic air; to Southerners, it seems, it defines the very atmosphere in which life is lived. Smith adds to it the grimness and tenacity of someone shaking life by the throat and commanding it to speak. The absence of any word from the death's-head within drives him to fury. What this Jacob will write when his wrestling with the angel of death finds its dawn is beyond conjecture.

6

Huge Pits of Darkness,
High Peaks of Light

Robinson Jeffers

The poet Robinson Jeffers (1887–1962) is periodically resurrected. Stanford University Press is bringing out his complete poems in four sumptuous volumes; and from the ashes of *The Selected Poetry* (1938), compiled by Jeffers himself, and of a second selection, compiled in 1965 by anonymous editors at Random House, there now arises a third, *Rock and Hawk*, selected by the Californian poet Robert Hass. Jeffers' own *Selected* ran to six hundred twenty-two pages, the second to one hundred eleven, and the new one—handsomely produced—is two hundred ninety pages long and contains over a hundred short poems. Hass has dropped Jeffers' swollen narrative poems (ranging from fifty to ninety pages apiece), which have now sunk in critical estimation, though in the thirties they made Jeffers' name and brought him the sort of adulation usually directed toward religious cult figures. Even reduced to his shorter works, Jeffers remains, it seems to me, a finally unsatisfying poet—coarse, limited, and defective in self-knowledge. Some modulation of intelligence or sensibility is missing from his writing. But because Jeffers was a man of very unusual linguistic equipment and literary training, because he felt so deeply compelled to poetry that he sequestered himself in Carmel and wrote obsessively, and because he achieved extraordinary fame in both poetry and drama, his work asks for a scrutiny no one would bother to give to amateur writing. He has had warm defenders of his craggy philosophy—Czesław Miłosz most recently—and impatient detractors, like Yvor Winters and Kenneth Rexroth (the California competition). It is not his opinions I would quarrel with. His descriptions of nature are made with an intent eye; his sensibility declares itself with apparent sincerity; his lexical range is enviable. And yet I resist grouping him not only with his greater contemporaries—Eliot and Frost—but even with such lesser contemporaries as Moore and Williams.

Robert Hass, in an earnest, intelligent, and winning essay prefacing this selection, gives an honest account of various unpleasant qualities he finds in Jeffers' work. Among the adjectives he resorts to are "pretentious," "repetitious," "bombastic," "humorless," "fuzzy," "obsessed," and "hysterical." Yet Hass's essay is fundamentally a defense of Jeffers, founded on his admiration for Jeffers' "truly obsessed and original imagination." Hass sets the internal imaginative power against what actually appeared from Jeffers' pen: "The most dangerous thing that can be said of him, I think, is that he was verbally careless." The risky division that Hass draws between imagination and writing may be dear to the heart of every poet; it is certainly, in some cases, dear to me. The extent to which any imaginative ardor outstrips its verbal after-image is commemorated in Shelley's vivid biblical image: "The mind in creation is as a fading coal. . . . When composition begins, inspiration is already on the decline." Beloved poets are valued for their imagination even in their less accomplished moments. But the distinction between fire and fading is rarely invoked for the whole of a poet's work. Hass seems to want us to take Jeffers' entire oeuvre as the work of a vivid imagination that never quite found its exact verbal body. Hass perhaps extrapolates backward to the glowing coal in Jeffers, while I see the embers, the extant works. It is not humorlessness or bombast I mind (after all, Coleridge accused Wordsworth of just these faults), nor is it hysteria and obsession (which are everywhere in, say, Eliot and Plath). Even pretentiousness and fuzziness might pass (they are not absent from Whitman).

In an attempt to explain objections to Jeffers, Hass suggests that modern critics, uncomfortable with poetic statement, were seeking, and not finding in Jeffers, the modernist hermetic symbol (Eliot's rose garden, Stevens' pigeons sinking downward to darkness). Yet that account is unsatisfactory: critics showed themselves willing to praise Frost's plain speaking and Eliot's long discursive passages in the *Quartets*. What, then, is it that fails to compel acquiescence to Jeffers' verse? My short answer would be "his moral timidity." Since I mean that phrase to apply to the morality of art, and not only to the morality of practical life, it may need some explanation.

Jeffers, though he seems not to have realized it, had a painful childhood. His father was a clergyman whose first wife died; he married again, and he was forty-eight when "Robin" was born. Biographers agree that Jeffers believed he loved his parents, and equally agree that behind the violent and incestuous family dramas that appear in his plays and poems there may have been some troubled Oedipal feelings toward his mother, who was in her twenties when she bore him. They also surmise that Jeffers as a child confused his father (a professor of Old Testament at the Western Theological Seminary of Pittsburgh) with God, and that his subsequent fierce atheism and his philosophy of scientific "Inhumanism" were the other side of the Presbyterian beliefs of his childhood. After severe paternal instruction in Latin and Greek and after European travel with his parents, the young Jeffers had become too unusual to fit in with other Pittsburgh schoolchildren, and he had a lonely youth. Between the ages of twelve and fifteen, he attended European boarding schools while his parents roamed about Europe and the Near East. Eventually, the family moved to Pasadena, and at eighteen Jeffers graduated from Occidental College. He went on to the University of Southern California and there met a young married woman, Una Call Kuster, whom he married eight years later, after she was divorced. He did graduate work in science, perhaps in an attempt to find a comprehensive world view different from that of his father. In 1912 Jeffers published his first book of poems, at his own expense; in 1913 he married Una; in 1914 they went by stagecoach to Carmel, built a house, and settled in for life. Their first child, a daughter, died; they then had twin sons. During the ten years after the publication of his fourth book, *Roan Stallion* (1925), Jeffers became an internationally famous man: a consciously Byronic studio portrait by Edward Weston ornaments the 1938 *Selected Poetry,* and Hass tells us that in the thirties Jeffers appeared on the cover of *Time* and in the pages of *Vogue.* His reputation, though it was somewhat resuscitated by Judith Anderson's 1947 appearance in his *Medea,* has since declined; his achievements (praised by Edwin Arlington Robinson and Mark Van Doren in the early years but disputed even then by Yvor Winters and later by R. P. Blackmur) continue to perplex evaluation.

Once Jeffers had found his free-verse style and his topics—the sublimity of nature, sexual violence, and the pettiness or degeneracy of mankind—nothing further seems to have happened fundamentally to his mind or his writing. This is agreed on by all. Hass sees some superficial mellowing in the later work. "The mind has relaxed somewhat," he says of the poetry of the last years, but he adds that Jeffers "still hammers away at his religious convictions." Not much, in short, has changed at the center. This permanent arrest at the point of youthful self-discovery is the central fact to be confronted by any commentator on Jeffers.

It is not that Jeffers did not work on his art. He learned to purge a good deal of his earlier grotesquerie, lines of the sort we find in, say, "Tamar," where Tamar asks the dead:

> What shall I ask more? How it feels when the last liquid
>   morsel
> Slides from the bone? Or whether you see the worm that
>   burrows up through the eye-socket, or thrill
> To the maggot's music in the tube of a dead ear? You stinking
>   dead.

More troubling than the surplus of the grotesque is Jeffers' never-purged sadism. Tamar's brother, sexually jealous, takes up a whip to flog her:

> Sickened to see the beautiful bare white
> Blemishless body writhe under [the whip] before it fell . . .
>   the coppery pad of her hair
> Crushed on the shoulder-blades, while that red snake-trail
> Swelled visibly from the waist and flank down the left thigh. . . .
>   From her bitten lip
> A trickle of blood ran down to the pillow.

Passages like these suggest that a braver artist than Jeffers would have dared to bring his sadistic impulses under some reflective scrutiny. Jeffers, instead, simply continued to act them out in verse, and, worse, to find in them a justified contempt for the human. His sadism is accompanied by a fascination with the socially deviant. Even when he does attempt some analysis of this obsession (he speculates, for instance, that some psychological deformity prompts figures such as Jesus and Buddha to form religions), the tone of hectic interest and covert excitement persists, unexamined. Jeffers' primary defense against his fantasies of sexual deviation, torture, dissolution, and sadism was an affectation of "coldness": while the narratives and plays run riot with incest, necrophilia, women sexually interested in stallions, and so on, the haughty poet watches aloofly. This Sadean reaction to sexual obsession and physical torture becomes a mechanical one in Jeffers—one by which he seems helplessly manipulated.

It is scarcely possible to prescribe a dose of intelligence to a poet so intelligent, or a dose of feeling to one so hopelessly trapped in a groove of feeling, or a deflection of obsession to one so obsessed. On the other hand, unanalyzed obsession is the opposite of moral intelligence, of aesthetic inquiry, and of that modulation of poetic rhythm and tone which makes for melody in verse as in music. Jeffers' anvil chorus is finally boring.

The argument against an *opera omnia* of dominant brasses and percussion is not—though it may appear so—solely a stylistic argument. A ceaselessly curious investigation of a chosen medium is the quality that above all distinguishes artists from the mass of other people (preachers, teachers, journalists) who spend time communicating thoughts, messages, and personal responses in prose and verse. It is true that Jeffers spent some years exploring language, and that he developed an early form of personal idiom. Whereas in *Flagons and Apples* (1912) and *Californians* (1916) he stumbles along in apprenticeship to Swinburne and Yeats, and especially to Robinson (the chief begetter of Jeffers' long narratives), by the time of *Tamar and Other Poems* (1924) Jeffers' long-breathed style has become recognizably his own. Hass's selection begins with poems from this book, which appeared when Jeffers was thirty-seven:

> The clapping blackness of the wings of pointed cormorants, the
>   great indolent planes
> Of autumn pelicans nine or a dozen strung shorelong,

But chiefly the gulls, the cloud-calligraphers of windy spirals
    before a storm,
Cruise north and south over the sea-rocks and over
That bluish enormous opal.

This is Jeffers at his spacious and lofty best. In his seventies, he is writing
lines that sound very much the same:

    The cormorants
Slip their long black bodies under the water and hunt like
    wolves
Through the green half-light. Screaming, the gulls watch,
Wild with envy and malice, cursing and snatching.

In short, from thirty-five to seventy-five Jeffers did not change his writing
in any artistically important way. By the time he was thirty-five, both his
parents had died, and he had acquired his lifelong wife, his lifelong
house, and his two children. Perhaps he was through with seeking, and
was preoccupied with recording.

In what Hass calls an "explosion of work," Jeffers wrote between 1920
and 1938 "fifteen narrative poems ranging in length from ten to two hun-
dred pages, four verse dramas, and almost two hundred lyric poems." A
writer he certainly was: a modest private income and timely gifts from
rich friends enabled him to live without a job, and he wrote every day.
After shearing the "rhyme-tassels" (as he called them) from his verse, he
devised his all-purpose unrhymed long line—a unit indebted, according
to one of Jeffers' private notes, to Greek quantitative meters and to tidal
rhythms. In this flexible line, which may also owe something to Whit-
man, Jeffers could say almost anything at any length, and did. The ab-
sence of a stanzaic exoskeleton sets problems for free-verse lyrics, since
all poetic structure—tonal, logical, visual—must then come from an in-
ner armature. Jeffers' turgid narratives (and Hass makes no brief for
them) were carried by their violent plots, but plots of this sort could not
govern his lyrics. In 1932, Jeffers sent some remarks on poetry versus
prose to a student at Berkeley—remarks that seem to convey absolutely
no idea of poetry as a form with a structure of its own, different from
structures appropriate to narration or exposition. For Jeffers, poetry was

simply more primitive, concrete, musical, emotional, imaginative, sensual, unspecialized, passionate, and celebratory than prose. It was, in fact, prose made rhythmic, intense, and exalted:

> Poetic content (the feeling, thought, and expression of poetry) may be found in prose also and is only distinguished from that of prose by having more of certain qualities and less of certain others. The thought is more primitive and less specialized. Language is more figurative, giving concrete images rather than abstract ideas and cares more for its own music. Poetry appeals rather to the emotions than to the intelligence and especially to the aesthetic emotion. It appeals more eagerly than prose does to the imagination and to the bodily senses. It deals with the more permanent aspects of man and nature.

When Jeffers pressed himself to go beyond such a feeble theory of poetic content, his remarks tended to be about what the poetic line should exhibit—rhythm and "singing emphasis," alliteration and assonance. It seems odd, given his long acquaintance with Greek and Latin poetry, that his comments never turned naturally to lyric genres, to larger compositional masses, to the structural supports of lyric, or to the modulation over time which is natural to a temporal art—not to speak of the qualities of concision, surprise, volatility, and intimacy so native to the lyric.

We can attribute Jeffers' indifference to such matters largely to the fact that he was not actually writing lyric. He was writing oratory—a rhythmic, emotional, sensual, and imaginative public prose he had absorbed from the Greek political tradition. And his oratorical stridency seems to me that of a timid man having to prove himself durable and masculine. Lyric for him is an oratorical sermon designed to persuade others—not a probe designed to investigate himself and his medium. A friend who was present at the reading Jeffers gave at Harvard in 1941 recalls that at the reception Jeffers turned to the wall, face averted from the crowd. The poet's attitude was at that time interpreted as hauteur; it could equally well be interpreted as the panicky ill-ease of a friendless, freakish boy (even though Jeffers was then over fifty).

Hass has omitted from his collection some poems once notorious—among them certain war poems of the forties, like "The Bloody Sire" and

"Cassandra." In "The Bloody Sire" Jeffers asks the question that exposes nakedly his instinctive conjunction of beauty, sex, religion, and murder:

> Who would remember Helen's face
> Lacking the terrible halo of spears?
> Who formed Christ but Herod and Caesar,
> The cruel and bloody victories of Caesar?
> Violence, the bloody sire of all the world's values.

And in "Cassandra" he places himself, as prophet, above both gods and men, who equally connive against "the truth" (a phrase, dear to ideologues, that comes easily to Jeffers' lips):

> Does it matter, Cassandra,
> Whether the people believe
> Your bitter fountain? Truly men hate the truth; they'd liefer
> Meet a tiger on the road.
> Therefore the poets honey their truth with lying. . . .
>   Poor bitch, be wise.
> No: you'll still mumble in a corner a crust of truth, to men
> And gods disgusting.—You and I, Cassandra.

Though the mellower Jeffers of the late sketches is an altogether more appealing fellow than this rigidly self-appointed denouncer of the degenerate mob, the essence of Jeffers' defensive and tormented personality lies more in the excessive poems (deleted, probably on grounds of taste, by Hass) than in the milder late woodnotes. Hass has also deleted the more maudlin of these, such as the posthumous speech of Jeffers' dead dog to him and his wife:

> I hope that when you are lying
>
> Under the ground like me your lives will appear
> As good and joyful as mine.
> No, dears, that's too much hope: you are not so well cared for
> As I have been.

By sparing us poems like this, Hass makes a better *Selected* than the 1965 one compiled by Random House. And in some late poems he shows us the Jeffers who had at the end of his life the grace to doubt the sufficiency of his aesthetic of brutality and its denigration of human life. In a glimpse of a sublimity not of nature (which he had always responded to) but of man, the old Jeffers speculated:

> The hawks are more heroic but man has a steeper mind.
> Huge pits of darkness, high peaks of light,
> You may calculate a comet's orbit or the dive of a hawk, not a
>   man's mind.

Perhaps he realized that all the California peaks and abysses he had spent his life describing were less "inhuman" and "objective" than he had suspected, since he transfers them here to interior steeps and pits, emblems of a perilous subjectivity like that admitted by Hopkins—"O the mind, mind has mountains; cliffs of fall / Frightful, sheer, no-man-fathomed." Late in life, in his most honest piece of self-examination, Jeffers mused on an anthology of Chinese poems—poems of a restrained aesthetic almost incomprehensible to him, since it got along without frenzied contempt, oratorical excess, lurid prophecy, or illogical lineation. His poem on the Chinese anthology is a genuine query, all defenses down. For the first time, Jeffers lifts his visor and gazes at Tu Fu and Li Po. In this most gentle of the late poems we see the Jeffers who might have been, relenting instead of relentless, curious rather than repudiatory, regretful instead of disdainful—damned, so to speak, to his own aesthetic of sublimity rather than boisterously electing it. Here is Jeffers' reluctant homage to discretion, gentleness, affection, friendship, and peace as aesthetic motives, and as a moral *summa* remote from his harsh Calvinism:

ON AN ANTHOLOGY OF CHINESE POEMS

> Beautiful the hanging cliff and the wind-thrown cedars, but they
>   have no weight.
> Beautiful the fantastically
> Small farmhouse and ribbon of rice-fields a mile below; and
>   billows of mist

Blow through the gorge. These men were better
Artists than any of ours, and far better observers. They loved
    landscape
And put man in his place. But why
Do their rocks have no weight? They loved rice-wine and peace
    and friendship,
Above all they loved landscape and solitude,
—Like Wordsworth. But Wordsworth's mountains have weight
    and mass, dull though the song be.
Is it a moral difference perhaps?

Jeffers' plaintive question "But why / Do their rocks have no weight?" is the cry of the Christian against the Confucian. Pound, contemplating the same Chinese poems, decided to try a weightlessness of his own, in phrases floating unmoored from the British solidity of blank verse. Jeffers, timid and unballasted among people, felt secured and ballasted by stone, weight, long lines, mass. His bluster—what Blackmur called "the flannel-mouthed inflation in the metric of Robinson Jeffers with his rugged rock-garden violence"—needs to be read as the long-maintained armor protecting him against an investigation into his own private terrors. Jeffers condemned "introversion" as the decadent practice of decadent cultures: "There is no health for the individual whose attention is taken up with his own mind and processes; equally there is no health for the society that is always introverted. . . . All past cultures have died of introversion." He added, in a moment of monumental self-delusion, "I have often used incest as a symbol to express these introversions." Perhaps what this really means is that when he practiced introspection he found incest, and that the price of introspection was consequently too high. It might have been too high for any of us; but the price of finding introspection too dangerous is in the layperson a self-stalled identity and in the poet a self-stalled art. Jeffers, it appears to me, will remain a notable minor poet, the first to give an adequate description in verse of the scenery of the California coast. His ambitions as a moralist and prophet were defeated by his lack of genuine moral curiosity and its counterpart, an original moral vision. If Jeffers' harsh contempt for human history had been tempered by personal insight, and framed in a flexible style, we might now read his poems as we read those of Miłosz.

7

New York Pastoral

James Schuyler

James Schuyler is that unlikely writer in contemporary New York, a pastoral poet. Though he has, understandably enough, been linked geographically with his friends Frank O'Hara, John Ashbery, and Kenneth Koch in what is called the New York School of poetry, his work, despite some superficial resemblances of form (short lines like O'Hara's, long lines like Koch's), is not like theirs. Schuyler is not radically allegorical, like Ashbery, but literal; he is not a social poet, like O'Hara, but a poet of loneliness; he is not comical and narrative, like Koch, but wistful and atmospheric. Though he has increasingly refused to write a "well-made poem," he is perfectly capable of the classic neatly turned lyric (he is an admirer of Herrick). I shall consider the short lyrics later, but any commentator on Schuyler must first deal with the strange long poems that are scattered through his work, from "The Crystal Lithium" through "Hymn to Life" and "The Morning of the Poem."

Schuyler's long poems, undramatic journals of daily life, have been his unshowy form of aesthetic refusal; they argue, implicitly and sometimes explicitly, that poetry is not a matter of the isolated Paterian moment or of important political or intellectual argument, but is rather coterminous with perception, reflection, and feeling, wherever they extend themselves. This practice has implications for living as well as for writing, and for thinking as well as for living. I associate it with pastoral because it values leisure, the sexual life, the "trivial" (as in Herrick), and retirement from the active life. The aesthetic of all-inclusiveness is particularly congenial, perhaps, to outlaws of all sorts as a displaced form of social demand: "Let me in; let all of me in."

The sumptuary laws of poetic tradition (bringing thoughts "to Church well drest and clad"—George Herbert) have been repeatedly challenged by new, intrusive voices of the "low" or "excluded"—Wordsworth's beggars, Frost's madwomen, Eliot's Wastelanders—but often, in a defensive gesture, authors have detached themselves (by means of intellectual evaluation or religious sublimity or narrative detachment) from their "outlaw" poetic surrogates. Schuyler, who is homosexual and writes openly about his homosexuality, creates no distance between himself as a writer and himself as the person encountering daily banality (as well as daily beauty):

> May
> Opens wide her bluest eyes and speaks in bird tongues and a
> Chain saw. The blighted elms come down. Already maple
>   saplings,
> Where elms once grew and whelmed, count as young trees. In
> A dishpan the soap powder dissolves under a turned-on
>   faucet. . . .
>   The sun sucks up the dew; the day is
> Clear; a bird shits on my window ledge. Rain will wash it off
> Or a storm will chip it loose. Life, I do not understand.
> Days tick by, each so unique, each so alike: what is that chatter
> In the grass?

"Confessional" poets have allowed the sordid, the tedious, even the depraved parts of their lives to compose the "low" strata of their theatrically disposed personal landscapes. "Realist" poets expose the gritty underside of modernity or heroism or civilized accomplishment. Schuyler, by unfolding to its full extent the component of banality in life and thought, reveals "confessional" and "realist" works as the operatically heightened things they are. Schuyler's long poems can set one's teeth on edge precisely because they do not avail themselves of the kinds of dramatic momentum that other apparently artless journal-poems depend on—Ginsberg's political oppositions, Ammons' transcendental buoyancies, Ashbery's quizzical metaphysics. The drama faintly visible behind Schuyler's long poems has to be deduced from his scattered allusions to several confinements in mental hospitals, periods of addiction to pills and alcohol, and an extreme nervousness manifesting itself in social silences, insomnia, and helplessness in practical matters. There are references to antidepressants, drinking, Antabuse, Alcoholics Anonymous. And yet, in spite of the bad biological hand that has been dealt him, Schuyler exhibits, especially in the long poems, a sunflower-like turning to life—a life hardly, it would seem, livable, but one represented often as ecstatic.

In fact, Schuyler's earliest chosen pastoral precursor, on the evidence of the youthful poems, was the rapturous Gerard Manley Hopkins; and anyone who has Hopkins' nature poetry by heart will hear its music beneath Schuyler's early work, rich in phonemic orchestration:

> the glorious swamp flower
> skunk cabbage and the tight uncurling punchboard slips
> of fern fronds. Toned, like patched, wash-faded rags.

Wallace Stevens' voice rises in Schuyler's landscape poems, too, shorn of its Tennysonian dying fall. Stevens will say, "The last leaf that is going to fall has fallen," his beautiful pentameter turning to falling trochees and dactyls under one's very eyes. Schuyler will be emphatically American, and say, "All the leaves / are down except / the few that aren't," a remark one could hear in Maine (where Schuyler used to stay with the Fairfield Porters). Stevens says with grammatical elegance, "It was snowing / And it was going / To snow." Schuyler says, in country tones, "No / snow yet but / it will snow." One could argue that the change from Stevens' lines to Schuyler's lines represents one more episode in the emancipation of American pastoral from English tones.

To Hopkins and Stevens, Schuyler added Gertrude Stein; she was useful to him because of her mixture of homely domestic nonsense with tenderness. In a poem that we could call a modern urban pastoral, Schuyler is steaming out wrinkles in some neckties, and writing a love song in his head to the faraway person who gave him the ties:

> Sometimes, even yet or now, I mean, I forget for a few
> sad minutes how unalone I
> am, steaming ties you gave
> me, ties are, yes even ties,
> are silk and real.

And Frank O'Hara's genial writing, urging the claims of the personal life, seems to have encouraged Schuyler to think that an unassuming voice might have a right to call itself poetic.

Helped in part by the example of such predecessors, Schuyler eventually found his own poetics lying just aslant from the way others—even his contemporaries—used words. An early love song in the form of a villanelle begins,

> I do not always understand what you say.
> Once, when you said, across, you meant along.
> What is, is by its nature, on display.

That third line could stand as an epigraph to all Schuyler's verse: How can one not see, or not grant the nature of what one sees, all of it? And yet the unnamed lover in the poem does not acknowledge by day what was done the night before. Schuyler's reproach to the lover is also a defense of the truth-telling urge of his own poetics of sexual acceptance:

> Words' meanings count, aside from what they weigh:
> poetry, like music, is not just song.
> I do not always understand what you say.
>
> You would hate, when with me, to meet by day
> What at night you met and did not think wrong.
> What is, is by its nature, on display.

Reticent though it is, this is a poem in defense of "coming out":

> I am as shy as you. Try as we may,
> only by practice will our talks prolong.
> What is, is by its nature, on display.

Schuyler called this villanelle simply "Poem"—a title poets invoke when what they have written seems to them to touch some rock-bottom sense of their own poetics. From this touching classic exercise, and its "naïve" and almost helpless admission that there is no way to keep the wraps on natural "inscapes," it is perhaps no great leap to late Schuyler and his revelations of the banal. Here is one morning's awakening on display:

> I'm no good at interpreting
> dreams. Hands fumble with clothes, and just at the delirious
>   moment I wake up:
> Is a wet dream too much to ask for? Time for a cigarette. Why
>   are pleasures bad for you?
> But how good the tobacco smoke tastes. Uhm. Blow smoke
>   rings if you can. Or
> blow me: I could do with a little carnal relief. The yard slopes
>   down to a swampy bit,
> then fields rise up where cows are pastured. They do nothing all
>   day but eat:
> filling their faces so they'll have a cud to chew on. I'm not
>   uncowlike myself: life as a
> continuous snack. Another ham-salad sandwich and then
>   goodbye.

This passage is neither so campy as some in Schuyler's writing nor so bittersweet as others, but it can stand as a fairly random sample of the problems raised by Schuyler's later work. Refusing the earlier charms of the insistent urgency and phonetic resonance that recalled Hopkins, it finds the humdrum more frequently on display than the momentous; it is suspicious of any transcendental explanation of life; it is relentlessly open to the more ignoble hints and nudges of the body; it is self-deprecating and joky; its flow of consciousness seems uncensored and nerveless.

The reader tempted to indict the later work on the grounds of poetic convention may find, however, a self-indictment waiting in the wings: Who is to say that wet dreams and being blown are ignoble? Is the sublime better than a joke? Are closure and drama indispensable to all aesthetic acts? To a reader enamored of reticence, intellectual phrasing, complex structures, or conspicuous ornament, Schuyler's talky, linear, patchy, pastoral daybooks, with their modest gamut of conversational tones, can seem diffuse and unsatisfying. To the admirer of Whitman, on the other hand, Schuyler can seem Whitman's legitimate heir (though without Whitman's astonishing imaginative flights—"I am stucco'd with birds and quadrupeds all over").

Schuyler's short poems often make an indelible impression. Among "The Payne-Whitney Poems" is one called "What," in which the misery of being confined in a mental hospital—groggy from medication, subject to loneliness and horrible noises, doubting even one's own vocation—is wonderfully and briefly rendered by the fretful questions (summed up in the title) of the first two stanzas. Then an unexpected grace is conferred by the eye's lighting on flowers:

WHAT

What's in those pills?
After lunch and I can
hardly keep my eyes
open. Oh, for someone
to
talk small talk with.
Even a dog would do.

Why are they hammering
iron outside? And what
is that generator whose
fierce hum comes in
the window? What is a
poem, anyway.

The daffodils, the heather
and the freesias all
speak to me, I speak
back, like St Francis
and the wolf of Gubbio.

It is Schuyler's long and honest investigation of how natural species speak to him, and in what human settings, that makes his work worth attention. The opulent landscapes of Darragh Park that have adorned Schuyler's book jackets—dunes, grass, and water on *Selected Poems,* purple loosestrife and rose of Sharon on *A Few Days*—point up the difference between the task, in this respect, of the painter and the poet: the painter trusts his shapes and colors alone to carry the weight of expressive feeling; the poet, even in a nature poem, generally must add some explicit description or analysis of a human situation. The visual speaks so forcibly by itself to Schuyler that he is almost tempted to try the painter's way, and some of his best poems restrain themselves from moral explicitness while presenting a moral insight through patterned and colored shapes. One such poem, "A Gray Thought," sets three natural greens (lilac leaves, lichens, and evergreens) against a gray autumnal sky:

In the sky a gray thought
ponders on three kinds of green:
Brassy tarnished leaves of lilacs
holding on half-heartedly and long. . . .
On a trunk, pale Paris green . . .
lichens, softly colored, hard in durance . . .
And another green, a dark thick green
to face the winter, laid in layers on
the spruce and balsam or in foxtail
bursts on pine in springy shapes
that weave and pierce
the leafless and unpatterned woods.

This is Schuyler's stoic meditation on the ways growth can persist in spite of intellectual bleakness and an absence of summer's patterns (a Stevensian theme par excellence). Life can be maintained by persistence (lilacs), by endurance (lichens), and by new kinds of interest (evergreens). The moral is drawn in painterly ways, rather than in philosophical ones. Each of the three tenacious greens grows on the eye, as the gray upper level closes all three in against a background of aesthetic deprivation—"the leafless and unpatterned woods." And although, as I've said, the theme may be Stevensian, the rhythms here are entirely Schuyler's, as springy as the evergreen shapes, and as vagrant and wayward as the tentative exchanges between instruments in chamber music.

A Schuyler poem almost always cherishes unplanned patterns. The delicate moment of the apparently aleatory, in poetry as in music, is an exquisite effect when it comes off, and can make "planned" poetry seem domineering, just as Schuyler's unemphatic gestures—light, unpossessive, relinquishing—can make others' tones seem melodramatic. Schuyler's romantic impressionism has a morality behind it—a morality of receptiveness and absence of ego:

> The day
> offers so much, holds
> so little or is it
> simply you who
> asking too much take
> too little? It is
> merely morning
> so always marvelously
> gratuitous and undemanding,
> freighted with messages
> and meaning.

The defects of Schuyler's qualities, especially in the long poems, are easy to list—chattiness, inconsequentiality, ingenuousness, banality, campiness. I have read him for years with the partial incomprehension of one less alive to visual effects than he, and one less willing to investigate the aleatory. Yet he can bring even a reluctant reader to admiration. A prose poem about a yard sale, "Used Handkerchiefs 5¢," sums up Schuyler's attractive openness, in which a Wordsworthian "wise passiveness" is rewarded by a treasure unasked for. In the middle of the random chaos of the yard sale (used handkerchiefs—"Clean used ones, of course"—postcards, an old Motorola gramophone) Schuyler sees his companion descend from the "trash-and-treasures loft" with what is to be today's chance sample of beauty:

> . . . a slab of undyed linen its silverness yellowing like a teaspoon from egg yolk, ironed with too cool an iron so the washing crush marks make a pattern over the weave and, above the thick welt of the hem, a cross-stitched border of spruce and juniper unstylized (unless style is simply to choose) in shades of drab that sink in, or emerge from: the hand towel of today, embroidered forty-some maybe years ago.

Hopkins would have liked this writing, with its exquisite texture of letters and sounds, its slipping from description to theory of style, its noticing of visual effects, both accidental (crush marks) and intended (cross-stitching). In this affectionate piece, Schuyler allies himself with an American pastoral aesthetic of the found, the cared-for, and the homemade—with Stevens' Tennessee gray jar and home-sewed, hand-embroidered sheet, with Elizabeth Bishop's doilies and hand-carved flute. "Home-made, home-made! But aren't we all?" says Bishop's Crusoe. Gradually, American poetry has become more authentically a home production, and James Schuyler's life work, now available in this handsome selection, has sought out and often found sights, idioms, and rhythms that are indubitably part of American cultural experience.

8

Imagination Pressing Back

Frank Bidart, Albert Goldbarth, and Amy Clampitt

The imagination—an ingredient as necessary to poetry as rhythm and active language—tends to be a faculty more often invoked than described, more often praised (as present) or lamented (as absent) than explained. It is the mind's pressing back against reality (Stevens), and it often takes the form of a casting beyond: the line of a fisherman or of the spider cast up, out, away, down—"till," as Whitman says, "the gossamer thread you fling catch somewhere, O my soul." The cast may be truly incomprehensible to others (as that of Blake was for a long time), and it is wished on the poet by destiny. The poet can try over a lifetime to expand its reach, to multiply the number of points it goes after, but the essential direction of its search may be as genetically determined as the instructions for the spider's web. The imagination is concerned not only to catch, or catch onto, something but to make its cast elastic, free, athletic, clean-lined, shapely, taut with the aim of the seeking line. What it seeks is the counterpressure to what threatens it. The imaginative cast of each poet can be seen most clearly by comparison. The three poets I compare here—Frank Bidart, Albert Goldbarth, and Amy Clampitt—have all by now defined themselves unmistakably through a series of books.

Bidart's *In the Western Night: Collected Poems, 1965–90* dares to claim as its imaginative terrain the philosophical dialectic of the West, now in disarray. This disarray affects Bidart the way a prolonged estrangement from a lifelong friend would pain someone else. (This is what I mean by the specificity of a poet's imaginative compulsion; Bidart's success or failure rides on how strongly he can make us feel his anguish over philosophical undecidability and power-hungry metaphysical egotism.) In the most ambitious of the new poems collected here, "The First Hour of the Night," Bidart describes yearningly the figures in Raphael's fresco *The School of Athens*, in which, with equable Renaissance symmetry and stability, Philosophy looks at Theology, Poetry faces Jurisprudence. But Bidart announces the end of

> the Neo-Platonic Christian-Humanist
> CONFIDENCE that the world's obdurate
> contradictions, terrifying
> unintelligibility,
>
>   can be *tamed* by CLASSIFICATION.

In a dream vision, Bidart enters the world of the fresco, but a nightmare follows, in which he sees many more figures crowd into the fresco: Descartes, Hegel, Schelling, Comte, D'Alembert, Kant, Luther, Sheherazade, Medusa. Instead of the poised balance of the Renaissance fresco, with Plato pointing up and Aristotle down (idealism countered by materialism), the scene degenerates into one of spitefully warring factions, described in Bidart's characteristically desperate typography:

> —What one thinker confidently
> ASSERTED,
>
>   another *spurned* as ILLUSION—.

Matter disputes Spirit for supremacy: hurrying back and forth between them, philosophical mediators negotiate in distress. Bidart's narration resumes with his central sentence:

> . . . indeed, I felt
> pain at this scene:—to see
>
>   PHILOSOPHY itself

divided, torn
    into three, or even *more* directions—;

. . . the unity of my being
torn.

The nightmare worsens: what had formerly seemed, in each group of
philosophers, a search for truth is now visible as yet another naked claim
to social power, and (after a vision of Christians slaughtering Jews during
the Crusades) Bidart's speaker concludes that the Kantian *"moral law
within"* is nothing but a rationalization of self-interest. That law

    is near to MADNESS—; everything terrible
    but buried in human motivation

    released, justified
        by SELF-RIGHTEOUSNESS and FANATICISM—.

And not only is "Truth" fatally embroiled with power; it is inseparable
from and dependent on historical change.

    These are, of course, postmodernist truisms, and only a device as dra-
matic, and as surprisingly concluded, as Bidart's increasingly phantasma-
gorical nightmare could take us through their dawning on a single mind,
undermining truth, disinterestedness, balance—all the concepts we
think with. As Raphael's Temple of Reason collapses, it swallows the very
structure of Western tradition:

    (—this *'tradition'* that I cannot
    THINK MY LIFE

    without, nor POSSESS IT within—;).

In explaining his agitated typography—seen at its full extent in these
lines—Bidart says (in an earlier interview reprinted at the end of *In the
Western Night*):

    I needed a way to embody the mind moving *through* the elements
  of its world, actively contending with and organizing them. . . .

Punctuation allows me to "lay out" the *bones* of a sentence visually, spatially, so that the reader can see the pauses, emphases, urgencies and languors in the voice.

The effort of reproducing the "mercurial and paradoxical" qualities of the human voice in trauma, and "the *volume* of the voice (from very quiet to extremely loud)," meant that "many words and phrases had to be not only entirely capitalized, but in italics." Bidart has, in short, applied to the page the sort of marks we are accustomed to in musical scores—rests, crescendos and decrescendos, tempo indications, marks for legato and rubato, and so on.

Bidart's longer poems—printed arias for solo voice—have almost always pressed language back against extremity: the suicide of Binswanger's anorexic patient Ellen West, Callas' self-destructive dieting in the service of art, Nijinsky's attempt (ending in madness) to encompass all of the First World War in a dance, and, in an early fictional poem, the feelings of Herbert White, child molester and murderer. Even Bidart's short first-person lyrics catch their speakers in unbearable situations, like the *odi et amo* of Catullus (in Bidart's stylish translation):

> I hate *and* love. Ignorant fish, who even
> wants the fly while writhing.

The torments of flesh and spirit mimed in Bidart's erotic poems and dramatized philosophically in "The First Hour of the Night" find their origin in Bidart's early, family poems, which can now be read, with the wisdom of hindsight, less as the "confessional" poems they once seemed than as the first examples of an obstinate and tenacious dissection of Western conceptuality. Freud was Bidart's original mentor in this anatomy of "reality," with reality, like charity, beginning at home. In the longer run, though, Bidart was after less corporeal game than the Oedipal riddle. His second mentor was Augustine, in whom the autobiographical (Oedipal, guilt-ridden) and the theological are inseparable. The theological is, in fact, the Augustinian "solution" to the Oedipal, and the most tragic moment in Bidart's collected poems turns on his having been unable to find with his own mother what the converted Augustine found with his mother in their common Christianity. In Bidart's "Con-

fessional," Augustine and his mother Monica, their earlier differences re-
solved, stand together ecstatically at a window in Ostia, contemplating
"what the saints' possession of God is like":

> —While they were thus talking of, straining to comprehend,
> panting for this WISDOM, with all the effort
>
> of their heart, for one heartbeat,
>
> they together attained to *touch* it—.

And nine days after the reconciliatory conversation, Monica was dead.
But Bidart's mother, as we see her in his poem, never understood her
life, its two failed marriages, its absence of profession or creativity; she
"felt she was here for some REASON,— / . . . but never found it." And
"Confessional," a modern poem of failed family romance and failed the-
ology, addressed to a psychoanalyst, ends with another intractable *odi
et amo:*

> *Man needs a metaphysics;*
> *he cannot have one.*

"Confessional" articulates epigrammatically the dilemma that issues
full-blown in "The First Hour of the Night": earlier, man could not,
though he needed one, have a metaphysics; now he can see that all previ-
ous systems of metaphysics, from Plato and Aristotle on, are both histori-
cally conditioned and politically self-interested. Most "confessional"
poets remain on the relational and psychological planes; Bidart is com-
pelled—or condemned—to the relational as an instance of the meta-
physical, and even of the theological.

The unsatisfactory homosexual experiences (no more unsatisfactory
than heterosexual experiences) that, together with the Oedipal bond,
provide the ground of Bidart's imagination show us Bidart's voice at an-
other level of suffering. Yet, lest we think that his is a solely masochistic
imagination, two idylls, both translations, suggest what might quiet its
exacerbations. One is the eternal Western fantasy, in Genesis, of a vege-
tarian and nonviolent Paradise; the other is John of the Cross's vision of

the erotic ecstasy that follows the dark night of the soul. Bidart's "Dark Night" is the best translation yet—in terms of independently realized poetic success—of the *noche oscura:*

> Winds from the circling parapet circling
>   us as I lay there touching and lifting his hair,—
>   with his sovereign hand, he
>   wounded my neck—
>   and my senses, when they touched that, touched nothing . . .
>
> In a dark night *(there where I*
>   *lost myself,—)* as I leaned to rest
>   in his smooth white breast, everything
>   ceased
>   and left me, forgotten in the grave of forgotten lilies.

Bidart's rage to be faithful to both sides of his divided nature leads him to pull roughly together—as if to insist on their inseparability—the two actions we disjoin by the words "love" and "sex"; he is exalted by "love" into quoting Plotinus, and is almost immediately fumbling for sex:

> First, I was there where unheard
> harmonies create the harmonies
>
> we hear—
>
> then I was a dog, sniffing
> your crotch.

Bidart dares us, with his outright bathos, to say if we are any different. Is not the mortifying bathos itself the "truth," rather than either side of the contradiction? In Bidart, extremes are not located on either end of a "decently" extended continuum; they are constantly jammed against each other, making a mockery of the very convention that assigns to them the word "extremes."

Bidart's imagination—to return to the place where I began—puts material desire in the same space as spiritual desire, and not in a Franciscan or Hopkinsian way, as the manifestation of the Platonic One in the many, but, rather, in an Augustinian way, as though the spiritual could find no path for itself except through the starving and gluttoning flesh and its "cauldron of unholy loves." But Bidart's imagination is characterized not only by its content; it is equally recognizable by its vocal motions, its cadenzas, its musical stops and starts (the heartbeats of the mind), its protestations and exclamations, its metaphysical leaps, the pantings of the soul, the uncontrollable erections of the body. Though I have previously invoked bel canto when writing of Bidart's improvisations for solo voice, the recent poetry seems more like oratorio: "'The School of Athens,' a cantata for male narrator and chorus." Deconstructive drama takes on, in Bidart's poem of philosophical collapse, a moral seriousness that it does not always exhibit in its didactic form. No poem can now exist for Bidart which does not question its own moral position-taking. To see oneself as a historically conditioned person of questionable motives and at the same time give lyric pathos to that skeptical vision is a hard task, and yet it is what is being attempted by several honest contemporary poets. Bidart is distinguished among them by his choice of the dramatic monologue, and by the pitch of the extremities that drive his imagination.

Albert Goldbarth is not, as Bidart is, a moral extremist. But, like Bidart, he is troubled by his historical position, and moves restlessly through the past, trying to see, on the one hand, its most unrepeatable specificities and, on the other, what, if anything, it exhibits in the way of similarity to contemporary reality. If the human "fraction" (Melville's term) is always searching tirelessly for its other half, as in Plato's myth, Goldbarth exhibits that search. More than once, he imagines the myth alive in himself. The attempt we all make, he says in his 1986 volume *Arts & Sciences*, is

> to be the wheel Plato says
> we all were in the days when man and woman formed a single-
> bodied
> being rolling breezily over the world.

      ... I
only know I've walked the darkness wanting more than any
Stonehenge to align with something bright. And then the lunar
dole of remnant sunlight touched me—here: an x between
the shoulderblades, those made-for-raising things. They stirred.
    Not
wings, no. More like the fossils of wings.

The title *Arts & Sciences* is true to the burrowing inquisitiveness that leads Goldbarth to read about everyone from the Egyptians to Madame Curie, and to speculate on past culture. His recent book, *Popular Culture*, faces up to the other primal material of his imagination—pop culture, the earliest source of the rich multiplicity that appeases the collector in him. In "novelties," comic books, and advertising he finds his first ripe satisfactions. He goes with his father, year after year, to a trade show at the World Trade Center, and finds enumeration crossed with nascent sex:

> Miss Cherry Harvest of 1954 is savvily bing-bedecked
> in snug red mounds of endorsement. Miss Home Hardware
> overflows a gray bikini-top (done as a wingnut). Miss
> Asbestos Insulation. Miss Kosher Franks. The Aluminum
> Siding Queen of 1957.

Though Goldbarth is now compelled (by women's liberation and his own reluctant adulthood) to imagine how Miss Home Hardware et al. actually *felt* (some loved the exposure, some hated the debasement), his ideological correction can't quite outdo the spell of the cornucopia of pop culture and its imaginary and buoyant transformations:

> We hate you. We're telling you now: we're ashamed,
> Miss Amalgamated Canning Concerns, Miss Taxidermy, Miss
>   Soybean Dealers. . . .
> We value you, with incredible passion. Miss Loosened Burnoose
> in the Deepening Desert Sunset, Miss Tonsils, Miss Lesbian
> Love, Miss Verdigris Glimmering Beautifully On A Hull Though
>   No One Sees It . . .

Do you
miss us? Miss Us. Miss You.

These few excerpts have to stand for the hundred-plus lines of the poem "The World Trade Center." Loquacity is a part of Goldbarth's act; his rhetoric is eager to mirror the number of things the world is full of, the unexpected fulfillments it holds in its arms. Goldbarth is a comic poet, and though his seriously undertaken and undeniably grieving poems on the deaths of his parents elicit sympathy, they don't bring forth his best tones, which are those of childlike absorption and of joy in plenty. He has, and understands, the true collector's mania. In one of his best poems ("Neologisms," from *Arts & Sciences*) we hear Darwin speaking in the *exaltatio ad absurdum* of the collector:

> One day, on tearing off some old bark, I
> saw two rare beetles, and seized one in each hand; then I saw a
> third and new kind, which I could not bear to lose, so that
> I popped the one which I held in my right hand into my mouth.

The zoological adventurousness of a Darwin, the devotion unto death of a Marie Curie, the choreographic inventiveness of a Loie Fuller, the heroism of the explorers who found the source of the Nile, the tenacity of a Champollion deciphering the Rosetta stone—these are for Goldbarth the exemplary virtues. They represent the imagination resisting the limitations of the known, and casting forth from the self into the uncharted: the direction of the cast and its cost do not matter; the imagination to conceive such a cast does.

The other half of Goldbarth's imagination hasn't yet, I think, found its adequate embodiment. It is what is usually called religious, and it leans toward New Age superstitions: that we have had past lives (he mentions examples of nonmusical mediums who wrote Schubert pieces, of nonarcheologist mediums who knew what human uses certain nameless prehistoric stone lumps had been put to); that there is a collective unconscious (he invokes Jung and mandalas); that one can address at least the possibility of angelic messengers and miraculous coincidences. Behind these casts of the imagination in Goldbarth (always accompanied by skeptical misgivings) lie the religious convictions of his childhood and his cousin's tales of the Baal Shem Tov (retold in his 1990 book of essays, *A Sympathy of Souls*). Goldbarth contemplates the religious imagination with an uncomplicated nostalgia—the enviable preserve, perhaps, of those to whom the religion of their parents has done no damage. Unlike Bidart, he does not interrogate religious sentiment with respect to what it may have produced in the way of mendacity, hatred, or oppression in the past. Goldbarth's tenderness toward the mystical does not, however, vitiate his enormous curiosity, or the momentum of his zest, or his sympathy of souls with the historical personages he resuscitates.

Here, for instance, are his urgent attempts to understand the withdrawal and chill felt by Mary Shelley (daughter of William Godwin and Mary Wollstonecraft) after her husband's drowning:

> As if the death of her mother
> 10 days after childbirth; and that ever-receding
> interest of the dispassionate father; and Fanny's
> laudanum suicide; and Harriet's
> drowning suicide; and the death of her own first
> daughter "less than two weeks, only"; and Willy
> gone, and Clara gone, reduced to two already
> lusterless locks in an album—weren't enough.
> So now the Gulf took
> him, too. No wonder she needed retreating,
> no wonder Trelawny once joked they should seat her
> at table "to ice the wine."

Unlike Bidart, who moves Augustine and Monica into his own metaphysical story, Goldbarth moves himself into Mary Shelley's historical life. Where Bidart spaces his minimalist sentences of confusion and distress far apart across the page, Goldbarth's montage here speeds up a woman's life into a cruel set of obituaries. This is at once Goldbarth's strength (his historical and fictional sympathy) and his weakness. He settles, perhaps too rapidly, into an unexamined ratification of his own choices (to remember life-affirming moments, to communicate across the static of distance and alienation), scanting the scathing self-examination so patent in Bidart. Nostrums—true and soothing ones—spring to Goldbarth's lips; I blame him not for thinking of them but, rather, for not finding better words for them. He recalls, for instance, the happier time when Shelley and Mary Shelley knew the intensity of early marriage and of writing to each other:

> I
> don't know if it sufficed.—And don't know what
> abiding strength
> a time of vital commonality provides, against
> the decimating powers. Maybe little. But it's all
> we can do, so should do—she did.

The clichés here ("abiding strength," "vital commonality") are drawn from an enfeebled religious language.

Goldbarth does much better when he finds a striking image for what he stubbornly clings to, the residue of religious faith. "That preliterate place faith comes from" is the subject of "Again," a poem on the death of Goldbarth's father, in which the poet finds himself, at his father's bedside, repeating like a mantra the words "Don't let him die." He recalls the age-old belief in the efficacy of pure repetition as prayer, and, characteristically, appends a historical incident:

> So I thought of Japan,
>
> the *Sheet of 1,000 Buddhas:* how a single woodblock stamp has
> meant
> so many duplications of the same small holy figure—each,
> its nimbus; each, its dole of glow to keep back its commensurate
> dole of benightedness. They finally make a pattern each is
> lost in: each a quantum of light, in light. In fact in 770 A.D.,
> the Empress Koken commanded one *million* prints of a
> Buddhist charm
> be stamped by copper blocks, "to ward off illness" says the story,
> which is
> this story as well.

Charms for the spiriting back of the dead (among the dead being Goldbarth's own child-self at ten or thirteen) besprinkle *Popular Culture.*

Even dead words are seduced back. A Sherlock Holmes poem lingers over words in the process of disappearing:

> *Landau* clattered by for the last time. *Brougham*
> followed close behind. These carriages . . .
>
> [would] never return to an *ostler,* never again. And he
> would never cumbersomely buckle into his *ulster.*
> Would people seek "lodgings" some time, announcing
>   themselves
> by "calling cards"? And what of "jollification,"
> what of "apoplexy"—both these bisque-red
> flushings of the cheeks were disappearing.

In the way certain poets care about the natural world, Goldbarth cares about the linguistic world, slowly vanishing into unintelligibility and extinction of species unless rescued by a Champollion or a poet.

The typical procedure of a Goldbarth poem, which gives it its quick, at first unsettling, transitions, is to keep two or three stories in mind at once, each of them somehow an analogue or a contradiction of another. In "Again," hoping against hope for his dying father's survival, Goldbarth recalls a story concerning a Japanese sailor shipwrecked on a coral reef in 1784; at the end of the poem, we learn that the bottle with the sailor's farewell message in it washed up a hundred and fifty years later, against all odds, on the beach outside the Japanese village where he was born. In between, there are stories of Goldbarth's divorce and of the night nurse's estranged husband as well as the passage about the Empress Koken and her million Buddha prints. As we read, we live, temporarily, in the restless and eccentrically furnished mind of the writer sitting at his father's bedside trying to account for his own unwilled chant, "Don't let him die."

Normally, lyric poetry longs to purge itself of the circumstantial, but Goldbarth resists that tendency. He is willing to go down with his ship and its cargo; if its almost random freight sinks it, he will sink with it, but he hopes that his message will, in any case, wash up on his native shores. His patient and exact salvaging of the past will move many read-

ers, who will remember, with him, in "Powers," the popular culture of
his boyhood:

> I read
> by flashlight under the covers: City Hall was being burgled
> of its Gems of the World display, and Captain Invincible faced
> a Mineral Ray (that already turned 2 bank guards and a porter
> into clumsily-rendered crystalline statues) . . .

> The Dynamo
> could will himself into a wielder of electrical jolts, and even
> invaders from Alpha-10 were vanquished. . . .

> I wasn't Me but
> an inchoate One of Them. With their Wave Transmitter
>   Wristlets,
> with their wands, their auras, their cowls. The Insect Master.
> Blockbuster. Astro Man.

The boy diving under the covers to lose himself in these conquering fic-
tions is attempting to forget the dismaying present, as we discover when
the poem ends. In a humiliating incident from the barely marginal life
his parents keep afloat, the boy hears his father heroically explain to the
landlady that he doesn't have the week's rent. The almost mindless obses-
siveness of a ten-year-old boy's fantasy justifies itself against the terrors
of a renter's world.

Goldbarth's poems still play out that earliest set of defenses. Horror
and death in the present set his responses spinning to the past, to reli-
gious speculation, to historical virtue, to fortifying stories, to art—to any
of its refuges: "Words / with one foot over the precipice, / called back /
to bodies again." What would happen if Goldbarth refused his sideways
skittering into myth, history, science fiction, and popular culture, and
faced, without eventual recourse to memory, the meanness of the here
and now and the relative impotence of the imagination? Perhaps it is the
very condition of his reclamatory profusion that he cannot.

It is metaphysics, as I have said, on which Bidart falters; metaphysics will not give him a stable, disinterested, and transhistorical "Truth," so he flees to the ethical realms of memory, loss, guilt, and the burdens of the past. But the spiritual impossibility of subsisting only on the frustrations of human connection sends Bidart's imagination back, again and again, to beat its wings against more stringent and absolute questions of truth and falsehood, eternity and time, politics and power. It is death and historical transience at which Goldbarth falters, turning away from them to other realms, alternative multiverses, hyperspace. Yet his imagination returns, compelled, to the black holes into which his fantastic creations, however elaborate, are relentlessly drawn.

For Amy Clampitt, landscape is the refuge to which, for its serenity, its visual variety, its biological laws, she turns in order to resolve questions of sexual identity, of unsatisfactory family relations, of the expectations of society, of the history of Iowa (whence she fled, in her twenties, to Greenwich Village). Reading, of course, was one resource of this bookish child, but nothing in her reading—not even Andersen or the Greek myths—ever gave her the pure wordless solace of the earth's changing sights and sounds.

Landscape was for Clampitt the first aesthetic realm, and in a central poem, "The Field Pansy," from her collection, *Westward,* she tells the story of all aesthetic people dismayed to discover that the beauty that so assuages and reassures them does absolutely nothing for someone else:

> Life was hard in the hinterland, where spring arrived
> with a gush of violets, sky-blue out of the ground of the
>   woodlot,
> but where a woman was praised by others of her sex for being
> Practical, and by men not at all, other than in a slow reddening
> about the neck, a callowly surreptitious wolf-whistle: where the
>   mode
>
> was stoic, and embarrassment stood in the way of affect:
> a mother having been alarmingly seen in tears, once only
> we brought her a fistful of johnny-jump-ups from the garden,
> "because you were crying"—and saw we'd done the wrong
>   thing.

The second stanza here is the final one of the poem, and, though all the others have five lines, it has only four, because the mother's rebuffing response shocks the child (and the later poet) into silence, represented by an aborted line of stifled feeling.

What, then, is the use of beauty, if it can heal oneself but not others? "What difference do the minutiae / of that seeming inconsequence that's called beauty / add up to?" It seems to Clampitt that some beauty-diffusing impulse in the universe itself is in question, an impulse that strews the earth with all the evolutionary varieties of pansy enumerated in the poem:

> . . . a gathering, a proliferation
>
> on a scale that, for all its unobtrusiveness, seems to be
> worldwide, of what I don't know how to read except as an
> urge to give pleasure . . .
>
> I know I'm leaving something out
> when I write of this omnipresence of something like eagerness,
>
> this gushing insouciance that appears at the same time capable
> of an all but infinite particularity.

Clampitt admires Hopkinsian inscape without seeking (as Hopkins often did) the best sunset, the most striking cloudscape, the most boister-ous weather. Her poetry crosses Hopkinsian "gush" ("He gushes, but he means it," a schoolmate of Hopkins said) with a Wordsworthian appreci-ation of the common and the unobtrusive: the field pansy is a cousin of the "violet by a mossy stone, / Half hidden from the eye."

In her Maine poems Clampitt notices the recrudescent mosses and sundews, everyday plants, as a stay against decay, and admires, in "High Noon," an elderly woman who is still bestowing, however faded herself, unfaded flowers on the young. The poem ends by reflecting on a photo-graph of the elderly woman in her youth:

> When the sun
> leaves the zenith (if it ever does) of that

> monochrome, it will utter its frivolous last
>   gasp in a smother of roses.

"Frivolous," perhaps, to those who do not understand a death accompanied by roses rather than by prayers, but a sentiment not unknown to Ronsard, watering a rose tree on a young girl's grave, *"Afin que vif et mort ton corps ne soit que roses"* ("So that, alive and dead alike, your body be naught but roses").

Violets and roses are the luxuriant, bright side of Clampitt's imagination, pressing back against the inhumanity of the social order. (Clampitt's father was a Quaker, and her first book included a poem in memory of a self-immolated Quaker martyr protesting the war in Vietnam.) In *Westward*, the symbol of social disorder is not war but the modern city. Clampitt's indictment of New York includes herself among the (relatively helpless) authors of "the general malfeasance." Here is the Dantesque description of "half-stupefied Manhattan" from the sinister opening of the long poem "The Prairie":

> The wind whines in the elevator shaft. The houseless
> squinny at us, mumbling. We walk attuned
> to the colubrine rustle of a proletariat
>
> that owes nobody anything, through a Manhattan
> otherwise (George Eliot's phrase) well wadded
> in stupidity—a warren of unruth, a propped
>
> vacuity: our every pittance under lock and key
> a party to the general malfeasance. Saurian,
> steam-wreathed rancors crowd the manholes,
>
> as though somebody grappled with the city's
> entrails: Laocoön, doomsayer, by a god
> or gods undone.

From the beginning of "The Prairie" in New York City, her own milieu, Clampitt traces, in a long and complicated arc, the parallel stories of her grandfather and Anton Chekhov, born in the same year. Chekhov wrote that the steppe cried out for a bard; Clampitt feels—in spite of her early escape to New York—the obligation to commemorate the prairie past that formed her sense of life. The flight of the poet from the "settled life" of the Midwest community takes place late in the poem, almost anonymously, in a reprise of the opening:

> Dreams of escape: out of the settled life's
> fencerow patrols, into their licensed overthrow:
>
> excess, androgyny, the left wing; anonymity-
> celebrity: escape achieved that's no escape,
> the waiting misstep, the glassy fjord-leap.
>
> Living anxious. The wind a suicidal howling
> in the elevator shaft. The manholes' stinking,
> steaming entrails. Dreams, now and again,
>
> lopsided fantasies of going back, weak-kneed,
> through the underbrush, and getting even.

Such brief selections from a lengthy poem give only a glimpse of Clampitt's rhythmic adroitness as she mimics the jump-starts and cowerings of the mind. In the end, she pursues the family line back to a house, dimly remembered from a snapshot, of a great-aunt in Pasadena: "The number / not quite right, the tenant an old / deaf Mexican who did not understand." The evanescence of personal history is palpable as the poem closes with the descendant of the homesteader unable to communicate with the Hispanic immigrant. This is a place where the American landscape, ever-changing under the soles of its westward-moving population, cannot give solace. Its failure to provide aesthetic reassurance is coupled with its failure to provide an enduring home for anyone.

Like landscape, femaleness has for Clampitt its disappointments; whatever the ultimate rewards to the contemporary woman artist, she and her forebears—Dorothy Wordsworth, Emily Dickinson—were unsuccessful girls, judged by the common standards of their societies. In "My Cousin Muriel," a cousin of the speaker is dying in California, and old memories arise while death, unspeakable, "stirs like a stone":

> The air of rural Protestant New England
>
>   . . . infused the hinterland
> my cousin Muriel and I both hailed from:

> a farmhouse childhood, kerosene-lit,
> tatting-and-mahogany genteel. "You
> were the smart one," she'd later say. . . .
>
> [She played] the whole trajectory of
> being female, while I played the dullard,
> presaged. She bloomed, knew how to flirt,
> acquired admirers. I didn't.

Clampitt has faced the question of being female before, mercilessly, in her elegy for her mother, "Procession at Candlemas"; here she confronts, in the frightening and frightened poem "A Hedge of Rubber Trees," what she herself might have become, uprooted in New York—a sodden recluse. She recounts her temporary alliance with a displaced eccentric:

> Unclassifiable castoffs, misfits, marginal cases:
> when you're one yourself, or close to it, there's
> a reassurance in proving you haven't quite gone
> under by taking up with somebody odder than you are.

Finally, the acquaintance with the elder eccentric founders. The poet does not excuse her own part in the separation:

> The West Village was changing. I was changing. The last
> time I asked her to dinner, she didn't show. Hours—
> or was it days?—later, she phoned to explain: she hadn't
> been able to find my block; a patrolman had steered her home.
> I spent my evenings canvassing for Gene McCarthy. Passing,
> I'd see her shades drawn, no light behind the rubber trees.
> She wasn't out, she didn't own a TV. She was in there,
> getting gently blotto. What came next, I wasn't brave
> enough to want to know.

Earlier, the recluse had dreamed that her own face in the mirror was "covered over . . . with gray veils." The lethal effacement of the spinster by society, partly because of her inability or refusal to compromise, partly because of the revulsion felt by the sexual for the asexual, is a theme not much treated in poetry. It is there in Clampitt, but unsentimentally; the recluse speaks of her cohort of roaches, "ruefully, as of an affliction that / might once, long ago, have been prevented." Landscape and "beauty" and "art," and even church (where the speaker and the recluse met), are powerless to cope with the disintegrative force of the city.

If, then, Clampitt's imagination at its most stringent cannot rest in landscape (whatever its exaltations), or in solidarity with women, or in institutional remedies, or in art, where will it find an anchor? The title poem of *Westward*, in partial answer, takes Clampitt to the island of Iona, off the western coast of Scotland. She goes there partly because Keats went there, partly because Lycidas drowned in the Irish Sea, partly because Saint Columba "made his pious landfall" there, partly because it is "the raw edge of Europe." On Iona, "the prospect / is to the west." At the same time, "the retrospect / is once again toward the interior." Facing both ways, back to Europe and forward to the New World, Clampitt imagines the dogged wanderings of what one can only call the Western religious imagination, guarding something that will be of use and solace to everyone (as art is not, as sexual identity is not, as even the beauty of the earth is not). Clampitt does not know where to locate the current home of the religious impulse, but she recalls its past, the trail of "the mind's / resistance to the omnipresence of what / moves but has no, cannot say its name." Naming and the religious impulse are for Clampitt (if I understand her correctly) the same. Carrying the Word has led, in the West, to all the "embarkations, landings, dooms, conquests, / missionary journeys, memorials" of human endeavor. *Westward* ends with a brilliantly entropic summary of those Christian journeyings from the Holy Land to Europe and on to the New World:

      Columba
in the skin-covered wicker of that coracle,

lofting these stonily decrepit preaching
posts above the heathen purple; in their
chiseled gnarls, dimmed by the weatherings

of a millennium and more, the braided syntax
of a zeal ignited somewhere to the east,
concealed in hovels, quarreled over,

portaged westward: a basket weave, a
fishing net, a weir to catch, to salvage
some tenet, some common intimation for

all flesh, to hold on somehow till
the last millennium: as though the routes,
the ribbonings and redoublings, the

attenuations, spent supply lines, frayed-
out gradual of the retreat from empire, all
its castaways, might still bear witness.

This Protestant witnessing to the Word is an old theme in American literature, but its belatedness (to use Harold Bloom's word) in "Westward" suggests that its frailty belies its reassurances. Nonetheless, Clampitt insists that the saving Word must be one available to all, not solely to readers of literature or people of one nationality.

Clampitt's formality in her prophetic moments, such as this one, means that her religious moments are estranged somewhat from the lines that speak of roaches and "getting gently blotto" and also from her botanizing lines. She is unwilling to give up on landscape or on the day-to-day (the deathbed journeys, the waits in clinics, the bus rides). Yet, above nature and above the quotidian, her imagination stubbornly aspires to something she cannot locate socially or institutionally, or even aesthetically. This "bearing witness" can be compromised or attenuated by circumstance, but it nonetheless stands all alone, "hugely politic" (Shakespeare's phrase). Clampitt, while recognizing the same tyrannies and historical corruptions in the pursuit of the absolute which so dismay Bidart, preserves a sense of the undamaged conscience reborn among human beings. It is for her a bulwark against the ultimate insufficiency of beauty and history alike. And though the power of her faith in that inner light is unmistakable, she does not always convince this reader of the reliability of a universal Word, reinvented by every culture.

In each of these poets there appears the documentary and autobiographical base that is natural to lyric. Bidart had a mother, and Goldbarth a father, and Clampitt a Cousin Muriel, no doubt; and the "Golden State" (Bidart), and New York and Texas (Goldbarth), and Maine (Clampitt) are all on the real map; and Augustine and the Empress Koken and Dorothy Wordsworth are all retrievable in the libraries. But the fierce torments of "The First Hour of the Night" and the luxuriant defenses of *Popular Culture* and the universal beneficence of natural beauty in "The Field Pansy"—these, as Stevens would say, "had to be imagined . . . / Required, as a necessity requires." Doubt, death, and corruption always threaten the stability of the imagination, which presses back in multiple forms. In these poets the American verse line seems to be getting longer, spreading out even to the margin, as if the imaginative counterpressure against entropy had to be as strong and as broad as possible. This proliferation of language is the reverse of the gnomic Word of religion: "I am who am"; "I am the way"; "My God, My King" (Herbert); "Yea, beds for all who come" (Christina Rossetti); "Yonder" (Hopkins). The "embellishments" of art and the plainness of the saving efficacious Word have always stood in an oblique and perplexed relation to each other. Each of these poets, representing the nostalgic afterglow of our three major religions (Catholic in Bidart, Jewish in Goldbarth, Protestant in Clampitt), declines to forgo the seductions of the absolute. Whether this position of the imagination can be authentically maintained, even if it is widely shared, remains in question.

9

Election and Reprobation

Donald Davie's *Collected Poems*

England and America were once closely allied in poetic life. Both Eliot and Frost published their first books in London, and when *Poetry* was founded in Chicago in 1912, with Pound as its London talent scout, it was as likely to publish W. B. Yeats or Ford Madox Hueffer (later Ford) as William Carlos Williams or Marianne Moore. But as the century wore on, American modernism began to set the poetic tone, and America no longer needed to direct its eyes toward London as the imperial capital of the English-speaking world. America, in short, began to act out the aesthetic rebellion against literary domination which other colonies—Ireland, India, the Caribbean, Africa—have also found necessary.

Modern American poets looking to do an end run around London— and around American Protestantism, too—turned first (as Longfellow had before them) to France and Italy, with notable results in the generation of Pound and Eliot. The brief vogue for Dylan Thomas and W. H. Auden among Americans who came of age in the fifties waned rapidly, and during the sixties most American poets went farther afield for lyric models—to South America, Germany, Russia, and eastern Europe. With the dissolution of the British Empire, English poets had definitively lost what cultural critics would call their literary hegemony. American publishers became less eager to publish English poetry, and American journals less eager to print or review it. In the long run, this may not matter: powerful poets are so thin on the ground in every country and in every generation that, eventually, they are eagerly sought out by readers worldwide. In the short run, though, it means that our young writers are ignorant of notable British models of poetry in English—models useful because culturally different. American readers may literally not know of the existence of a Philip Larkin or a Donald Davie.

Larkin's *Collected Poems* came out posthumously. We are fortunate to have Davie's *Collected Poems* while Davie is still alive. Davie was born in Yorkshire, in 1922, and was educated at Cambridge; his readable and outspoken autobiography, *These the Companions,* takes the reader through his youth, service in Murmansk and Archangel as a communications officer in the Royal Navy during the war years, and his return, after marriage, to the Cambridge of F. R. Leavis. ("*Scrutiny* was my bible, and F. R. Leavis my prophet.") Davie took a Ph.D. at Cambridge, and afterward there were many teaching years: first at Trinity College, Dublin, then at Cambridge, the University of Essex, Stanford, and Vanderbilt. However, his main activity through these years was writing a poetry of mingled fierceness and self-contempt. This curious mixture is what keeps the reader of Davie alert. Davie says in "Puritans," the last chapter of his autobiography, "The Calvinist doctrines of election and reprobation may be false and brutal in every other realm of human endeavour; in the arts they rule. . . . In the arts, as between the genuine and the fake, or between the achieved and the unachieved, there cannot be any halfway house." Even those who agree with him on this point may not be as confident as he in personal judgments of genuineness, or as joyously eager in battle on these issues.

Davie says of himself that "if there is one sort of rhetoric for which I have been fitted by nature as well as nurture, it is the Jeremiad," and he continues:

> I have made a comfortable career out of crying in saturnine tones, "Woe! woe!" or "It is later than you think," or "Things are going from bad to worse." And a whole generation of English writers grew up along with me in this modestly profitable skill. The best of us are those, like Kingsley Amis or Bernard Levin or Anthony Burgess, who mock their own gloomy irascibility even as they articulate it.

Davie's voice—judgmental, ironic, epigrammatic, humorous, self-lacerating—speaks always with reference to an inhuman perpendicular standard that itself goes unquestioned. It is not a standard of Beauty or Truth; Davie is a poet of the third member of the Platonic triad, Justice. Born of Dissenting stock, he distrusts fluency, loquacity, "charm," and permissiveness, and sides with taciturnity, measure, strictness, and law. Yet he himself is often unmeasured, irritable, and quarrelsome, rather than equable, while in another dimension he allows himself to be genial—even "charming." Davie's sense of both public and private sin is the source of his desire for public and private justice. These inner conflicts—as the poet plays both reprobate and judge—give Davie's best poetry its tension, its constriction, and its self-blaming force.

Here, for instance, is a poem of acid self-analysis comparing his behavior with his wife's:

> I assert that such is the case:
> I seem to have more resources;
> I thrive on enforcing the more
> The less naked the force is.
>
> Mutinies, sulks, reprisals
> All play into my hand;
> To be injured and forgiving
> Was one of the roles I planned.

His own roles, planned or not, are baffling enough to Davie to make him cast round for illuminating comparisons of himself with others. One of those others is Piranesi, repetitively drawing his claustrophobic prisons:

> The effect remains, as ever, gaunt and fierce.
>
> Those were his true proclivities? Perhaps.
> Successful in his single narrow track,
> He branches out, but only to collapse,
> Imprisoned in his own unhappy knack,
>
> Which, when unfailing, fails him most, perhaps.

Even Perfection, if it is perfection in a "narrow track," can be judged deficient, and Davie thrashes even against his own double. On the other hand, he finds more heartening doubles, one of them the blind and deaf Helen Keller. It might seem, Davie says, that the twentieth century has abjured language:

> The Gutenberg era, the era of rhyme, is over.
> It's an end to the word-smith now, an end to the Skald,
> an end to the erudite, elated rover
> threading a fiord of words.

And yet Keller stands as an example of one who reclaimed wordlessness with language:

> You were by force of circumstance, by force
> of your afflictions, I suppose, the most
> literary person ever was.
> No sight nor sound for you was more than a ghost;
> and yet because you called each phantom's name,
> tame to your paddock chords and colours came. . . .
>
> You, who had not foreseen it, you endured it:
> a life that is stripped, stripped down to the naked,
> asking what ground it has, what has ensured it.
> Your answer was: the language, for whose sake it
> seemed worthwhile in Tuscumbia, Alabama,
> month after month to grope and croak and stammer.

For Davie as a poet, language is reclaimed only by the "grope and croak and stammer" of those who, following Pound's injunction, try to "make it new."

Davie is frequently grim, about himself and poetry alike, but he can also relish happiness—the happiness of prospective travel, for instance, in "A Spring Song" (with its epigraph from Pope, "Stooped to truth and moralized his song"):

> Spring pricks a little. I get out the maps.
> Time to demoralize my song, high time.

> Vernal a little. *Primavera*. First
> Green, first truth and last.
> High time, high time. . . .
>
> High time and a long time yet, my love!
> Get out that blessed map.
> Ageing, you take your glasses off to read it.
> Stooping to truth, we potter to Montoire.
> High time, my love. High time and a long time yet.

This is one of the more contented marriage poems. Others yield a powerful narrative of a life lived within the mutual devotion and mutual injuries of a long companionship—a difficult narrative to sketch from the inside, especially if the poet subscribes to discretion. "Penelope" is Davie's meditation on constancy in a time of marital "dryness":

> Charity for
> A while; then, grace withdrawn;
> The flow, and then the ebb.
>
> What wove the web
> Now frays it, with as much
> Devotion in each breath.
>
> Long-absent Death
> Veers in the offing; nears
> And goes off, to-and-fro.
>
> And all right, so;
> This being out of touch
> Alone tests constancy.

The epigrammatic distance in such a passage is a legacy from the stubborn astringency of the North, from which Davie comes:

> For one who espouses the North,
> I am hazy about it, frankly. It's a chosen
> North of the mind I take my bearings by,
> A stripped style and a wintry.

One might find this a deflected sort of self-praise if Davie did not add immediately:

> The style is decadent almost,
> Emaciated, flayed. One knows such shapes,
> Such minds, such people, always in need of a touch
> Of frost, not to go pulpy.

The pulpy, the "warm" (in the vulgar sense), and the inner coarseness of a consciously adopted "common touch" are all anathema to Davie; distrusting the organic, the vegetative, and the luxuriant, he prefers the Poundian metaphor of the poem as sculpture. Poems are "a space / Cleared to walk around in":

> Their various symmetries are
> Guarantees that the space has
> Boundaries, and beyond them
> The turbulence it was cleared from.

This is from Davie's "Ars Poetica," an elegy for the sculptor Michael Ayrton. Reluctantly, Davie adds that we are now unlikely to encounter again "the enormous / Louring, resonant spaces / Carved out by a Virgil."

The wish to be spacious in epic panorama has led Davie to his least successful vein—the topical historical poem. Versified meditations out of Francis Parkman and brief biographies of historical personages are so condensed as to be (as similar passages in Lowell sometimes were) unintelligible. Here is an anticipation of Cooper's novels out of Scott, in the poem called "Frontenac":

> Heart of Midlothian, the milky mother
> (Sir Walter's Doric) of sane masterpieces
> Fed at that flaccid udder, Walter Scott,
> Great lax geometer, first plotted them,
> Triangulations that explode
> The architect's box of space, and by a torsion
> As bland as violent sprain
> Narrative time and the archives' single slot.

Verbal torsions and sprains like these sometimes result from Davie's wish to be terse, "plotted," witty. Always, his verse pits rhythm against compression, trying to constrain them into mutual accommodation. When the accommodation works—as in Davie's greatest poem, the self-portrait "In the Stopping Train"—the accomplished grudging voice (halting, like the local "stopping" train) finds its rhythmic equivalent in trimeters bearing a musical rest, or stop, after each line:

> I have got into the slow train
> again. I made the mistake
> knowing what I was doing,
> knowing who had to be punished.
>
> I know who has to be punished:
> the man going mad inside me. . . .
>
> Torment him with his hatreds,
> torment him with his false
> loves. Torment him with time
> that has disclosed their falsehood.
>
> Time, the exquisite torment!
> His future is a slow
> and stopping train through places
> whose names used to have virtue.

This poem of murderous self-accusation exhibits Davie's "emaciated, flayed" style at the height of its powers. But it is not by any means his last self-portrait. Here is a different, more self-forgiving view, in an elegy for his friend Kenneth Millar (Ross Macdonald):

> Walking about the emptied house I
> jangle softly at each heavyish step,
> an old plough-horse, some parts of his harness upon him,
> who strays, tired out but happy with that, through musky
> honey-shot glooms of a barn where, though he
> strays only idly towards it, sweet hay will be found in a crib.

These looser meters of Davie's, accompanied by "the chink of pocketed coins" remembered from his father's similar walks through the house, reflect something less dismal, less tidy, than the self-flogging trimeters of "In the Stopping Train." Davie fears that such relaxation may be merely the sloth of age, but we may also see it as a sign of benignity:

> [Sloth] does no harm; it spares
> The inattentive world
> One more triumphant play
> Out of my one strong suit,
> Sardonic paradox.

Yet, as though to rebuke the dilation of middle-age complacency, Davie entitled his last full collection (based in large part on the Psalms) *To Scorch or Freeze*—those two unlovely Christian visions of the end of the world. Davie's religious adherence (which shifted from Baptist to Anglican) may be incomprehensible to some of his readers, but the vehicles it offers him are old and deep ones for rendering experience. And they provoke new reflections from Davie. Why, he wonders, does the Holy Spirit, represented by Jesus as the Comforter, descend on the apostles as a blast of wind? Davie's poem "The Comforter," the strongest in *To Scorch or Freeze*, represents the Comforter as that wind of alienation and disorientation known to every *déraciné*, to everyone who is "not at home in the grid."

That grid of the ordinary, first felt as home, becomes—to the person fated to be reformer, saint, artist, eccentric—an intolerable Procrustean bed. The first intuition of the *déraciné* is one of a devastating loneliness, the disintegration of "home." Only later will the exceptional person see loneliness as the first sign of vocation, the first breath from the world to which he will eventually belong. Whereas the Father and the Son are perhaps God's "masks / compassionately adapted / to our capacities," the Holy Spirit is frightening:

> And indeed He is the strangest
> of the Three Persons,
> the most estranged. . . .

Integration, fulfilment
have nothing to do with this Person;
cure, or harmony—nothing
like that is intended.

Invasion is His note:
disintegration.
A wind from the outside corners
of the human map;
disorienting;

His strangeness for the comfort
of those not at home in the grid.

A poem as spare as this depends almost entirely on its succession of *mots justes:* "strangest," "estranged," "invasion," "disintegration," "disorienting," "strangeness"—all set off against that resonant and etymologically rich word "comfort." "Stay me with flagons, comfort me with apples"; "The Father . . . shall give you another Comforter"; "Comforter, where, where is your comforting?" As a poem about the wind of poetic inspiration in its devastating instead of its comforting aspects, this ranks as one of the most penetrating analyses of that withering and revivifying wind named by Shelley "destroyer and preserver." To those "not at home in the grid," the lines offer the courage and encouragement of a poet who has encountered the wind and its painful enlightenment.

Much of Davie is perhaps too English for many Americans—his volume called *The Shires,* for instance, summons up in turn each shire in England. Or an American may balk at Davie's unrepentant respect (part of a long quarrel, it's true) for Pound. The mentally ill Pound in the Pisan cage may be a figure of pity, but hardly, as Davie will have it in "Ezra Pound in Pisa," of "excellence":

Excellence is what
A man who treads a path
In a prison-yard might string
Together, day by day,
From straws blown in his path
And bits of remembering.

Yet most of Davie is not inaccessible to Americans, and he should have a place in our anthologies as a remarkable modernist poet. When Davie has been noticed in the United States, it has usually been by other Poundians (a sect unto themselves) or by neo-formalists, those who advocate regular poetic measures as a principle of absolute value, saving the world from the depravity of free verse. Davie, though loyal to a "sculptural" aesthetic, and a frequent practitioner of counted measures, deserves better than these supporters. He has never sequestered himself from experiment in free as well as in formal verse.

Davie has been a notable apologist for Russian poetry; and though his technical debt to Pushkin, Mandelstam, and Pasternak can be judged only by those who know Russian poetry in the original, the elegance and worldly sangfroid of Pushkin can be seen in him, as can Mandelstam's terseness of imagery and Pasternak's capacity for sketching a mood in a few lines. The chief modern British influences on Davie are the awkward but unyieldingly honest Hardy (on whom Davie has written with passion and discernment), Yeats (whose trochaic trimeters Davie has transformed into something far more spondaic, angular, and resistant), and Auden (whose political poetry resonates through all modern British verse). If Davie cannot reach the yielding, pliant, glowing strength of poetry at its most incandescent, he at least knows clearly where he stands, rebuking the aesthetic dance as "always / a self-abuser, glassed / in the pond of its own procedures." Yet he immediately contradicts his own disapproval, granting that sometimes, "God-induced," the dance "shakes free and runs loose . . . to high meadows." If his rhythms are more punitive than liberating, his poetic intelligence more abrasive than sympathetic, these characteristics make his pages more purely his own. In "Brantôme" he runs through the words by which he will symbolically describe himself before we can use them against him: "rarefied," "severe," "four-square," "austere," "fierce." We can urge against him a line from his own "Abbeyforde": "Clement time brings in its / Amnesties."

Fine though it is to have Davie's *Collected Poems,* it is a crime that the University of Chicago Press has not provided the book with an index of titles and first lines. Has there ever before been a modern *Collected Poems* stinted of such things?

10

A World of Foreboding

Charles Simic

Charles Simic's riddling poems, for all that they reproduce many things about his century (its wars, its cities, its eccentrics, and so on) in the end chiefly reproduce the Simic sieve—a sorting machine that selects phenomena that suit Simic's totemic desire. There is no escape hatch in a Simic poem: you enter it and are a prisoner within its uncompromising and irremediable world:

> The trembling finger of a woman
> Goes down the list of casualties
> On the evening of the first snow.
>
> The house is cold and the list is long.
>
> All our names are included.

This short poem, entitled "War," from the collection *Hotel Insomnia* (1992), exhibits all the hallmarks of the Simic style: an apparently speakerless scene; an indefinite article establishing the vagueness of place and time—"a woman" somewhere, anywhere, on a wintry evening; then a menacing definite article focusing our gaze, in this instance on "the" list; then a late entrance of the personal pronoun engaging the speaker's life and ours. This coercive poem of war excludes everything else that might be going on in "real" wartime (people eating, drinking, going to school, manufacturing guns, and so on) in favor of a single emblem—the domestic Muse enumerating the many war dead—followed (as in emblem books) by a motto underneath: "All our names are included." The motto broadens the emblem from the war dead to all dead.

Thus, Simic's poems, even when they contain a narrative, can almost always be "folded back" into a visual cartoon accompanied by a caption. I say "cartoon" at this point rather than "emblem" because Simic is a master of the mixed style, with vulgarity cheek by jowl with sublimity. Simic's interesting memoir of his youth, "In the Beginning," included in his collection of essays called *Wonderful Words, Silent Truth* (1990), suggests that both the working-class origin of his joking and hard-drinking father and the middle-class origin of his musical mother exerted Oedipal claims on his sensibility. The poems abound in working-class litter, both rustic and urban: pigs, kitchens, newspapers, dishes, gum machines, butchers, sneakers, condoms, grease; but they also exhibit the furniture of the maternally espoused ideal realm—monarchs, clouds, angels, Madonnas, martyrs, palaces, and saints.

Simic's work demands that we cohabit with both classes, with pigs and angels alike. "To think clearly," he says in the poem of that name in *Hotel Insomnia,* "What I need is a pig and an angel." Then the fate of the pig and the task of the angel are sketched in:

> The pig knows what's in store for him.
> Give him hope, angel child,
> With that foreverness stuff.

This is where some will part company with Simic. "I don't mind admitting that I believe in God," he said in an interview almost twenty years ago (reprinted in *The Uncertain Certainty* of 1985), and although the injunction to the "angel child" has a good deal of irony attached, Simic cannot do without the presence of the angel. To describe the world as it is, without the backdrop of the ideal, is to be a collaborator in the world's injustice. As Simic says to his angel, "Don't go admiring yourself / In the butcher's knife / As if it were a whore's mirror." The butcher and the pig alone do not a poem make.

Simic's mockery is aimed at the pig, the angel, and himself; the sardonically comic side of his nature alternates with the remorselessly bleak. Life is a vulgar joke; life is tragedy. Perhaps for one who as a child saw World War II in Yugoslavia, life will always be overcast by horror; yet for one who escaped destruction, life will also seem charmed, lucky, privileged. Simic is not unaware of appetite, relish, and gusto. Yet it is in the coercive nature of his writing, as I have described it, that I find the deepest truth about him: "I have you trapped and you can't get out." Think how different from his the lyrics of Wordsworth or Keats are, always leading you from hill to vale, from bower to nook. In them, alternative universes abound, with elbowroom, legroom, headroom; styles meander, migrate, elevate you high and beckon you low. Attention tightens and slackens, lyric solos are followed by choral effects (as in the "Grecian Urn"). All of these fluidities disappear in Simic. An unbearable tension darkens the air. "No one is to be let off," says the punisher. No air. Few windows. No key. Minimal furniture; the bread is stale. The view is circumscribed.

I deduce that this was Simic's fundamental experience of the world for so many years that he was destined to immortalize himself by finding a form that reproduced it exactly, as in this extract from *The Book of Gods and Devils,* (1990):

> Outside, the same dark snowflake
> Seemed to be falling over and over again.
> You studied the cracked walls,
> The maplike water stain on the ceiling,
> Trying to fix in your mind its cities and rivers.

The persistence of the definite article marks this symbolic scene as an iconic one, to be exfoliated into poem after poem. Simic has been annoyed that critics have spoken of his works as "parables," saying, in *The Uncertain Certainty,* "I don't write parables. If I say 'rats in diapers,' that's to be taken literally." Simic's inclination is indeed to present deeply literal details, but they take on parabolic or emblematic significance because so much has been erased in order to isolate those details in a glaring beam of pitiless interrogation. The first poem in *Hotel Insomnia* reads, in its entirety, as follows:

EVENING CHESS

> The Black Queen raised high
> In my father's angry hand.

Like many other Simic poems, this one depends on a verbless sentence fragment, its past participle suspending forever the father's wrath. Everything else has been suppressed—the chessboard, the table, the mother, the brother, the father's face; we are not told the motive for, or the object of, the father's anger. The largest suppression of all is that of the frightened little boy sitting opposite the angry father. Perhaps we are to understand that the parents are quarreling. Or perhaps the father is angry at his son. In any case, the cowering child, so fully implied and necessary to the scene, is effaced except in his personal pronoun, and the hand grows immense as it occupies the whole world of the poem. The poetics that generates such a poem, dependent on a single detail, is one of ruthless extirpation. What remains on the page is monumentalized, pregnant with signification, a cartoon "hand" that all by itself can be "angry."

The two books of poems under scrutiny here, while preserving Simic's coercive style, vary its content. *The Book of Gods and Devils* is often autobiographical, sometimes covertly (as is Simic's wont) but at other times overtly so. There is, for example, a touching glimpse of Simic's first reading of Shelley in a "dingy coffee shop" in New York: the poem alternates between urban wreckage—drunks, the homeless, broken umbrellas—and the visionary reaches of Shelley's social prophecies:

> How strange it all was . . . The world's raffle
> That dark October night . . .
> The yellowed volume of poetry
> With its Splendors and Glooms
> Which I studied by the light of storefronts:
> Drugstores and barbershops,
> Afraid of my small windowless room
> Cold as a tomb of an infant emperor.

What distinguishes this excerpt, and makes it something more than a reminiscence of adolescent idealization juxtaposed with urban banality, is the presence of two startling phrases—"the world's raffle," and "the tomb of an infant emperor." Neither of these is at all expectable, and one halts in coming to them as before a surrealist effect. Neither is strictly speaking surreal; both can be parsed into sense. But the essentially lawless nature of Simic's imagination, darting against his coercive structures, is continually escaping the very prisons he has himself built.

A comparable poem of adolescence ("Crepuscule with Nellie") chooses as its moment of escape the writer's unearthly sense of joy while listening to jazz at the Five Spot; there follows a jolting comedown at closing time, with "the prospect of the freeze outside," and the disappearance (no doubt because her partner found the jazz more interesting) of the Nellie of the title. But the autobiographical reach of *The Book of Gods and Devils* goes back further than adolescence. There are also reminiscences stemming from Simic's wartime childhood ("We played war during the war, / Margaret. Toy soldiers were in big demand"). One of the best of these, "The Wail," recounts, I believe, the arrest of Simic's father by the Gestapo, recalled in the memoir "In the Beginning" (collected in *Wonderful Words, Silent Truth*):

> One night the Gestapo came to arrest my father. This time I was asleep and awoke suddenly to the bright lights. They were rummaging everywhere and making a lot of noise. My father was already dressed. He was saying something, probably cracking a joke. That was his style. No matter how bleak the situation, he'd find something funny to say. . . .
>
> I guess I went to sleep after they took him away. In any case, nothing much happened this time. He was released.

Here is "The Wail," complete, in which the atmosphere of that night is recreated. The child Simic, his brother, and their mother wait to see if the father will return:

> As if there were nothing to live for . . .
> As if there were . . . nothing.
> In the fading light, our mother
> Sat sewing with her head bowed.
>
> Did her hand tremble? By the first faint
> Hint of night coming, how all lay

Still, except for the memory of that voice:
Him whom the wild life hurried away . . .

Long stretches of silence in between.
Clock talking to a clock.
Dogs lying on their paws with ears cocked.
You and me afraid to breathe.

Finally, she went to peek. Someone covered
With a newspaper on the sidewalk.
Otherwise, no one about. The street empty.
The sky full of gypsy clouds.

Simic here shows us nothing followed by nothing; fading light, coming night; stillness, silence, suspended breath; fear, no one about in an empty street. This is the classic Simic: a landscape or a room full of vague menace, a sinister light hovering above a clustered huddle of victims. The wail as title and caption is the unheard melody of the scene.

Though there are "persons" serving as dramatis personae or addressees in some of these poems—the "Nellie" of the jazz bar, the "Margaret" of the toy soldiers, a "Martha" here, a "Lucille" there, these women, otherwise unidentified, seem to serve only as rhythmic pretexts in a line—"Bite into [the tomatoes], Martha"; "Better grab hold of that tree, Lucille"—and have none of the human power of the mother and her terrified children in "The Wail." I'm not clear about Simic's purpose in resorting to these women's names as vocatives of address; they seem inert, pointless, and in some odd way useless to the poem. Their colorful particularity seems an affront to Simic's bleached-out negations; but they may be his way of affirming the verbal color of life even in the absence of situational color.

In *The Book of Gods and Devils,* for all the fascination of the quasi-realistic scenes retrieved from Simic's childhood and youth, it is the poems of slightly surrealist malice that still seem to me Simic's best. I can give only one example, for reasons of space: it is his Black Mass parody of the religious quest, called "With Eyes Veiled":

First they dream about it,
Then they go looking for it.

The cities are full of figments.
Some even carry parcels.

Trust me. It's not there.
Perhaps in the opposite direction,
On some street you took by chance
Having grown tired of the search.

A dusty storefront waits for you
Full of religious paraphernalia
Made by the blind. The store
Padlocked. Night falling.

The blue and gold Madonna in the window
Smiles with her secret knowledge.
Exotic rings on her fat fingers.
A black stain where her child used to be.

This poem displays Simic's characteristic anticlimaxes of disappoint-
ment falling after line breaks: we see icons "Made by the blind. The
store / Padlocked." This is deflationary, but worse is to come. The degra-
dation of the Madonna into fallen woman, "exotic rings on her fat fin-
gers," is followed by the macabre replacement of Innocence by "a black
stain." The successive images here—each one worked, significant, mem-
orable—are "locked into" their respective lines by their placement. Sim-
ic's alternation of full sentences and sentence fragments mimics the ac-
quisition of knowledge: an original main-clause existential statement ("A
dusty storefront waits for you"; "The . . . Madonna smiles") is followed
by one or more short "takes" of perceptual noun-phrase noting: a pad-
lock; dusk or exotic rings; a black stain. Once one has felt the point of
these placements—both the anticlimactic line-break ones and the "no-
ticing" noun-phrase ones—the poem is by no means exhausted; the se-
mantic freight of its "paraphernalia," the implications of words like "se-
cret," "fat," and "stains," send forth ripples of suggestion in ever-
widening circles. The achieved Simic poem is itself often a "black stain"
of innocence destroyed, and, like a stain, it spreads and deepens.

 Hotel Insomnia, the volume following *The Book of Gods and Devils,*
reminds us that Simic (as he tells us in "In the Beginning") suffers from

"lifelong insomnia." This book is more an evolving sequence than a collection of separate poems. What makes it a sequence is the inscribing, on every page without exception, of several words from the repeated epistemological master list that forms a backdrop to the whole. The accompanying table shows the words comprising the master list, and the rough categories into which they fall.

Like Trakl, Simic moves counters such as these into new configurations within each poem. Each poem becomes a new chess game, but the pieces are often invariant. Here is "Romantic Sonnet," played with some twenty of the magic counters, which I have underlined:

> *Evenings* of sovereign clarity—
> *Wine* and *bread* on the *table,*
> *Mother* praying,
> *Father naked* in *bed.*
>
> Was I that skinny *boy* stretched out
> In the field behind the *house,*
> His *heart* cut out with a *toy knife?*
> Was I the *crow* hovering over him?
>
> *Happiness,* you are the bright *red* lining
> of the *dark winter coat*
> Grief wears inside out.
>
> This is about myself when I'm *remembering,*
> And your *long insomniac's* nails,
> O *Time,* I keep *chewing* and *chewing.*

After reading sixty-six pages in which words like these are heard again and again, chiming with and against each other, one has a comprehensive picture of the mind in which they keep tolling. Simic's world has aged. About one poem in three has something old in it—an old dog, a blind old woman, old snow, shoes grown old, a crippled old man, an old cemetery. In Simic's insomniac nights, the world shrivels, wrinkles, dwindles, both physically and metaphysically. The fly on the pale ceiling enlarges its sinister web, the meadows themselves become a theater of cruelty,

Closure	_Menace_	_Home_	_Nature_
evening	black	father	rain
dark	scream(ing)	child	fire
shadow	red	table	cloud
empty	match	mother	moon
sleep(less)	deaf	door	view
insomnia	blood(y)	wall	sky
death	flame	room	flowers
silent(ce)	unhappy	mirror	eternity
shuffle	candle	corner	time
secret	strange	love	light
night	cross	dream	wind
winter	white	happy	morning
end	list	house	sun(light)
snow	blind	book	sea
afternoon	long	window	leaves
late	fallen	bed	woods
storm	broken	coat	bird
fate	chilly	name	quiet
unknown	dumb	roof	beautiful
whisper	pale	watch	truth
	mute	scribble	infinite
	strange(r)	pencil	life
	greasy	memory	world
	knife	wine	golden
	chewing	boy	day
	slaughter	toy	air
	scream	kiss	
	spike	doll	
	funeral		

Body	_People_	_City_	_Subhuman_
hand	old men	hotel	fly
naked	murderer	street	spider
eye	old woman	sidewalk	web
head	prisoner	city	mice
fist	fortune-	(dime-)store	crow(ing)
heart	teller	window	pig
mouth	poet	building(ers)	dog
hair	nun	ceiling	
breasts	homeless	prison(er)	
tongue	preacher	school	
	glove	cage	
	shoe	shop	
		shutter	
		glass	

children and pigs alike are led to slaughter, a nun carries morphine to the dying.

Even the poems recording a moment of happiness or appetite—"Country Lunch," for instance—are shadowed by foreboding: "A feast in the time of plague— / That's the way it feels today." *Hotel Insomnia* celebrates the "funeral of some lofty vision," according to "Miss Nostradamus," one of its many seeresses, Muses, and fortunetellers. And the lofty visions go by, in cultural history, almost too fast to count. "Gods trying different costumes / ... emerg[e] one by one / To serve you"; Hellenism, Christianity, and Materialism fuse in "Aphrodite with arms missing dressed as a nun / Waiting to take your order." It is in this sort of philosophical shorthand that Simic sketches the unnerving persistence of the past into the present.

My favorite poem at the moment in *Hotel Insomnia* is a tour de force called "Tragic Architecture." With the reverse prophecy of informed hindsight, Simic now knows what his elementary school classmates became when they grew up—madwoman, murderer, executioner. The potential cruelty of all children is laconically remarked: "The janitor brought us mice to play with." The children have "hearts of stone." And though Simic is a grown man on another continent, he is also forever imprisoned in his past, a boy left behind, forgotten by Time. "Tragic Architecture" is a circular poem, framed by its past/present trees in the wind:

> School, prison, trees in the wind,
> I climbed your gloomy stairs,
> Stood in your farthest corners
> With my face to the wall.
>
> The murderer sat in the front row.
> A mad little Ophelia
> Wrote today's date on the blackboard.
> The executioner was my best friend.
> He already wore black.
> The janitor brought us mice to play with.
>
> In that room with its red sunsets—
> It was eternity's time to speak,

So we listened
As if our hearts were made of stone.

All of that in ruins now.
Cracked, peeling walls
With every window broken.
Not even a naked light bulb left
For the prisoner forgotten in solitary,
And the school boy left behind
Watching the bare winter trees
Lashed by the driving wind.

The achieved musical form of this poem—solitary sentence-quatrain of the "I"; inventory of schoolmates; sentence-quatrain of the "we"; inventory of memory done in the third person—is typical of Simic's studied arrangements. The more extended sentences serve for reverie; the short declarative sentences serve as bricks to build a world. The entire impossibility of jettisoning a wretched past is more starkly exhibited in Simic than in any psychological treatise. Yet he does not treat his past in a "confessional" way; the material, we may say, remains psychologically unanalyzed while being thoroughly poetically analyzed (by image, by placement, by narrative). Simic's stylistic arrangements of experience suggest that tragic memory has found its appropriate architectural form.

It is not surprising, given Simic's gnomic forms, that he found the boxes of Joseph Cornell—mysterious formal arrangements of synecdochic objects—peculiarly congenial. His homage to Cornell's art—*Dime-Store Alchemy* (1992)—could have, as its motto, the closing sentence of one of its prose poems: "The clarity of one's vision is a work of art." Admirers of Cornell's constructions will be drawn to Simic's "versions" of the boxes illustrated here. One Cornell box, for instance, contains a standing doll obscured by a hedge of twigs taller than she is. Needless to say, there could be many "readings" of this silent form, and perhaps only Simic would give this one:

The chubby doll in a forest of twigs. . . .
    A spoiled little girl wearing a straw hat
about to be burnt at the stake.

This prose poem might be better without its final line—"All this is vaguely erotic and sinister"—but Simic likes to embroider mottos under his emblems. It seems to me we would have known that the doll-scene, as he has described it, was both erotic and sinister without being told.

Dime-Store Alchemy offers more, though, than poetic versions of Cornell boxes. It is a book of art theory, full of obiter dicta on how to construct an artwork, a vehicle of reverie, an object that would enrich the imagination of the viewer and keep him company forever. There are reflections on toys, dreams, fetishes, symbolic objects: "Two sticks leaning against each other make a house." Cornell's art of the scavenger is composed out of "the strangest trash imaginable"; it is an invitation to a labyrinth. The successive alternatives offered in the poem "Matchbox with a Fly in It" (deriving from Vasko Popa's "The Little Box," reprinted here by Simic) are as applicable to poems as to Cornell's art-boxes:

> Shadow box [phenomena]
> Music box [the Muses]
> Pill box [Apollo as healer]
> A box which contains a puzzle [poetry as enigma]
> A box with tiny drawers [stanzas; secret contents]
> Navigation box [a directive]
> Jewelry box [poem as ornamental]
> Sailor's box [vital supplies]
> Butterfly box [preserved specimens]
> Box stuffed with souvenirs of a sea voyage [memory and
>   displacement]
> Magic prison [the presentness of the past]
> An empty box [art as illusion]

The reader of any Simic poem has to stop—not to "translate," as I've done in shorthand here, but to feel the individual pressure of each modifying phrase, and to construct the sequential interrelations of the whole. Perhaps the order of some of the phrases above could be shuffled, but the restriction and disillusion of the last two namings in "Matchbox with a Fly in It" make us see them as unalterable parts of its closure. The fly of the title is mortality itself, found inside all the boxes, no matter what their aspectual surface. Simic's fly, like Stevens' blackbird, inserts itself everywhere.

For Simic as for Cornell, "the city is a huge image machine," and Cornell's daily wanderings through New York, picking up cast-off objects which he would transform into his profoundly meditated arrangements, match Simic's own observant walks through streets full of cinemas, penny arcades, stores, vending machines, newspapers, and mirrors. No other book by Simic transmits so strongly as *Dime-Store Alchemy* what New York must have meant to him when he first arrived from Europe— "A poetry slot machine offering a jackpot of incommensurable meanings activated by our imagination. Its mystic repertoire has many images."

Myself, I draw the line at words like "incommensurable" and "mystic," but that is perhaps my loss. I really do find poetry commensurable with life—not "mystic" (which for me would lessen its wonder) but rather entirely within the realm of human power, however rarely that power appears. Chirico is quoted by Simic a few pages earlier, uttering a sentiment with which Simic explicitly agrees ("He's right"): "Every object has two aspects: one current one, which we see nearly always and which is seen by men in general; and the other, which is spectral and metaphysical and seen only by rare individuals in moments of clairvoyance." I could understand such a statement if it were put in terms of ascribed value. After all, a perfectly bad painting is to its maker a beloved object, as it is to some of its viewers (see, for example, Bishop's "Poem," on the bad painting by her great-uncle); and even an unlovely house is someone's castle. Perhaps the ascription of value to any object is a form of "clairvoyance," because objects look different seen with the eye of love or the eye of poetic scrutiny. But Chirico doesn't seem to be talking about this sort of invisible halo, which we all can confer on many objects. No: some other claim is being made here. The "rare individuals" that Chirico and Simic have in mind are artists. But is there some aspect of objects seeable only by artists? And if so, is the right word for such an aspect "spectral"? Or "metaphysical"? And if so, is a reader or viewer then privileged to see this "spectral" aspect through the eyes of the artist? Artists make us see many aspects of being, but none of them seem to me either spectral or metaphysical, nor do I feel admitted to a form of "clairvoyance," in the usual occult sense of that word. I am wary of vaguely mystical claims made for poetry and the other arts—as wary as I am of ethical and civic claims, and of truth claims. There are better ways of making good citizens, or laying down laws of ethics, or providing a defense of truth claims, than lyric poetry. Poems, like all human fabrications, from straw huts to theology, are made to our measure and by our measure, and are not above or beyond us. We do not need to ascribe more to art than we ascribe to unaided human powers elsewhere. Language and paint are not metaphysical and forms are not spectral. Patterning is a universal human act; and even when it is extended to the most complex and imaginative and individual patterning, it is still ours and of us, no more. The wonder of art, for me, is precisely that it does *not* belong to some rare or spectral realm. As Stevens said of the poet, "As part of nature he is part of us, / His rarities are ours."

Simic is still enough of a surrealist to want to claim some realm that is edgily outside nature—in nonsense, in philosophy, in paintings like Chirico's, or in boxes like Cornell's. It probably seems like reductionism to him if a critic wants to describe, in knowable human terms, that edge of unreason, that irrational element of poetry (as Stevens called it). The weird angles and colors of Chirico, his mute and looming forms, do indeed want to intimate a realm other than the known world, and the same is true for Cornell's tiny environments, which the eye enters into and lives within. Perhaps critics are of two kinds: those who rest in the strangeness of such environments and truly regard them as alternate forms of existence—"spectral and metaphysical"—and more empirical critics who will not rest until they find the link between those environments and the human ones from which they sprang. Like others, I prize Simic for his stanzas of the eerily inexplicable (manifested in his wonderfully varied means of menace and his formally laconic manner), but I would be very unhappy if the stylistic imagination in them were not intimately linked to recognizable human predicaments. The Language Poets have sometimes made common cause with Simic, and he with them; but where they are often merely clever, he is clever and horrifying and heartrending. He is also down-to-earth and mockingly skeptical, especially with respect to himself; he never forgets the dime store when he is about his stylistic alchemy. He is certainly the best political poet, in a large sense, on the American scene; his wry emblems outclass, in their stylishness, the heavy-handedness of most social poetry, while remaining more terrifying in their human implications than explicit political documentation. In his plainness of speech, he is of the line of Whitman and Williams, but in the cunning strategies of his forms, he has brought the allegorical subversiveness of eastern European poetry into our native practice. The next generation of political poets will need to be on their mettle if they want to surpass him.

11

American Zen

Gary Snyder's
No Nature

Gary Snyder is more widely known as an ecological activist than as a poet, and indeed the jacket copy on his *No Nature: New and Selected Poems* makes a heavy-handed pitch to the ecologically minded sector of his audience: "We are a people, as this century ends, desperate to recapture the feeling of being at home in the world. *No Nature* offers us guidance along this path. Snyder's poems invite us to observe nature carefully, and to see ecology, bioregionalism, and sustainable culture as intrinsically bound to our own human fate." This offers us Snyder as guru, and it is a role he has not avoided. "My political position," he has written, "is to be a spokesman for wild nature. . . . And for the people who live in dependence on that." Gurus may live by their messages alone, but poets do not. And though Snyder has earned the seriousness of his views, which he presents not only in political debates over the fate of the California landscape, for instance, but also in the example of his own frugal way of living, his moral seriousness by itself would not earn him the title of poet. But he has also changed what we consider the lyric self to be.

Modern dismantlers of the notion of selfhood have pointed out that each of us is less a "unified self" than a site traversed by the discourses to which we have been exposed. The amalgam of multiple discourses in you "is" you; consciousness is coextensive with the languages in which it is conceived. The free-will or constructivist version of this idea gives you some agency in picking and choosing your discourses, whereas the determinist version finds you helplessly passive in your absorption of the discourses of your cultural and environmental moment.

There is an element of plain common sense in all this; of course one's selfhood is bounded by the available discourses of conceptualization during one's existence—a fact that ought to prevent the sort of anachronistic blame that accuses the Bible of "sexism" or Shakespeare of "racism." But a more acute question follows: what would a self that really believed itself to be just a site of crisscrossing transient discourses (and no more than that) sound like when it opened its mouth? It would have to sound both more provisional and more self-effacing than the encapsulated "I" that has represented, successively, the Christian soul, the rationalist self, and the Freudian ego. It would know that it once did not exist, and would soon not exist again; it would be less anxious about the lifelong continuity of selfhood than was, say, Wordsworth. It would have to be self-conscious about the discourse realm in which it was moving at any given moment, and of its exits and entrances as it moved from one realm to another.

Such a self would not regard itself as distinct from other matter in the universe. It would be part of nature, but not in the pantheistic way that projected a soul into nature. Instead, the self would be situated in an unremarkable continuity with other inorganic and organic clusters of natural forms. It would not occupy a position superior to other beings but would see itself in a horizontal landscape, touching other beings left and right. It would know that it constitutes its world by means of its own limited perceptual apparatus, but it would also acknowledge that the world seems to us a solid given thing, and that it impresses itself upon us in realist guise.

What would this sort of selfhood look like in lyric? It would look like Gary Snyder. And how did a poet born in 1930, the contemporary of the confessional poets (Plath, Sexton) and the prophetic poets (Ginsberg, Rich), think up this selfless self and its distinctive style of writing? The complete answer will not appear until we know more of Snyder's life (there is as yet no biography), but the central experience from which his adult poetry derives seems to be his study of Zen Buddhism, both as a young man and then during the twelve years (1956–1968) when he lived mostly in Japan, studying with Zen masters.

Snyder was born in San Francisco, where his father was a housing administrator for the government, but spent his childhood on his parents' "feeble farm" north of Seattle; he suffered from rickets as a child because of his insufficient diet. His father's father had been an organizer for the Wobblies, and it was presumably from that line of the family that Snyder derived his social concern; he still quotes the old I.W.W. slogan, "Forming the new society within the shell of the old." After his parents' divorce, he lived in Portland, Oregon, with his mother, who was a journalist; she sent him to the best public high school, and he won a scholarship to Reed College, where he majored in anthropology and literature, writing a senior thesis on a myth of the Haida tribe of British Columbian Indians. He also taught himself to sit in meditation, and studied Far Eastern culture, to which he had been drawn by Chinese painting: "When I was eleven or twelve, I went into the Chinese room at the Seattle art museum and saw Chinese landscape paintings; they blew my mind. My shock of recognition was very simple: 'It looks just like the Cascades.'"

Even before Snyder graduated from Reed, he had restlessly shipped out from New York as a merchant seaman and had worked as a logger and forest lookout in Oregon. (Pictures of him at every stage of his life show a rangy, lean, handsome, cheerfully smiling and physically fit man handling tools, climbing mountains, and trekking through wilderness.) He went briefly to graduate school in linguistics and anthropology at Indiana, but returned to the West Coast to study Japanese at Berkeley from 1953 to 1956, in order to prepare to study Buddhism in Japan. He turned up regularly at the poet Kenneth Rexroth's open house on Friday evenings, and in 1955 was one of the participants in the famous San Francisco poetry reading that launched the Beat movement. (In 1958, Jack Kerouac put him in *The Dharma Bums* as "Japhy Ryder.") During the years in Japan that followed, he endured the rigors of long hours of sitting, menial work, and listening in cold study halls to lectures by Zen masters.

Snyder came back to America two years after his Zen teacher, Oda Sessō Rōshi, of the Daitoku-ji Monastery in Kyoto, died; convinced that some action in the world was necessary, he decided against the purely contemplative life of study and meditation. In biographical dictionaries he lists his politics as "Radical" and his religion as "Buddhist of the Mahayana-Vajrayana line." He has had four wives, and two sons by the third of these, but this aspect of his life remains obscure; the first three wives do not appear among the more than sixty contributors to the informative 1991 Sierra Club book *Gary Snyder: Dimensions of a Life.* Since 1970, he has lived in California, in the foothills of the Sierras near Nevada City on a hundred-acre tract of remote land that he bought together with Allen Ginsberg and their friend Richard Baker. Though he has taught at both Berkeley and Davis, he has avoided for most of his life regular engagement in the academic world; since 1986, though, he has held a part-time professorship at Davis. (To teach a real poetry workshop, he once said spiritedly, "there would have to be a sauna right there, and a quarter of an acre of garden plot, and a good kitchen, and some musical instruments, and God knows what-all.")

In spite of such moments of mockery, Snyder, as a learned person himself, does not disparage the university; on the contrary, like a good anthropologist, he defines its social function: "The University has the function of reassessing our tradition, our body of lore, every generation. . . . The professors in the English department are like kiva priests, priests of the kiva that we have to go to from time to time to say, 'Now why was it that there are three lines painted at the top of this eagle feather, with a little bit of red fluff on it? Now what was the reason for doing that?' Somebody who keeps that in mind for us." It is because Snyder has read so widely in the canons of East and West alike that he can write, "A great poet does not express his or her self, he expresses all of our selves."

A committee of which I was a member awarded the 1975 Pulitzer Prize to Snyder's *Turtle Island,* and I recall wondering at the time who the person was who sang these impersonal songs. Here, for example, is the now famous poem "The Real Work" (about rowing with friends by Alcatraz, as the epigraph tells us):

> sea-lions and birds,
> sun through fog
> flaps up and lolling,
> looks you dead in the eye.
> sun haze;
> a long tanker riding light and high.

sharp wave choppy line—
interface tide-flows—
seagulls sit on the meeting
eating;
we slide by white-stained cliffs.

the real work.
washing and sighing,
sliding by.

There's an impersonal "you" here and an amorphous "we," but no "I."
Instead, the reader meets a montage of noun phrases, and along with
them come verbals in *-ing:* the sun lolling, the tanker riding, the tide-
flows meeting, the seagulls eating, the "real work" of the sea washing and
sighing, the "real work" of the observers sliding by. A hidden hand has
taken a good deal of trouble to arrange these and other visual and aural
effects, bringing about what the poet Alan Williamson has called "little
defiant rescues of pure momentariness from the grid of generalized time
that is built into grammar itself." But the cinematographer of this scene
prefers to obscure himself, letting us follow his "camera eye" alone, just
as the moralist of this poem, defining what "the real work" is, prefers to
couch it in metaphorical rather than conceptual terms.

This method of composition was named metaphorically by Snyder
himself in his first volume as "riprap"—the stone cobble laid on a moun-
tain trail to prevent erosion: "Lay down these words / Before your mind
like rocks." It is painstaking and heavy work. The poetics of riprap owes
something to Pound's notion of the poem as sculpture, and to Pound's
phrasal organization, but Snyder, more than Pound, is attached to syn-
tactic effects as well as phrasal ones. In "The Real Work" there are real
sentences: the sun looks you in the eye, the seagulls sit, and the rowers
slide by cliffs. That is, there is statement and closure as well as timeless
phrasal presentation of visual effects. The morality of the end echoes
Keats's "moving waters at their priestlike task / Of pure ablution round
earth's human shores," but Keats would not have written in terms of the
easygoing "sliding by."

Back in 1975, I preferred the elegantly arranged cinematographic
poems in *Turtle Island* to the heavy-handed protest poems, and I still do.
Here is an example of the latter:

> How can the head-heavy power-hungry politic scientist
> Government   two-world Capitalist-Imperialist
> Third-world Communist paper-shuffling male
>   non-farmer   jet-set bureaucrats
> Speak for the green of the leaf? Speak for the soil?
> (Ah Margaret Mead . . . do you sometimes dream of Samoa?)

There was more of this sort of political-tract boilerplate in the eight volumes from which *No Nature* has been selected. And there were failed attempts to speak with a tribal voice, as in "Praise for Sick Women," a poem not collected here that was printed in the influential 1960 Donald Allen anthology *The New American Poetry*. "Praise for Sick Women" begins with an unfortunate reminiscence of Pound ("The female is fertile, and discipline / (contra naturam) only / confuses her"); it continues with an attempt to represent early tribal views which considered menstruation unclean:

> Where's hell then?
> In the moon.
> In the change of the moon:
> In a bark shack
> Crouched from sun, five days,
> Blood dripping through crusted thighs.

Inept though this is, it is suggestive of the sort of experiment Snyder wanted to make.

A list of poetic imperatives in the mature Snyder would go something like this: to reenter the archaic, but not in such a way as to sound foolish; to utter protests, but not in such a way as to become solely a propagandist; to efface "personality" in favor of a mostly perceptual being-in-the-world; to arrange words like cobble ("granite; ingrained / with torment of fire and weight"; to use restraint in tone and form alike. Snyder does wonderful things with and within these imperatives. He often registers the passage of time with an impersonality full of wonder: the vividly appreciative evolutionary poem "What Happened Here Before" traces the geological and ecological changes in the California landscape from three hundred million years ago till 1825, retelling each epoch, sometimes in the present tense, sometimes in the past. Three hundred million years ago: "soft sands, muds, and marls." Eighty million years ago: "warm quiet centuries of rains . . . / volcanic ash . . . piles up the gold and gravel." Three million years ago: "ground squirrel, fox, blacktail hare, ringtail, bobcat, bear, / all came to live here." Forty thousand years ago: "And human people came with basket hats and nets." This part of the poem closes with the nineteenth-century gold rush:

> Then came the white man: tossed up trees and
>   boulders with big hoses,
>   going after that old gravel and the gold.
> horses, apple-orchards, card-games,
>   pistol-shooting, churches, county jail.

For the duration of such a poem, we are given, on loan, a time-sense that we ourselves may live in rarely, but that Snyder lives in always—the opulent time-sense of a luxuriously unfolding evolutionary dynamic in which we are very late comers. When reproached for the "impracticality" of his ideas on how to live, Snyder is fond of pointing out that he is in synchrony with the large evolutionary picture, whereas his critics live too narrowly in the present: "It's only a temporary turbulence I'm setting myself against. I'm in line with the big flow . . . 'Right now' is an illusion too." In poems like "What Happened Here before," Snyder takes on the archaic tribal role of storyteller, but instead of telling cosmological tribal myths of sky gods and earth women, he relates our commonly accepted narrative of geological and evolutionary change in successive phases ("I was there to see it") of exquisitely chosen detail, musically modulated into what are, it is not too much to say, lovable stanzas.

The later Snyder can allow himself a relaxed political diction, as in a poem dedicated to Jerry Brown, "Talking Late with the Governor about the Budget," where, "tired of the effort / Of thinking about 'the People,'" he leaves the building and sees overhead the moon, a planet, and a star, "And east, over the Sierra, / Far flashes of lightning— / Is it raining to-night at home?" The glimpses of personal feeling here—of weary Arts Council efforts in unpromising directions, and of momentary homesick-ness—are nevertheless chastened by the presence of the regal and imper-turbable processes of the cosmos. Politics cannot be everything to Snyder. His Buddhism has always existed in sharp and productive tension with his inherited socialist utopianism and its negative consequence, bitter political protest. Insofar as Buddhism proclaims such engagement a form of illusion, Snyder knows that he should not let it disturb his inner quiet: "To take the struggle on without the least hope of doing any good." Asked whether poetry makes anything happen, Snyder once replied, "Well in that sense poetry does no more than woodchopping, or automobile repair, or anything else does because they're all equally real." And so he drives himself resolutely back from protest to his poetic function: to be a link in the transmission of what there is to be seen and known in the world. (He remarks, suggestively, in one interview, "My father . . . was a smart man, a very handy man, but he only knew about fifteen different trees and after that he was lost. I wanted more precision; I wanted to look deeper into the underbrush.") He wants to be a channel for what he calls, in the early poem of that name, "High Quality Information." It is the earnest and eager poem of a young man, and in it Snyder makes clear that much must be repressed in order for the new imperatives to arise:

> A life spent seeking it
> Like a worm in the earth,
> Like a hawk. Catching threads
> Sketching bones
> Assessing where the road goes.
> Lao-tzu says
> To forget what you knew is best.
> That's what I want;
> To get these sights down,
> Clear, right to the place
> Where they face
> Back into the mind of my times.
> The same old circuitry
> But some paths color-coded
> *Empty*
> And we're free to go.

To forget what you knew; to color-code some of your mental paths "Empty" and never go down them again: this resolve accounts for some of what is missing in Snyder's work.

Snyder is not unaware of the dangers in taking too remote and geolog-
ical a view of human affairs. He voices that danger in the poem "Word
Basket Woman," commenting on the American poet nearest him in eco-
logical vision, Robinson Jeffers:

> Robinson Jeffers, his tall cold view
> quite true in a way, but why did he say it
> as though he alone
> stood above our delusions, he also
> feared death, insignificance,
> and was not quite up to the inhuman beauty
> of parsnips or diapers, the deathless
> nobility at the core of all ordinary things.

Because Snyder fears the tonal extremes of prophetic denunciation
and an indifferent Olympianism, because he wants to include parsnips
and diapers, the tonal range he allows himself in his best poetry is rather
narrow: it runs from curious observation to cheerful enjoyment to genial
hospitality. Because he is so steady in his self-control, the more denuncia-
tory and chaotic moments in the poetry strike the reader as off key. Yet
one suspects that chaos may be more "natural" to Snyder than order, the
mid-range tonality more "controlled" than spontaneous. This control
can be seen in the tightness of his poetic structures.

There is an obsessive concern with arrangement in Snyder's best
work—a concern one wants to call "Japanese"—as all the cobbles in the
riprap begin to take on mutual relations like those between the famous
stones in the Ryoan-ji garden. The stones that we repair to, in a visual
zigzag, as we traverse "Surrounded by Wild Turkeys," a beautiful late
meditation on parental and filial generations, are the words "call," "pass,"
"through," and "like":

> Little calls   as they pass
> through dry forbs and grasses
> Under blue oak and gray digger pine
> In the warm afternoon of the forest-fire haze;
>
> Twenty or more, long-legged birds all alike.
>
> So are we, in our soft calling,

passing on through.

Our young, which trail after,

Look just like us.

The other "stones" successively placed in the poem are its gentle adjectives: "little," "blue," "gray," "warm," "long-legged," "soft." They make up the tonal climate. In many poems, Snyder represents himself and his family as leading what one must call a mammalian life, really not much different in its needs and instincts from the herd life of bears or sheep; but here he extends the comparison even to birds. Of course, even Snyder's organic sympathies have limits; he is not likely to compare himself and his family to a hive of termites. But a poem like "Surrounded by Wild Turkeys" (in which the baby turkeys "trailing" after their parents confer their verb on Snyder's mental image of his own children) suggests a way of being in the world—unassuming, honest, untranscendent, self-deprecating, tender, and open to delight—which is quietly exemplary, without aggressively urging itself on others.

Formally, Snyder has stuck pretty conclusively to his main tools— noun phrases, present participles, an emphasis on the visual, and a care for musical phrasing. Every so often, he'll do something deliberately striking, as in a Zen poem of earthly revelation. This poem bears an enormous title, and is dated from an origin over forty thousand years ago, when human life first appeared on earth:

24:IV:40075, 3:30 PM,
N. OF COALDALE, NEVADA, A GLIMPSE THROUGH A
BREAK IN THE STORM OF THE SUMMIT
OF THE WHITE MOUNTAINS

O Mother Gaia

sky cloud gate milk snow

wind-void-word

I bow in roadside gravel

This is a densely constructed poem of both vertical and horizontal orientation. Mother Gaia, the earth, is found on the highest hierarchic level; sky, snow, and summit on the next level down; wind and discourse below that, while the humble disciple on the humble pebbles defines the lowest level. So much for the "vertical plot." The "horizontal plot" of landscape does not, and cannot, exist at the highest level, that of conceptuality: there, Mother Gaia lives alone. Below her, we see the broad horizontal revelation described in the title: a gate opens in the milky clouded sky, and one glimpses a snowy summit. (Naturally, the gate opens in the middle of the scene, framed by cloud-milk in the proximate position, by sky and snow in the remote position.) The horizontal plot at the next level, expressed in words linked by hyphens, tells us that the natural "word" of the universe (the wind) and the real word of human discourse, cannot be separated from the Buddhist void, the gap in meaning, occupying the same place in the "discursive plot" on this level as the glimpsed gate in the "higher" visual plot preceding it. Finally, the last horizontal plot presents the human figure "I" on the left, balanced by the humbling gravel on the right. This is a poem that takes up the challenge of the pagan and Christian shaped lyric and renews the form, while renewing as well the classical apostrophe to the genius loci in the theophany, or manifestation of the god or goddess.

Snyder is one of the many modernist poets to have brought English lyric into conjunction with Chinese and Japanese poetry. The long history of Western fascination with "the Chinese written character as a medium for poetry" (Pound out of Fenollosa) has reached its apogee with Snyder, if only because Snyder (unlike Amy Lowell, Pound, Stevens, Williams, Rexroth, and others) really knows Japanese and Chinese. His economy and fastidiousness in poetry would please, I should think, not only the ghosts of American Imagism and Objectivism but also those Zen masters with whom he studied; they would recognize the metaphorical weight borne by his apparently artless visual lists, and the historical passion distilled into the words retelling his evolutionary chronicles.

In this way, Snyder offers a worthy counter-possibility to the American passion for explanatory confession. His poems convey remarkably little about his own views of his psyche. Perhaps he doesn't believe he has one—or, at least, one available to reliable inspection. He compels his reader into a rather shocking redefinition of what makes an interesting poem—a definition that goes not only against the confessional norm prevalent in Western lyric since the *Vita Nuova*, and the witty metaphysical poetry that has been the chief lyric rival to the confessional strain, but also against the third major stream of lyric, the "nature poetry" where one might think to locate him. What would the providential Emerson of "The Rhodora," the yearning Frost of "Birches," or the stern Jeffers of Big Sur make of the unembarrassed opening of Snyder's "Right in the Trail," a humorous but admiring poem about bear droppings:

> Here it is, near the house,
> A big pile, fat scats,
> Studded with those deep red
> Smooth-skinned manzanita berries,
> Such a pile! Such droppings,
> Awesome.

Snyder's attempt to see as a Native American might, his de-Christianized gaze, his Buddhist reverence for all life, are the efforts authenticating the stanzas of his nature poems, good and bad alike, and make for his indubitable originality. Especially in the nature poems, we see the suppression of a confessional and introspective self, and the adoption of a self that is perceptually alive, one which allows the discourses appropriate to successive phenomena to appear through him, as through a medium, on the page.

The losses in adopting such an attitude, with its allied formal techniques, are real. The volatility, anguish, and self-questioning of the passionate self, together with certain of its appropriate vocabularies and tropes, vanish. The stories of Snyder's four marriages (and the three divorces) go untold, as does his loss, by divorce, of his father (the cause, perhaps, of his attachment first to Rexroth and next to a succession of Zen masters). The quite fantastic confection that is Snyder's life (measured against the American male norm) makes him a genuine American eccentric, living naked with his naked family (as a visitor reports in the Sierra Club book), and building not only a house but also a Zen meditation hall for himself and his neighbors. His life may be his greatest work of art. Its raggednesses (such as every life must possess) have been pruned and espaliered; the beautiful and chastely decorated Japanese-style timber house, the fine plain utensils, the orderly division of the days and months into travel time and work time, the neatness of all his visual arrangements—these are the outward signs of an inner discipline that may work to hold some disorder at bay. One must respect Snyder for keeping the constraint equal to the disorder. His discretion about personal suffering suggests that the chaos and violence he attacks in the industrial world outside his careful precincts of pastoral retirement may be in part a projection from within, causing that occasional disequilibrium in tone that mars some of his poems.

Snyder remarked in an interview that he could sing approximately two hundred folk songs by heart. The simplicity of oral poetry is what he aims to preserve in his far more tersely organized written poetry. "The poem or the song," he says revealingly, "manifests itself as a special concentration of the capacities of the language and rises up into its own shape." Such a poem rebukes, by its authenticity, poems of no compactness, of no individual shape: "There is an intuitive aesthetic judgment that you can make that in part spots phoniness, spots excess, spots the overblown, or the undersaid, the unripe, or the overripe." Snyder usually walks the tightrope between these extremes with a clearly judged balance; the true poem, he has said, walks "that edge between what can be said and that which cannot be said." It is just that fine edge that is missing in his prose: "If we are lucky we may eventually arrive at a totally integrated world culture with matrilineal descent, free-form marriage, natural-credit communist economy, less industry, far less population and lots more national parks." Yes, no doubt, but who will remember this paragraph in fifty years? It is a good thing we have poetry to protect us from expository prose at its most *bien pensant*. And although *No Nature* is annoyingly arranged (with some early poems stuck in the latter part, interrupting what is otherwise a chronological order) it is good to have most of Gary Snyder's poems available in one volume. He has been claimed by virtuous ecology, but let us claim him for virtuous poetry, too; by getting rid of "too much ego interference, too much abstract intellect, too much striving for effect," he has constructed in verse a remarkable self resolutely different from the perennial lyric "I," a self in which archaic and modern discourses alike can meet. Of course, it then takes Snyder's genius to make riprap of them, until they make a trail for us into his myths and texts.

12

A Steely Glitter
Chasing Shadows

John Ashbery's *Flow Chart*

What is John Ashbery's single-poem book *Flow Chart?* A two-hundred-fifteen-page lyric; a diary; a monitor screen registering a moving EEG; a thousand and one nights; Penelope's web unraveling; views from Argus' hundred eyes; a book of riddles; a ham-radio station; an old trunk full of memories; a rubbish dump; a Bartlett's "Familiar Quotations"; a Last Folio; a vaudeville act. It is maddening, enthralling, and funny by turns; its sentences are like chains of crystal alternating with jello. It makes Ashbery's past work (except for those poems in *The Tennis Court Oath*, his experiment in the surreal) seem serenely classical, well ordered, pure, shapely, and, above all, *short*.

Since the sixties, Ashbery has consistently been writing experimental poems that have both continued and revised American lyric. In interviews he has professed a bland astonishment that his ruminations should seem to his readers different from their own. He is probably right in assuming that what Stevens called "the hum of thoughts evaded in the mind" must be, in a given time and place, rather alike from mind to mind. In my own case, by entering into some bizarrely tuned pitch inside myself I can find myself on Ashbery's wavelength, where everything at the symbolic level makes sense. The irritating (and seductive) thing about this tuning in is that it can't be willed; I can't make it happen when I am tired or impatient. But when the frequencies meet, the effect on me is Ashbery's alone, and it is a form of trance.

Ashbery is, above all, a poet of the moral life, but his means are the means of farce: pratfalls, absurd scenarios, preposterous coincidences, a Chaplinesque wistfulness, and—something often absent in farce—a hatful of colored scarves of language. He says awful things about life, but he puts a comic spin on them, a double take of irony. He excels especially in the fertility with which he imagines catastrophe:

> Then the fun begins in earnest, blows rain
> down from all over, chopping-block sounds,
> you think mechanically of Mary Stuart and Lady
> Jane Grey, holding on to your forelock, cap in hand, of course.

In Ashbery's amiably malign universe, however, no sooner is the speaker crushed by circumstance than he's up and running again. As if in a speeded-up film, we are allowed a brief frame of comedy—

> Yet certainly
> there are some bright spots, and when you listen to the laughter
> in the middle of these it makes for more than a cosmetic truth

—but no sooner does cheerfulness break in than something silently menacing heaves into view: "The hangar gets unbearably hot and very smelly."

Like the continually recycled rolling theatrical backdrop used to simulate a landscape seen from a train, Ashbery's recurrent farce of naïve hopes rudely demolished keeps being run past us throughout *Flow Chart*. A mimicry of innocence-constantly-turning-into-experience is hardly new in literature, but Ashbery rewrites the theme in slang and slapstick, and creates, against that music-hall background, various silhouettes of love, landscape, and art. There he is, "like a daisy on muck," as the pristine poem rises out of the slime of life and language.

There's a brave despair in *Flow Chart*—more, I think, than in Ashbery's earlier books. Philosophically, he has always been a skeptic, and his incorrigibly comic side precludes the satisfying comfort of gloomy skepticism of the German variety. His pretense is always one of genial chat, but the chat increasingly includes moments of guilt, dismay, self-reproach, sadness, and exhaustion. The superficial camaraderie eventually seems a treble ostinato against which we hear more clearly the sighs and screams from the torture chamber. To present torture in terms of farce is a Beckettian ideal that Ashbery shares: "And behind / the barn it behooves us again to take up the principle, so like the art / of tragedy and so unlike." It is not quite tragedy, because it has no ultimate sanction from God or Fate: "I see / far, in looking, out over a life, the strange, wrenching mess of it." And Ashbery is a master of the unexplained mess, here the dissolution of a former bond:

> Patiently you again show me my name in the register where I
>   wrote it.
> But I'll be off now, there's no point in thanking me for what I
>   haven't done, nor in
> my thanking you for all the things you did for me, the good
>   things and the less good.
> In riper times of trial we stayed together. But in this kind of
>   bleached-out crisis-
> feeling, the best one can do is remain polite while dreaming of
>   revenge in another key.

Just when something in life has acquired "variation, texture," then "the sanitation department decreed / it was coming through," and, helpless, one sees one's possessions—friendships, loves—ground up in the hopper of Fate's garbage truck.

The despair in Ashbery is peerlessly matched by his superb dramas of the complacent self-justification we all resort to. There is very little to be said for life, for its listless or agonized days followed by an inevitable execution:

> Still, life is reasonably absorbing
> and there's a lot of nice people around. Most days are well fed
> and relaxing, and one can improve one's mind a little
> by going out to a film or having a chat with that special friend;
>   and before
> you know it it's time to brush your teeth and go to bed.

Not that this pabulum of self-reassurance can last long. Truth breaks in:

> Why then, does that feeling
> of emptiness keep turning up like a stranger you've seen dozens
> of times, out-of-focus
> usually, standing toward the rear of the bus or fishing for coins
> at the newsstand? . . .
> Unfortunately we must die, and after that no one is sure what
> happens. Accounts vary.

Yet ostrich-like defenses against the truth recur, as a heaven is supposed after death:

> But we
> most of us feel we'll be made comfortable for much of the time
> after that, and get credit
> for the (admittedly) few nice things we did, and no one is going
> to make too much
> of a fuss over those we'd rather draw the curtain over, and
> besides, we can't see
> much that was wrong in them, there are two sides to every
> question.

If a *frisson* of emptiness follows our perception of oncoming death, then the excuses of self-regard immediately obscure the *frisson*. In this way Ashbery traces the flirtings of the mind with moral awareness, and exposes its quick scurrying to its preferred and pathetic holes of security.

Perhaps no other recent lyric poet has so swallowed the entire range of the spoken and written language of his time and then, like a mother bird, regurgitated it (delicately rearranged) as food for readers. Eliot, Pound, and Moore all incorporated "low" language of the sort that fin-de-siècle lyric had tried to do without, but Ashbery has taken the modernist experiment to its end point: to boilerplate, advertising, doggerel, obscenity, technology, media talk—the subliterary of all kinds. At the same time, he adds piquancy to his offered dish with the condiments of the past: archaisms, the dated language of flappers and lounge lizards, quotations from the canon, ancient children's books, nursery rhymes.

This happens not only at the level of words but at the levels of grammar and syntax. Rarely has an exquisite writer deliberately written so banally.

At the level of genre, Ashbery is a joyous parodist. There is scarcely a received genre that doesn't emerge here doing a comic turn as a parody of itself. Most of these passages in *Flow Chart* are too long to quote: a nice one can be found on pages 106 and 107 parodying parataxis—a syntax in which sentences are joined by connectives such as "and" or "then" or "but." This is the interminable linear syntax in which most of us tell our dreams or the plots of movies. Yet a nobler paratactic style descends to us from the grand simplicities of Genesis, the Gospels, and fairy stories, and interference from these transmissions keeps breaking into Ashbery's modern broadcast:

> And Joan she said
> too it was like being dead only she didn't care, she might as well
>   be anyway, for all
> she cared, and then someone came back with beef. And said
>   here
> put a rose on this, you're not afraid, you do it, and someone
>   said, O if the law
> decree it he must do it. . . .
> And then in the shade they put their heads
> together, and one comes back, the others being a little way off,
>   and says, who
> do you think taught you to disobey in the first place? And he
>   says, my father.
> And at that they were all struck dumb . . . and it was all over for
>   that day.

Ashbery's absurdly long lines seem to say that the nutrients in this contemporary paratactic language are so thinned out that we need a lot of words to get anywhere at all. The miraculous concision of "real poetry" is thereby laid bare as the highest "artificiality" (in the best sense).

The necessity of recording everything, of being "one of those on whom nothing is lost" (Henry James, in one of Ashbery's raisin-quotations elaborating the pudding), is a theme to which Ashbery often returns. "Did it ever occur" to preachers, he says, that we human beings "aren't /

as they imagine us, or even as we imagine ourselves, but more like bales / of hay, already harvested but still sitting around, waiting for someone to put them / in the barn before rain and rodents have their way with them?" The labor of the Keatsian harvester—to shelter, in the "rich garners" of poems, himself, his readers, and their culture before the rains and rats get them—is never-ending. If Ashbery is convinced of anything under his affable skepticism, it is that tomorrow won't be like today. His poetry is a continual approximation of Zeno's paradox: No matter how you hasten toward your goal, you will always be unable to reach it.

As Ashbery waits for "my / boulder that rushes to me yet hangs suspended / like mistletoe," he harvests his bales, his gathered stacks of paper. The daily burden of living in constant awareness is now (Ashbery is over sixty) harder and harder labor:

> The page
> that was waiting to be turned had grown heavy as a barren
>   mountain range, and armies
> of civil engineers equipped with the latest in pulleys, winches,
>   sprockets, and windlasses
> were just at that moment attempting to negotiate its sheer sides,
>   with little success.

One feels reading these lines a pulse of buoyant recognition that someone has here recorded the sullen effort of shifting, in late middle age, into a new phase. At the same time, one recognizes that Ashbery (whose lexical range is enormous, and who rarely repeats a word) is absolutely delighted to have found a use in lyric for the unlikely words "civil engineers," "pulleys," "winches," "sprockets," and "windlasses." The old metaphor of the soul's multiple powers (intellect, will, imagination, reason, and so on) pulling together has been Napoleonically updated to the technology of empire, retaining just enough old-fashionedness to be charming, and given just enough metallic modernity to quell all that nonsense (so Ashbery implies) of medieval psychology.

Flow Chart, though it is divided into six sections, and though it masquerades as a narrative, is really a lyric poem, in that it imitates the structure of narrative while not having a narrative theme. There is no real end to the flow of the flow chart, and no one ever progresses in it except in circles. It is true that the beginning of each section of the poem acts like a beginning, and the end like an ending, but there are any number of mini-beginnings and crypto-endings scattered through the whole book. At times, Ashbery even seems to be telling us that this is his last work, that henceforth we are on our own:

> I have no further bread and cheese for you; these days I count
>   little
> but the linens folded in my scented cedar closets, folded up
>   against time, in case
> I ever have a use for them; and you, you others, have only to
>   break away
> like chunks of ice from the much larger iceberg to accomplish
>   your destiny, that day in court
> the monkeys and jesters seemed to promise you—or was it a
>   bad dream?

The infrastructure of all this—folded sheets of poems in closets ("presses," in the old sense), the Melville/Bishop iceberg, the vaguely Shakespearean monkeys and jesters, the ambiguous Keatsian "or was it a bad dream?"—is constructed from the flotsam and jetsam of culture. While Arnold and Eliot tended to quote their poetic touchstones directly, Ashbery, though perfectly willing to insert the odd line of "The Castaway," prefers to embed his allusions in weird and funny ways. The Bible, Homer, Virgil, Dante, Shakespeare, Marvell, Cowper, Blake, Keats, Arnold, Hopkins, Whitman, Lewis Carroll, Edward Lear, Henry James, Stevens, Eliot make cameo appearances here, but chimerically altered: Hamlet's "slings and arrows of outrageous fortune" turns up, for instance, as "the snakes and ladders / of outrageous fortune." Both the stately "Game of Chess" and "What the Thunder Said," from "The Waste Land," appear in parodic form:

> Even in my late forties I patiently awaited
> this. After dinner she played Kjerulf. We sipped tea, looking at
>   each other. . . .
> Another day we read the thunder its own prepared statement.

Datta. Dayadhvam. Damyata. The sheer effrontery of Eliot's incorporating a "prepared statement" for thunder amuses Ashbery, and his wit at Eliot's expense marks a deep debt to and love for Eliot. But a scavenger hunt for manhandled quotations is not what Ashbery's reader is in the game for. Rather, the reader receives a highly idiosyncratic introduction to the contents of what Stevens called the "trash can at the end of the world," where all culture comes eventually to rest as pieces of itself.

In the past, the symbolic code that all poets resort to has usually been a fairly self-consistent one, no matter how heterodox. Scholars have felt that they could figure out Blake's or Yeats's "system," and make reasonable deductions about the author's symbolic intent. Ashbery of course has to write partly in the inherited code—the autumn of life, harvest as one's final ingathering, palaces as elaborate constructions, earthquakes and storms as catastrophe, and so on—but he also departs from old poetic codes for a freakish one of his own. In his code, "the sanitation department" stands temporarily for whatever mysterious extinction-machine vacuums up relationships; the next time the force of destruction shows up, however, it will be called "rain and rodents," or a dam that overflows, or the fate that makes you "wash up like a piece of polyester at the gulf's festering edge." Metaphors in Ashbery succeed each other vertiginously. One reads on the qui vive, riding the crests of ever-new imagery while, on some subliminal level, doing the decoding and relishing the sport.

The code is not always breakable. Ashbery feels free to use private information inaccessible to his reader (if only so that his autobiography in verse can be an intimate one, and the reticence that means so much to him will remain unviolated). We know that he will not reveal personal particulars; when he speaks, in one of his characteristic mixed metaphors, of "the skein of secret misery lobbed from generation to generation," we will not be told what went wrong among the Ashberys. But we are grateful to have the secret misery named as the shameful burden it is, and to see noted the parental insouciance with which it is passed down: "Here, it's *your* serve; *you* knit something with it." And when the code works it becomes a wonderful shorthand.

Here, in shorthand, is something about (so I gather) growing up among adults, and growing up gay, and changing by night (in one's own mind and perhaps in that of others) into a monster, and (another source of adolescent embarrassment) shooting up to over six feet. A recollection of adult advice opens the passage:

> Retreat, retreat! was all they ever
> said, and seemed sometimes not to know what they meant.
> Thus night
> appears to have existed always, and to one's surprise one finds
> oneself
> adapting to it as though one had never known anything else,
> and growing fangs and howling
> at the moon and avoiding questions from loved ones and
> overreacting.
> Now it was time to be tall too, a further complication.

This sort of disguised autobiography runs all through Part IV of *Flow Chart.*

It is discouraging to be Ashbery, because the very culture of which he is the linguistic recorder cannot read him, so densely woven is the web of his text. His very effect—that one is gazing down through a stream of transparent words into pure consciousness—depends on the reader's noting, at least subconsciously, the whole orchestral potential of the English language, high and low, sufficiently to register the oboes here, the triangle there, the snare drums somewhere else. *Flow Chart* is like one huge party line, with everyone in the English-speaking world, past and present, from Chaucer to Ann Landers, interrupting each other in incessant fragments. This apparently aleatory music is conducted by an invisible master at the synthesizer. The whole is too big to be subordinated to criticism; no critical essay could hope to control, except in very general terms, the sheer volume of linguistic and psychological data presented by the poem.

A couple of years ago, I came across (in *Poetry New York 3*, published by the CUNY Graduate Center) a poem written by a philosopher named Frank White; it is called "On First Looking into Ashbery." It recognizes how uninhibited Ashbery is, and how stuffy he makes his academic readers feel:

> When you read the real thing,
> A living poet speaking your language,
> Colloquial, but in the poet's own give-away tones,
> Picking over your common existence
> Like a practiced hand at a rummage sale,
> You almost choke on your own discourse,
> Wonder how you can ever wear it in public again—
> So out of date, so over-worn, so ill-suited to the occasion
> It somehow suddenly seems.

And yet the philosopher-speaker bounces back, realizing that Ashbery's unfettered voice has the exhilarating effect of altering his own constricted one:

> But only for a moment. The panic passes.
> Soon you are having your say again,
> Scared but talking back,
> Accent barely detectably affected,
> Having added one more high-fidelity speaker
> To your sound equipment.

All poets are "high-fidelity speakers," transmitting what Hopkins called "the current language heightened"; but Ashbery, like such narrative or dramatic writers as Chaucer and Shakespeare, and unlike most lyric poets, has made this linguistic fidelity to the entire current language a notable area of experiment. His total "Sonata of Experience" has by now had such a sing-along effect that the literary magazines are full of his imitators, trailing inconsequence, slang, and jokes. But the imitators don't have Ashbery's inexhaustible vocabulary, and they don't have his Proustian syntax, not to mention his rueful self-mockery and his lavish decorativeness. *Flow Chart* contains, for example, a double sestina; its end words, according to Ashbery, are borrowed from a double sestina by Swinburne. (And with the mention of Swinburne another Ashbery affiliation is revealed. Both poets are makers of a liquid cascade of words:

"Come speak with me," says Ashbery, "behind the screen of the water-fall's Holophane.")

For all his appearance of decadence and camp, Ashbery is rendering an account, at once strict and voluminous, of a naked contemporary moral consciousness that most of us still shrink from, and doing so in a language more ample than most of us can wield as our own. Poetry, says Ashbery, usually appears as "this purple weather / with the eye of a god attached, that sees / inward and outward." That definition speaks of poetry's psychological acuteness and also of its claim to render the objective world.

But there is another poetry, written in what Keats called "a finer tone," which passes beyond both psychology and description, and leaps into a savage and thrilling authority of language. No more than any other poet would Ashbery assert that such poetry is in his voluntary power, but, in the single most transfixing passage in *Flow Chart*, he imagines it:

> And then everything you were going to say and
> everything they were going to say to you in reply would erupt
> in lightning, a steely glitter chasing shadows like a pack
> of hounds, once they tasted the flavor of blood, and then this
>   light would gradually
> form prickly engraved letters on a page—*but who would read
>   that!*

Lightning-letters—let him read them who dares. But also engraved, formal; the letters of an invitation. And prickly—they draw blood. Who would not want to read that?

13

A Dissonant Triad

Henri Cole, Rita Dove, and August Kleinzahler

Ringing declarations—about God, politics, sexism, parents—go down well with unsophisticated audiences, but in our present climate they sound tinny and false, especially when they concern political struggles in other countries. The language of national or familial violence flaps its tattered vocabulary with no more than a melodramatic effect. The question for an American poet, living in relative personal and national peace and plenty, is how to find the imaginative interest in life without invoking a false theatricality, how to be modest without being dull, how to be moving without being maudlin.

Henri Cole has I think not given his satirical strengths enough space in *The Zoo Wheel of Knowledge.* For me, the most enlivening moments in it—even though they risk stereotype—are those where Cole takes a slyly knowing tone. Here, from "The Roosevelt Spa," is military authority, absurd in undress:

> The winter I was nine
> Father took me swimming
> at the Pentagon. Bald and pink-
> faced, ears in an upsweep,
>
> even the grim Colonels swam naked
> in the steamy natatorium.

This, of course, could not have been written without *Life Studies,* but elsewhere Cole finds a more decorated style for his satire, as in an equally absurd tableau of patient and doctor, from "Papilloma":

> Naked, horizontal, marooned
> 　　beetlelike on my spine,
> a snow-white scroll of tissue unwound
> 　　beneath me, I lie puffy-eyed
>
> on my M.D.'s examination bed.
>
> . . . . .
>
> 　　He knocks on the doors of my chest,
>
> pushes gently into my abdomen's
> 　　little pillows of liver
> and spleen, his hands pink as a doll's . . .

Cole's observant eye and careful hand find satisfactory packages of sound, like the squishy "little pillows of liver." He is not always idiomatic; does anyone say "my M.D."?

And here, in a more lethal satiric vignette, are the rich; they appear in a poem called "Tuxedo":

> After espresso six spiral-haired
> ladies, coquettish as girls,
> "go pee" in tandem. Pearly
>
> white, the powder room sees
> their lives pass through its mirrors, . . .
>
> 　　A fleet
>
> of hearses, the tycoons
> idle in the china-blue ballroom,
> their petroleum-black lapels glossy
> as new-buffed fenders. Exhaust
>
> snakes from their awful Havana

cigars, setting the wives sneezing
on return in a heliostream
of taffeta and organza.

The coquettishness and power mask frigidity; the couples go home to
Embassy Row,

where their homes have mighty
wings with electric eyes and tiny
twinbeds unwrapped like mints
for them to sleep in, each in each.

Like all satire, this is "unfair," but it is imaginatively exact, with a relish
like Pope's for miniature social detail.

Yet it seems that Cole thinks his vein is principally a "tender" or "lyric"
one. His attempts at graceful compliment in "The Best Man" (written
on the occasion of his brother's wedding) sound, however well meant, in-
sincere:

Godspeed, brother and sister. Swim with the armor
of arctic fish. As the hour's quarters
dong past, dandle the axis of your devotion,
learn the million nuances of your hearts.

It is Merrill who is the baleful predecessor here. And Cole's elegy for
David Kalstone, "Lost in Venice," suffers from a too-Jamesian (too-
Merrillesque?) wish for the perfect sweetness of the perfect moment:

We lingered at sunset with drinks
in the library beneath a vaulted
cavernous ceiling of gesso washes
and ornate stuccos to recount each
day's aquatinted discoveries,
the canal's rosy surfaces peeking
in upon us. . . .

. . . . .

My host
lifted his tumbler, toasting the rooms
and his seclusion there. A halo
of white hair, turbanlike, illumined
his head in a vertical ray . . .

A complacency in these lines, unintended perhaps but disturbing, returns at the end of the elegy:

In the darkening
night, black gondolas skimmed beneath us,
and a tenor's silver crescendo touched
the air like a shepherd boy's sweet harping.

Sweetness needs astringency to be aesthetically believable, and there isn't, to my taste, enough astringency here. Cole's gift for the phrase is still in evidence (in for example, "a tenor's silver crescendo"), but the stanza cries out for a counter-movement like the ones Herbert put in his "sweet" poems, where a "sweet rose" is at the same time "angry and brave." The tartness of "season'd timber" lets Herbert get away with his "sweet spring, full of sweet days and roses." A little iron (or seasoned timber) never comes amiss amid sweetness, and a thorn-pricked eye (the rose's red is a visual thorn) is prevented from doting overmuch. A good dash of eroticism is also a counter to lyric "sweetness," and this Cole does find in "Cape Cod Elegy":

an untainted summer long ago,
such throat-swallowing
nakedness, inexorable as the sun, him

swimming towards me,
a hairline of copper, his torso
new-minted from the sea.

. . . . .

Let me recall
in the life to come the sudden

saline wave of his embrace.

The formal principles of Cole's poems, except for slant rhymes, aren't salient. He is not writing syllabics or metered lines, so the elaborate indentations in the Kalstone elegy seem to have no real justification, unlike their predecessors in, say, Herbert (where indentations precisely indicate which lines are tetrameters, which trimeters) or in Keats (where indentations suggest the beginning of a new movement in the odes). Nor do the "stanzas" in many of Cole's poems have a clear rationale, since the sentences continue over stanza breaks. I accept that something can "feel right" to the poet—a stanza break here, an indentation there—but if it does not demonstrate its own reason for being to a willing reader, it may remain formally inert on the page. I say this while recognizing how vague formal principles have become. Perhaps some commanding period style is waiting in the wings, as unavoidable as Dryden's couplets or Wordsworth's blank verse, but if so it has yet to declare itself. Meanwhile, Cole emphasizes his homage to the past by his use of stanzas, slant rhymes, and indentations. When he uses them to suggest a formal shape (like liturgical antiphonal singing), his typographic arrangements become convincing, as in "Ascension on Fire Island":

The floor creaks beneath us
like the hull of a ship,
   and the surf purrs in the distance,
confounding us with place,
   till a cardinal alights, twig-flexing,
anchoring us with his featherweight.

Cole's subjects—family, boyhood, death, nature—would be conventional were it not for the willingness to convey within them some ugly or grisly detail. In his title poem, he goes with friends to the zoo, and recognizes his kinship with the animals by anthropomorphizing them:

> Above us the ape's lips are cracked and bleeding,
> his pink tits pumped up from swinging
> in the canopy. . . .

He also recalls neighborhood boys killed when they trespassed into the polar bears' den. Yet the ugly and the nonhuman are finally assimilated into a prayer of analogy:

> Oh Lord, make us sure as the beasts
> who drink from the pond, their shaggy manes
> dappled with air; who see those that flee
> from them, yet wait and breathe accustomed
> to the night; and who listen tirelessly
> for grasses to blow on the plain again.

The combination of "shaggy" and "dappled," of "tirelessly" and "grasses," carries the music of the prayer. Cole seems to me, finally, to be a poet of "sensibility" but also—if he would value it more—a potential poet of satire.

Rita Dove, on the other hand, looks for a hard, angular surface to her poems. She is an expert in the disjunctive, often refusing the usual discursive signs of "the meditative." Crosscutting and elliptical jumps were her chief stylistic signature even in her first volume, *The Yellow House on the Corner*. *Grace Notes* is her fourth book, and represents both a return to the lyric from her successful objective sequence *Thomas and Beulah,* and an attempt to make her poems weigh less heavily on the page. Her poems are rarely without drama, however, and she has done a remarkable thing in making even the routines of motherhood become dramatic in the best poems in this volume, a sequence occupying Part III of *Grace Notes.* Here is "The Breathing, the Endless News":

> Every god is lonely, an exile
> composed of parts: elk horn,
> cloven hoof. Receptacle

for wishes, each god is empty
without us, penitent,
raking our yards into windblown piles. . . .

Children know this: they are
the trailings of gods. Their eyes
hold nothing at birth then fill slowly

with the myth of ourselves. Not so the dolls,
out for the count, each toe pouting from
the slumped-over toddler clothes:

no blossoming there. So we
give our children dolls, and
they know just what to do—

line them up and shoot them.
With every execution
doll and god grow stronger.

This is at once mock-horrific (the angelic daughter lines up her dolls and
shoots them) and culturally unnerving. The actors of the poem—the
gods and ourselves, the godlike children and their not-godlike dolls; the
picture of life as the successive killing of successive "dolls" by emergent
"gods"; the declining parents; the fetishistic nature of consciousness and
its gods (part noble elk horn, part indecent cloven hoof)—all these are
immensely suggestive without ever becoming quite explicitly allegorical.

In "Genetic Expedition," Dove (a black married to a white man) con-
trasts her own looks to those of her blond daughter, with a frankness
that sentimentality would blush at:

Each evening I see my breasts
slacker, black-tipped
like the heavy plugs on hot water bottles;

. . . . .

   My child has
her father's hips, his hair
like the miller's daughter, combed gold.

Though her lips are mine, housewives
stare when we cross the parking lot
because of that ghostly profusion.

You can't be cute, she says. *You're big.*
She's lost her toddler's belly,
that seaworthy prow. She regards me
with serious eyes, power-lit,
atomic gaze
I'm sucked into, sheer through to

the gray brain of sky.

The disturbing ending—an atomic extinction of the parent back into
the mind of the universe—draws the sensual immediacy of the opening
into its component gray quanta, raw material for the next invention of
the sky.

As these poems suggest, Dove's lines and stanzas are carefully aligned
into dovetailed wholes. (The pun, unintended, seems legitimate.) Her
"Ars Poetica" doesn't deal with the making of poems, only with the stance
from which they are made. This is contrasted to the large ambitions,
satirically presented earlier in the poem, of two male straw men:

What I want is this poem to be small,
a ghost town
on the larger map of wills.
Then you can pencil me in as a hawk:
a traveling x-marks-the-spot.

This doesn't get to the heart of Dove's talent. Her true *ars poetica* in this
volume is a harsh poem called "Ozone," which is about arrangement and
what it yields—which is precisely nothing (if you choose to see it that
way). Life, says the poem, is "suckered up / an invisible flue"; it "disap-
pear[s] into an empty bouquet." The maddening aspect of art is that life
disappears into it once you've cleared out the space for life to fit into it.
The weirdness with which, as Stevens said, "Things as they are / Are
changed upon the blue guitar," is both the despair and the triumph of
artists. Thinking to express feeling, they make a hole in reality:

Everything civilized will whistle before
it rages—kettle of the asthmatic,
the aerosol can and its immaculate awl
perforating the dome of heaven.

We wire the sky for comfort;
we thread it through our lungs for a perfect fit.
We've arranged this calm, though it is constantly
unraveling.

. . . . .

The sky is wired so it won't fall down.
Each house notches into its neighbor
and then the next, the whole row scaldingly white,
unmistakable as a set of bared teeth.

Dove hasn't always this angry fatality, but there is an electricity (whistling, raging) about this wiring and notching and scalding and perforation that makes "Ozone" unforgettable. The poem speaks to the pain underlying Dove's work: the barely contained nervous tension which can be appeased only by notching one bared tooth into the next, carefully blowtorching a hole in the sky with awl-like precision, fixing the hole like "a gentleman [who] pokes blue through a buttonhole." Dove's combination of the domestic kettle, the artisanal awl, the aesthetic boutonniere, and the passional bared teeth convinces a reader that Dove's inner factions are in intense communication with each other.

Dove is interested by intransigence and its discontents. In one of the lesser poems here, a set of students respond to what they (and Dove, their teacher) take to be racism in a (white) lecturer (who may be William Arrowsmith; the poem is called "Arrow"):

. . . We sat there.
Dana's purple eyes deepened, Becky
twitched to her hairtips
and Janice in her red shoes
scribbled [a note of rage]. . . .

> My students
> sat there already devising
>
> their different ways of coping:
> Dana knowing it best to have
> the migraine at once, get the poison out quickly
> Becky holding it back for five hours   and Janice
> making it to the evening reading and
> party afterwards
> in black pants and tunic with silver mirrors
> her shoes pointed and studded, wicked witch shoes:
> Janice who will wear red for three days or
> yellow brighter
> than her hair so she can't be
> seen   at all

Janice's way, we suspect, is Dove's way; anger and tension are released in the scribbling of a note, the flaunting of color, the disappearance of self into raiment. The comparative slackness and "realism" here are a mode Dove carries off less well than she does her fierce and laconic "symbolic" mode. Here is her splendidly suggestive "Medusa":

> I've got to go
> down where my eye
> can't reach
> hairy star
> who forgets to shiver
> forgets the cool suck
> inside
>
> Someday long
> off someone will
> see me
> fling me up
> until I look
> into sky
>
> drop his memory

My hair
dry water

Resistant though this is to analysis, it feels right, at least to me. That "hairy star," the eye, forgets (because of its visual and cerebral way of being) the shiver and the suck of the passional life. By descending into her subaqueous realm, Medusa gains the snaky locks that symbolize her knowledge. When another eye sees her, she is stellified and turned into the "dry water" of art. The beholder forgets his other life, stands rooted. This, too, is an *ars poetica*, though not only that.

I admire Dove's persistent probes into ordinary language, including the language of the black proletariat. Here, the most successful experiment in that genre is "Genie's Prayer under the Kitchen Sink"—a monologue by a grown son (Eugene, the "Genie" of the title) summoned by his mother to unclog the kitchen sink. The touch becomes uneasy here and there, though, as Dove wants a decorativeness in her poem that the voice of her protagonist can't sustain:

. . . I came because I'm good at this, I'm good

with my hands; last March I bought some 2 by 4s
at Home Depot and honed them down
to the sleekest, blondest, free-standing bar
any mildewed basement in a cardboard housing tract
under the glass gloom of a factory clock
ever saw. . . .

One can believe in the first four lines of this, but not the last three.

Dove's youth, in this volume, is already shadowed, and one can see her trying to peer out of her present emotional riches into a savorless future. She visits an old poet in "Old Folk's [*sic*] Home, Jerusalem":

So you wrote a few poems. The horned
thumbnail hooked into an ear doesn't care.
The gray underwear wadded over a belt says So what. . . .

Valley settlements put on their lights
like armor; there's finch chit and my sandal's
inconsequential crunch.

Everyone waiting here was once in love.

The flatness of "my sandal's inconsequential crunch" betokens a Dove to
come, looking at intransigence become inconsequential, though still held
in the unyielding principle of her angular stanzas.

As for August Kleinzahler, in *Earthquake Weather* he comes heralded
by approving words from Ashbery and Wilbur, among others—words
which, unlike most blurbs, bear some relation to the poems inside.
Kleinzahler—who seems, by internal evidence, to be somewhere in his
forties—has learned a lot from the unlikely combination of Ammons
and Stevens. Here is his Ammons side:

Peaches on top of the compost, sitting pretty
rot from underneath blue
—jays swoop
down for poppyseed then curl
back up to the fencepost
because cat
he's got a lot of tricks . . .

This charming run-on-at-the-mouth style has more in view (as Am-
mons' does too) than a weather report on the back yard. The poem it
comes from is one of three composing an accomplished sequence called
"Before Winter," recording various atmospheres of the past and present:

voices issuing from those faces
running up&down
the vibraphone of me in dissonant
sheets and there's my
own voice, somehow
got separated in the crowd

> I say
> *Let me see down from a*
> *very high place.*
> *not tethered here by need*

This (a version of Dove's hawk image for the poet) is as close to an ex-
plicit *ars poetica* as Kleinzahler will come. The image by no means covers
his art. Closer to his combination of the raffish, the marginalized, the
feckless, the sentimental, and the affectionate, is his fey song-of-himself,
"The Lunatic of Lindley Meadow":

> At nightfall, when the inquisitive elves in elf-pants
> wander over the ridge with chummy screed,
> the snaps of the beak your hand becomes cease,
>
> and evening's last fungo dwindles
> high over the spruce, for an instant getting lost
> in one band of sky turning dark under another,
>
> falling back into view falling
> out of the sky, *pop,* a dead wren in his mitt. *Let's*
> *get home,* the big boy says, *Mom'll holler.*
>
> The car horns along Fulton subside with the dark,
> the big felt-lined dark: bright little logos and cars
> set in black felt while still pulsing light,
>
> a lid on top. And see, here he comes now,
> Conga Lad, pleasing the elves who come close but not too,
> making the birds go way. Time to start home,
>
> so clean it up nice and blow germs off your pouch—
> the nice warm room, the smell in the wool.

This seems to me perfectly realized, and full of entrancing touches, like
the "felt-lined dark" and the "elves in elf-pants." Like cummings,
Kleinzahler has that light touch rare in literature. At the same time, he
can be intense over the loss of his cat (who is, in the book, his only
companion), In "Outing," the cat

> peeks out
> from under my hat and runs off
> to prowl, keep
> low or go wild in the lot
>
> overgrown with foxtail, then stays
> away two nights
> and a day don't let's not . . .
>
> Just dim the lights, draw
> the blind
> and give us a bagatelle in F
>
> yes, F would be nice
> till you hear a scrrr-atch at the back
> door and lookie
>
> see.

Kleinzahler's loneliness gives life in the Bay Area a derelict air; the "earthquake weather" of the title poem is in him as well as in "Mrs. B / she forgot her medication / now she's *on*." Elsewhere there are skinheads in "their concrete shell, over the fence / screaming *break your face*, smashing empties." In the bay, "foghorns / lowing like outsize beasts / shackled to cliffs" accompany Kleinzahler's thoughts. In all this, Kleinzahler drinks, drifts, and wanders, finding new words to put into poems: "check the boxscores"; "way the hell away"; "making the furnace kick on"; "beamed off satellite"; "twi-night doubleheaders"; "the smush-faced bus." These pieces of ordinary talk are Kleinzahler's strong suit only because they occur in his glancing, alert rhythms. These often turn into bitter little songs with a comic edge, or comic little songs with a bitter edge.

Kleinzahler too often falls over the edge into tough-guy sentimentality, as in "On the Way Home to Jersey One Night":

> And the two guys from Chicago,
> Algren and Farrell—
> I'm always imagining them out there
> in the shadows and doorways,

at every window and busted skylight,
keeping the ledger,

taking the last soiled scraps of it in.

Nonetheless it's an adventurous leap, to try to bring the seedy world of Algren and Farrell into speaking distance with "the delightful origami of an exiled prince," to have "Hootie Bill Do Polonius," to write "A Birthday Bash for Thomas Nashe." Against the dreary explicitness of so much of the "new narrative," Kleinzahler's jaunty skips and riffs solace the ear.

14

The Black Dove

Rita Dove, Poet Laureate

When she was a Fulbright student in Germany, the most recent American Poet Laureate, Rita Dove, came across a portrait of two Berlin sideshow entertainers of the twenties. The painting, by the artist Christian Schad (1894–1982), was painted in 1929; its title is *Agosta the Winged Man and Rasha the Black Dove*. The painting is reproduced on the cover of Rita Dove's second book of poems, *Museum,* and shows Agosta, his naked torso deformed by a bone disease that has caused his ribs and scapulas to point out through his skin like wings, and, seated below him, his fellow circus freak—a perfectly normal and handsome woman, whose only freakishness (in the Berlin of 1929) was that she was black. Rita Dove, who is black, found herself confronting Rasha the Black Dove; it's no wonder that the portrait generated one of Dove's most gripping poems.

The poem, with the same title as the painting, is voiced indirectly through Schad, the painter. At first, he thinks that his scrupulous and dispassionate eye is "merciless," as it sees and reproduces, in unadorned and unconcealed directness, the two figures set aside as spectacles by his society. But then he repents, and thinks, "The canvas, / not his eye, was merciless." It is the exactions of the medium, the stylized accuracy demanded by the art form, that guarantees the mercilessness of the portrait. But at the close, as Schad decides on his composition, he changes his mind yet again:

> Agosta in
> classical drapery, then,
> and Rasha at his feet.
> Without passion. Not
> the canvas
>   but their gaze,
>   so calm,
> was merciless.

It is the stigmatized figures, frontally posed, gazing out forever at those who gaze at them, who are "merciless." True, the artist's eye, with its absence of distorting "passion," plays a role; true, the canvas, which confers, in its recollection of the history of portraiture, classical drapery on this "ignoble" subject, also plays a part; but it is *what* is rendered through eye and style—the position of Agosta and Rasha in 1929 Berlin—that indicts its culture. As Dove saw her painted counterpart-Dove—doomed to dance in a circus with a boa constrictor to make a living—she knew *something* had to be merciless. In deciding on subject matter, she does not discount either eye or style, but she knows they have to bend their attention on deep and consequential things.

It is evident from such a poem, and from its attention to a painting by a white artist of a black woman, that Dove has thought hard about medium, message, and artist as they cooperate to make a piece of memorable or striking art. No black artist can avoid the question of subject matter; no black American poet, drawing on an overwhelmingly white tradition, can avoid a special case of what Harold Bloom called "the anxiety of influence." The same is true, to a lesser extent perhaps, of the woman artist. Yet if these important subject matters are not seen by a dispassionate eye and presented by a trained hand, the result will not be art. Dove becomes a very interesting case of a poet who is committed to these and other subjects (notably family history, love, politics, and motherhood) and whose gift for geometric stylization rivals, in its power, the seriousness of her topics.

The Laureateship, its title deriving from the English lifetime laureateship (now held by Ted Hughes), is, of course, something of a joke in an American setting. Even though poetry is almost wholly absent from American elementary and secondary education, and absent from university education except in the training of English majors, the Library of

Congress retains a job with which to honor poets. The poet appointed to the post used to be called Consultant in Poetry to the Library of Congress, and a string of notable people—the most recent being Joseph Brodsky, Mark Strand, and Mona Van Duyn—have inhabited the office, with varying results. The two-year stint makes the job essentially powerless and ceremonial, and consequently distressing to the poets, who see only too clearly the invisibility of poetry in America to all but the converted. Rita Dove, the youngest Poet Laureate, has reached for a larger connection to the Washington, D.C., community. Joseph Brodsky, during his tenure, famously said that poems should be sold in supermarkets—as indeed they should be, but who is to do the publishing and the marketing? And who would buy them unless a cultural training that made Americans thirst for poetry was there underpinning such a venture? "It is difficult / to get the news from poems," said William Carlos Williams (who himself did a lot to make the news easier to get), "yet men die miserably every day / for lack / of what is found there." That sentiment, or something like it, is one reason that even a democracy can still use a Poet Laureate.

The present Laureate is the author of four excellent books of poems, of which the third, *Thomas and Beulah,* won the Pulitzer Prize. Dove grew up in Akron, where her father was a chemist for the Goodyear Tire and Rubber Company. She went to Miami University on a National Merit Scholarship, graduated *summa cum laude,* and, after her Fulbright to Tübingen in 1974–75, took an M.F.A. at the University of Iowa. In 1980, when Dove was twenty-eight, Carnegie-Mellon published her first book, *The Yellow House on the Corner.* Like other first books, *The Yellow House* had its share of workshop poems, but it also had supremely finished poems, among them one that shows the young not-yet-poet discovering in her high school geometry homework a first inkling of the divine elation of formal pattern:

> I prove a theorem and the house expands:
> the windows jerk free to hover near the ceiling,
> the ceiling floats away with a sigh.
>
> As the walls clear themselves of everything
> but transparency, the scent of carnations
> leaves with them. I am out in the open

and above the windows have hinged into butterflies,
sunlight glinting where they've intersected.
They are going to some point true and unproven.

The Yellow House on the Corner also began a series of experiments, still
going on in Dove's poems, on how to write as a black. One early notion
was to take on history and write in a historically inflected slave's voice,
as in "Belinda's Petition," set in 1782, requesting manumission from the
United States Congress:

> I am Belinda, an African,
> since the age of twelve a Slave.
> I will not take too much of your Time,
> but to plead and place my pitiable Life
> unto the Fathers of this Nation.

And so on, with a creaking historical progress. Dove was more successful
in "The House Slave," in which the speaker feels guilty over the fate of her
sister the field slave. This is written in a neutrally contemporary voice:

> The first horn lifts its arm over the dew-lit grass
> and in the slave quarters there is a rustling—
> children are bundled into aprons, cornbread
>
> and water gourds grabbed, a salt pork breakfast taken.

Dialect, too, uneasily mixed with lyricism, was one of Dove's ventures in
the slave poems:

> Ain't got a reason
> to run away—
> leastways, not one
> would save my life.
> So I scoop speculation
> into a hopsack.
> I scoop fluff till
> the ground rears white

and I'm the only dark
spot in the sky.

These and other experiments—a prose poem, a poem mixing prose and verse, poems studded with bits and pieces of history from newspapers, pamphlets, memoirs—show Dove going persistently back to black material, uncertain of the best way in. The most daring poem taking on black life was "Nigger Song: An Odyssey," spoken collectively by six excited teenagers out for a good time in a car, feeling the marvelous invulnerability of youth:

> We six pile in, the engine churning ink:
> We ride into the night. . . .

> We sweep past excavation sites; the pits
> Of gravel gleam like mounds of ice.
> Weeds clutch at the wheels. . . .

> In the nigger night, thick with the smell of cabbages,
> Nothing can catch us.
> Laughter spills like gin from glasses,
> And "yeah" we whisper, "yeah"
> We croon, "yeah."

This is not entirely believable, but not unbelievable, either; the mood of unleashed speed and giddy freedom carries the poem. Here and in the poems called "Adolescence," Dove is notably apt at catching the volatile moods of puberty.

Both the deep theme of geometric form and the high, if flawed, ambitions of the many poems on blackness remained visible in Dove's second book, *Museum*, which also exhibited, as continuing concerns, questions of gender and of artistic creation, as in "Agosta the Winged Man and Rasha the Black Dove." Yet this superbly formal poem coexists in *Museum* with such colloquial epigrams as "Eastern European Eclogues," of which the fifth reads, in its entirety:

> Who?
> Of course not.

Why should they.
Of course not.

The reader is left to infer the story, one only too familiar.

In "Parsley," Dove's penetratingly imaginative mind took on the task of trying to conjecture why Rafael Trujillo, dictator of the Dominican Republic, ordered (as Dove's note to the poem tells us) fifty thousand migrant Haitian cane cutters killed because they could not pronounce the Spanish *r* properly: the test was the word *perejil,* or parsley. The poem, too long to quote here, summons up both the exhausted workers (in a quasi-villanelle) and the demented Trujillo (in a quasi-sestina); their vocabularies intertwine, so that we see that murderer and victims share a world. In her sinisterly plausible account of Trujillo's decision for genocide, Dove interrogates the extent to which aesthetic or libidinal attachment to language (Trujillo's obsession with "correct" Spanish, which he associates with his dead mother) can itself—as a poet knows— become vicious. Dove's rebukes of others are believable because they are also warnings to herself.

By the time she composed *Museum,* Dove had forsaken historical fustian for a language that is analytic, reflective, and thoroughly meditated. The poems are not "confessional," though they are often autobiographical. Experience has been reviewed, mastered, and controlled into intelligibility. The procedures of the poems leave little to chance; they are colloquial, jagged, and flexible, but there is nothing sprawling, messy, or incoherent about them. They aim to be structurally crystalline in form, but often laconically opaque in language. They halt the reader, and challenge a decoding.

It was the next book, *Thomas and Beulah,* that won the Pulitzer Prize. The book springs from the history of Dove's maternal grandparents, who migrated north, each from a different southern state, and married in Ohio. The life they made in Akron between marriage and death is the subject matter of the poems (which have been translated into a very well done videocassette by Video Press, of Cave Creek, Arizona). Dove solves the "color question" in *Thomas and Beulah* by having everyone in the central story be black, so that daily life is just daily life. (Every so often, the white context appears on the edges.) The gender question is treated evenhandedly, as Dove writes in sympathy with both Thomas and Beulah, often reproducing their own sense of themselves in free indirect discourse, and giving each a separate sequence of poems (first Thomas, then Beulah). History remains in play, no longer as antebellum slave history but as the history of industrial and domestic servitude in the earlier twentieth century. The problem of "high" art ("Agosta," and so on) and "low" art ("Nigger Song," and so on) is solved by keeping the two sequences—Thomas' and Beulah's—as elegant in structural form as a lieder cycle while letting colloquial talk run freely through them.

Dove ekes out the slender family information about her dead grandparents with her own invention, so that in the poem "Daystar," for instance, we perceive Beulah's experience as a mother in a double exposure with Dove's own. (Dove is married to the German novelist Fred Viebahn; they have a daughter.) Thomas and Beulah have had four children, all daughters ("Girl. Girl. Girl. Girl," Thomas reflects glumly); the burden of their upbringing falls on Beulah:

> She wanted a little room for thinking:
> but she saw diapers steaming on the line,
> a doll slumped behind the door.
>
> So she lugged a chair behind the garage
> to sit out the children's naps. . . .
>
> She had an hour, at best, before Liza appeared
> pouting from the top of the stairs.
> And just *what* was mother doing
> out back with the field mice? Why,
>
> building a palace. Later
> that night when Thomas rolled over and
> lurched into her, she would open her eyes
> and think of the place that was hers
> for an hour—where
> she was nothing,
> pure nothing, in the middle of the day.

The story of Thomas and Beulah unrolls through such brief glimpses, as the reader fills in the gaps between the snapshots. It is a common story in the great industrial migration of southern blacks to the North—both parents working at marginal jobs for low pay, Thomas' Depression layoff and illness, the constant, almost unspoken presence of discrimination. But the sequence is by no means all bleak: it is punctuated by the ordinary satisfactions—making hair pomade, planning a daughter's wedding, buying (at a church rummage sale) an encyclopedia with "One Volume Missing":

> Werner's Encyclopedia,
> Akron, Ohio, 1909:
> Complete in Twenty-Five Volumes
> minus one—
>
> for five bucks
> no zebras, no Virginia,
> no wars.

Thomas and Beulah, with its individual poems strung on the two names, sums up Dove's rethinking of the lyric poet's relation to history. No longer presenting a narrative in a single continuous fabric, she lets the raw data of life become pieces for a reader to assemble. But the sure hand of form supports each momentary glimpse; cunningly counterbalancing each other into stability, the tart and touching individual poems add up to a sturdy two-part invention, symbolizing that mysterious third thing, a lifelong marriage.

And what has happened to geometry, gender, blackness, history, and "high" and "low" art in Dove's recent Grace Notes (1989)? They continue in what has now become Dove's most characteristic style—the throwaway utterance that leaves a corrosive trace. A mother gives her child a doll and reflects:

> we
> give our children dolls, and
> they know just what to do—
>
> line them up and shoot them.

A Florida picnic of Dove's childhood, held trespassingly on a whites-only beach, leaves only one indelible memory, that of "the scratch, / shell on tin / of [the] distress" of crabs in a bucket, harvested for boiling. But the rest of the poem, though invented, dwells on black self-contempt and universal human defenses against the unpleasant. Aunt Helen looks at the scratching struggling crabs, and the child is bewildered by her comment:

> Why does Aunt Helen
> laugh before saying "Look at that—
>
> a bunch of niggers, not
> a-one get out 'fore the others pull him
> back." I don't believe her—
>
> just as I don't believe *they* won't come
> and chase us back to the colored-only shore
> crisp with litter and broken glass.

The observant and truth-telling child speaks up:

> "When do we kill them?"
> "Kill'em? Hell, the water does *that*.
> They don't feel a thing . . . no nervous system."

One hears the echo of the long series of white excuses for oppressing blacks: "They don't feel a thing . . . no nervous system"—another acid biting its way through the page, but aimed at blacks as well as whites.

Dove has moments, not always unwarranted, of giving in to sentiment, but her stock-in-trade is a dry, unsparing accuracy, as strict toward herself as toward others:

> Each evening I see my breasts
> slacker, black-tipped
> like the heavy plugs on hot water bottles;

each day resembling more the spiked fruits
dangling from natives in the *National Geographic*
my father forbade us to read.

This poem, "Genetic Expedition," owes a debt to Elizabeth Bishop's "In the Waiting Room," but the vertiginous horror of the little girl in the Bishop poem, when she realizes she is female, is not a factor in Dove's sequel. Instead, the poem looks down through the female line to the next Dove—Rita Dove's daughter:

My child has
her father's hips, his hair
like the miller's daughter, combed gold.
Though her lips are mine, housewives
stare when we cross the parking lot
because of that ghostly profusion.

To Dove, revising her precursor, anatomy is not destiny, and her daughter's "atomic gaze" (fission? fusion?) offers a crucible of power for an unreadable future.

The ambitions of lyric are no less serious—though they are sometimes thought to be—than those of drama or epic. Just as a solo partita reflects a mind, a temperament, and a universe within its own self-set compass, so lyric does within its generic means. Dove's unsettling themes are "stapled down with every step" of her poems, compressing large and complex feelings, both personal and political, into an outwardly restricted but internally expansive space. Technically, her poems "work" by their fierce concision and by an exceptional sense of rhythmic pulse. (Dove used to play the cello, still plays the viola da gamba, and is a trained singer.) No matter how painful her stories, no matter how sharp-edged her lines, her poems fall on the ear with solace. There are, of course, emotions not yet expressed in her repertoire—personal hatred, marital jealousy, shame of inadequate motherhood, who knows?—or, if they are here, they have been sublimed into refinement, beyond personal visibility. The anxiety that manifests itself as her taut control has so far precluded certain forms of the comic, the genial, or the insouciant; but her poems know reproach, irony, and a terse impatience very well. They also know a surprising surrealism, which turns out to be realism:

> From the beautiful lawnmower
> float curls of evaporated gasoline;
> the hinged ax of the butterfly pauses.

The *beautiful* lawnmower? The *ax* of the butterfly? By such almost assaultive means, Dove trains her reader into original perception.

It is an unusual mind that makes itself known in Dove's poems—acute, well-read, observant, reflective, formal. It refuses naïveté, and prefers a scalpel to a paintbrush. It is not a comfortable mind: aloof, watchful, it scrutinizes its readers and demands an answering intensity in return for its own. It is a pity that the Poet Laureate's office has no budget to speak of, no staff to speak of, and no lobbying power. It cannot act broadly to restore poetry to the young, who have in this country been so unaccountably deprived of their heritage. (What child any longer knows hundreds of poems by heart, as my mother, educated in public schools, did two generations ago?) "To have great poets," said Walt Whitman, "there must be great audiences too." If our human seedlings had the childhood nourishment they deserve, we would be growing a veritable forest of appreciators of poetry, and a fair number of potential Laureates. As it is, we have at present a stunning incumbent, who deserves the honor of the title.

15

Drawn to Figments and Occasion

Lucie Brock-Broido's *A Hunger*

Lucie Brock-Broido, in her first book, *A Hunger,* says of herself:

> Given my disposition, I will always be
> circuitous, precocious, an Embellisher. . . .
> Given my character, I will always be mercurial,
> a little sentimental, star-shaped & terrestrial.

The description rings true. Her poems are indeed circuitous, chiefly in their regression to childhood or girlhood; precocious, in their suffusing of a child's surreal perceptions with an adult knowingness; and embellished in fantastic and mercurial ways. She is terrestrial enough to write poems about (and in the imagined voices of) celebrities—Marilyn Monroe, Jessica McClure (the baby in the well), Birdie Africa (a child survivor of the police fire bombing of the MOVE cult in Philadelphia). And she is sentimental enough to write about lovers and relatives. But even these presumably mundane subjects have been tilted oddly toward a brazen freakishness:

> This work of mine . . .
>   It's peopled by Wizards, the Forlorn,

The Awkward, the Blinkers, the Spoon-Fingered, Agnostic
    Lispers,
Stutterers of Prayer, the Flatulent, the Closet Weepers,
The Charlatans. I am one of those.

This list of capitalized categories escapes self-parody only by espousing it, in a deliberately stylized version of Anne Sexton out of Disney. Brock-Broido is intent on an apparent factuality (history, the newspapers, quotations from *People*) but is all the while skittering off into the more unreliable forms of pictorial, fabular, and linguistic distortion. The poems leap off the page.

Brock-Broido was for five years a Briggs-Copeland Lecturer in Poetry at Harvard, where an appointment committee, of which I was one, hired her on the basis of the manuscript of *A Hunger*. Among other things, we liked her slangy and morose self-mockery, as in "Autobiography," which is set in a rented room:

It is only three o'clock & already I'm alone
Listening to the lovers next door
Like Patsy Cline & her Man
Throwing barebacked wooden furniture
Like the real life bicker of true love.
I love that hands-on,
Die-while-you're-dark-haired-still
& young, fists curled to desire,
Take Me kind of love.
They'll make love without apology
& I'll be left to the afternoon
& the autoerotic sounds of my American voice
Getting it all down.

The poet could just as well be the quarreling, love-driven girl next door—or maybe she once was. The ruefulness of self-inquiry saves the satire. Elsewhere, the poems often take on, by a hypnotic ventriloquism, the imagined voices of desperate or abandoned children. Here is Birdie Africa, child of the MOVE cult, holed up against the police:

There are other children now.
We run like wild
animals. We let our hair go
into puzzles which will never be unraveled.
We let our teeth go fierce.
We leave dirt in our palms
& sleep without nightclothes.
We pee in the yards & eat raw things.

Throughout *A Hunger*, Brock-Broido offers a witty running commentary on the clichés and terrors of contemporary America—ozone holes, the eschatological fantasy of Rapture, the taming of the American male:

There's a puncture in the southern reaches
Of the earth's protective atmosphere. I'm trying
To be moved by this, but I'm more piqued by Rapture now. . . .

Your new woman is Easy on the Eye, you say. Since this recent
Nomenclature for the Wind Chill, the world's a colder place . . .

　　　You Montana
Boys will marry one day after all, in small vehicular domiciles.

And yet, for all this contemporary chic, the poems are capable of suddenly sliding off the rails of "English" entirely, in ways that hope to reproduce the mind of the murderous or the mad. In the following quotation we see both, as one of a pair of identical twins imagines murdering the other:

　　First of all, I wept to God
—when world is wet & shy, under the bridge, I hold her
head down under
water & I feel her thrash
against me, just this once, I murder her,
it's a once in a lifetime thing you know?
You have no idea
how much I love her, I am she.

Some of the hazards of Brock-Broido's enterprise are easily seen: preciousness, exaggeration, a histrionic use of the more sensational edges of the news. Other hazards, less immediately apparent, take an insidious toll in the long run—chiefly the persistent use of a few obsessive words, among them the adjectives "small," "little," "tiny," "frail," "fragile"; the nouns "child" and "girl"; the verb "curl." Brock-Broido's infant or adolescent personae, frail, vulnerable, or ill, are curled in a fetal self-protectiveness, forbidden full extension. They master their author—and are, in turn, partly or wholly mastered by her. The apparently unconscious repetition of the self-deprecating adjectives suggests an as yet incomplete control over psychic material.

Brock-Broido's talismanic words open into a magical territory of "Domestic Mysticism" (the title of the first poem). The "domestic" part is represented by the recognizable furnishings of our world, from saxophones to Sno-cones, and among these furnishings women will recognize the apparatus of growing up as a girl: teacups, Dresden china, velvet curtains, bedroom windows, sewing, plants, eyelet-cotton dresses—to cite only the list from the opening poem. The "mystic" part of domestic mysticism appears in the slightly off-key manipulations of commonplace things, usually by metaphors (which I've italicized below) drawn from registers of reality which are radically different from the things they describe:

> I could watch . . .
> >   the quarries
> > *Churning* great chunks of marble.

> >   Those of us whose eyes
> > By chance, genetics, *aptitude,* go down
> > On the ends will be perceived as perpetually sad.

> >   The wanderers are still *avenging*
> > their insomnia in the dark
> > false *hellebore* red of poolhalls,
> > in the allnight pastel *caves* of laundromats

> The anorexic soul
> In *spandex tights* slips out of bed with me
>
> My sister & I would move *like spiders*
> into the nests of our dotted swiss nightgowns

Brock-Broido may inherit some of her domestic mysticism from Theodore Roethke, who specialized in the elusive and evasive intuitive movements of a little child-soul alive in a world of greenhouse domesticity, a tendril-spirit baffled by the motions of an as yet uninterpreted fate. Roethke, I think, wanted to remain unconscious, but Brock-Broido's preverbal personae struggle crazily toward consciousness and, consequently, toward language. They find this struggle libidinally exciting. It is their means of individuation, their path toward what the Jessica McClure poem calls "personal geometry." After all, what happens to the self is arbitrary; it is only by following, interpreting, naming the affronts to the sensibility, living them over again, that the self establishes control over them. The poem "After the Grand Perhaps" traces affront—sensuous, sensual, or imaginative—as part of the passage toward consciousness:

> After what is arbitrary: the hand grazing
> something too sharp or fine, the word spoken
> out of sleep, the buckling of the knees to cold,
> the melting of the parts to want,
> the design of the moon to cast
> unfriendly light, the dazed shadow
> of the self as it follows the self. . . .
> After life there must be life.

This diction—with its unobtrusive debts to Keats and Yeats—is distanced by its ghostliness from what Northrop Frye would call the "low mimetic" style of American poetic realism (recently overworked); yet it is perfectly intelligible, without any fanciness of reference or surrealism of manner.

Brock-Broido's revelations about herself in *A Hunger* tend to be made obliquely, often by crosscutting. Some of these disclosures deal with anorexia. "I, myself, as you know," says the protagonist of the prose poem

"Ten Years' Apprenticeship in Fantasy," "have been starving alternately for a decade." "The anorexics," comments the speaker of "After the Grand Perhaps," "have curled into their geometric forms." And Baby Jessica, in the well, complains that she has wedged her right leg in "a notorious and irredeemable position," saying, "I hate to be unnatural, especially in personal geometry." Nonetheless, she adds, she will survive, like "the small mythic creature I have always known I ought to be."

Baby Jessica is Brock-Broido's most complete, if most occluded, self-portrait. She boasts that she "can make the well's walls glitter / back at me." This may sound innocent enough, but the voice that Jessica eventually manufactures during her ordeal in the well has a jeering and sexually precocious awareness:

> Big gangly weepy gamey men, Sweethearts & Insomniacs,
> keep prodding me   *to sing.*
> And I sing.
>
> And: *Move your foot for me, Juicy.*
> And I wiggle it back for the man.
>
> And: *How does a kitten go?*
> And I go like kitten goes, on
>
> & on in that throaty liquid lewd bowlegged
> voice like kittens make.
> Then shut these big ole eyes.

It is a vulgar voice, a sardonic voice, a hardboiled voice:

> In the matter of my toes, there has been damage done
> but when I come back, they'll pinken up I'm sure.
> In America: *Hard Work & Prayer.*

It is even the voice of a priestess, one of Plath's queen bees:

> Surrounded by jelly, an accoutrement of eros for ascent
> from the well, I am born.

> Wide eyed & swaddled in white linens, I emerge
> pristine & preserved, like some Egyptian form.

Needless to say, this fantasy voice, damaged and preening, bears no mimetic relation to the real Jessica McClure. The incident of the baby in the well, one feels, was, like other *incidents provocateurs* in the book, the key that unlocked a Bluebeard's chamber in the poet's linguistic unconscious. There is a Grand Guignol relish in the act, as the perverse newborn speech breaks out:

> I am born into the dark
> rococo teratogenic rooms of the underground.

The deformations of language in the child-poems hint at the swollen terrors of the crushing birth-journey into identity, represented at its most sinister in the poem "Elective Mutes," about (actual) criminally insane identical female twins, who invented a private language by which to communicate with each other, remaining mute to the outside world. The poem could be called a violently skewed portrait of the female poet and her Muse, a hyped-up version of Stevens and his interior paramour, locked in a soliloquy "in which being there together is enough":

> In summertime, when we were little, I remember we
> walking with synchronized steps, a four-armed girl . . .
> We were eleven, a shadow & a shadow
> of her shadow.

Though the girls are British, Brock-Broido has them imagine an American adolescence—going to a drive-in, for example:

> All the convertible tops
> are down & the speakerbox hangs
> on the rear view mirror like a locust,
> slow & distorted like that
> & you climb in back to have a boy
> inside you, that's what I want, on the back seat
> sprawling in the noises like an animal

he makes, but you're shy, you're bourgeois, you talk
American which I sort of like but it's kind of sleazy, you know?

The rhythmic momentum of this piece of Americana and the audacity
of throwing it into a poem about mad English twins suggest the driven-
ness of Brock-Broido's imagination, which at other times can be delicate
and lyrical. Here, for instance, is a spookily lyrical portrait of two Ameri-
can hands, one making change in a gas station, the other dealing drugs
from behind a shop curtain in Harlem:

> I love
> these things too, the self serve
> filling station where a pale hand
> sneaks out making silver
> change, or the one dark palm
> in the meat shop on Amsterdam & 110th
> behind the curtain handing out
> the little envelopes of *Heartbeat.*

Something in Brock-Broido likes stealth, toxicity, wildness, neon—
"perfect mean lines." This part valuably adds astringency to her passion
for the beautiful. In the long farewell to a failed love affair, "I Wish You
Love"—which is at the same time an elegy for her father—the sensa-
tional and lyrical halves of Brock-Broido's sensibility meet. A broken
heart, death, the exhumed body of Mengele, ecological disaster, commer-
cial slaughter, the humdrum, the extravagant, the technological, the dis-
torted, the lyric all lurch together into an eclectic postmodern elegy:

> After a death in the family
> Gadgets go wrong for awhile; it's nothing
> You shouldn't expect, the near-collapse of anything electrical
> Or bound by heat or light. This is the gospel truth.
>
> In the evangelic dusk
> Way past the Bible belt, they're killing off
> Large common beasts, shackle & hoist method.

Don't you think they know what's going on?
All of those old prophets were the same: doom, doom.
But most of all, When snowflakes fall

I wish you love.

These deaths, glitches, butcherings, and song snatches go on in terse
but unstoppable six-line stanzas. Other hazards and griefs in *A Hunger*
are presented within the manicured paragraphs of prose poems. The
sheen of the arranged is lovingly applied to the fissures, accidents,
crimes, and corpses of life, as if to say defiantly, "Well, that's what art is,
isn't it?" To which the answer is yes and no: yes when the disjunction
between the hysterias of life and the formalities of art is to be empha-
sized, no when the equally true continuity between consciousness and
composition is the point to be made. Brock-Broido, now in her early
thirties, will perhaps in other books make up different versions of the
answer, putting her threatened and terrified childhood in a less varnished
and steely cage. In this volume she tells us what she is up to:

I am the medieval child in the basket, rocking.
Feigning sleep, up all night listening for secrets:
why there are punishments,
what news bad weather brings,
how things get winnowed out.

Will the child leave the rocking basket? Will she leave the restless, shelter-
ing automobiles that are her grownup version of the basket? Will she
loosen the tight stanzas that are the metrical equivalent of the basket?
Will she become someone other than the little-small child-girl? The in-
terest shown here in "getting it all down" suggests she will. "The psychic,"
as she says, "leaves the past":

sand covers Egypt,

Moves constantly to arrive at the streak
Of the yet-to-be.

This poet, "drawn to figments & occasion," has ornamented her book jacket with Carpaccio's *Dream of Saint Ursula*, in which the saint, asleep in her virginal four-poster (her relinquished book open on the reading table near the entrance to her chamber), is visited by an angel, forebodingly bearing toward her the palm of martyrdom. Saint Ursula (already inserted into modern poetry by Stevens) seems to stand here for the virginal "domestic mysticism" associated with fasting, prayer, and meditation. To be fair to its own brilliant inspiration, this book should have borne on the other half of its jacket the beautiful, equally aloof, but awake and ravenous face of the Medusa.

16

Second Thoughts

Seamus Heaney's
The Haw Lantern

Here are thirty-two new poems by Seamus Heaney—the yield since *Station Island* (1985). Heaney is a poet of abundance who is undergoing in middle age the experience of natural loss. As the earth loses for him the mass and gravity of familiar presences—parents and friends taken by death—desiccation and weightlessness threaten the former fullness of the sensual life.

The moment of emptiness can be found in other poets. "Already I take up less emotional space / Than a snowdrop," James Merrill wrote at such a point in his own evolution. Lowell's grim engine, churning powerfully on through the late sonnets, did not quite admit the chill of such a moment until *Day by Day:*

> We are things thrown in the air alive in flight . . .
> our rust the color of the chameleon.

It is very difficult for poets of brick and mortar solidity, like Lowell, or of rooted heaviness, like Heaney, to become light, airy, desiccated. In their new style they cannot abandon their former selves. The struggle to be one's old self and one's new self together is the struggle of poetry itself, which must accumulate new layers rather than discard old ones.

Heaney must thus continue to be a poet rich in tactile language, while

expressing emptiness, absence, distance. *The Haw Lantern,* poised be-
tween these contradictory imperatives of adult life, is almost peniten-
tially faithful to each, determined to forsake neither. Here, from "Bann
Clay" *(Poems, 1965–1975),* is the younger Heaney writing fifteen years ago
about moist clay:

> They loaded on to the bank
> Slabs like the squared-off clots
> Of a blue cream. . . .
>
>   Once, cleaning a drain
> I shovelled up livery slicks
> Till the water gradually ran
>
> Clear on its old floor.
> Under the humus and roots
> This smooth weight. I labour
> Towards it still. It holds and gluts.

Image and sound both bear witness here to the rich fluidity of the natural
world. Now, in *The Haw Lantern,* Heaney finds he must, to be truthful
to his past, add manufacture to nature. When he looks with adult eyes
at his natal earth, he finds machinery there as well as organic matter; and
he writes not with fluidity but with aphoristic brevity:

> When I hoked there, I would find
> An acorn and a rusted bolt.
>
> If I lifted my eyes, a factory chimney
> And a dormant mountain.
>
> If I listened, an engine shunting
> And a trotting horse.
>
> . . . . .
>
> My left hand placed the standard iron weight.
> My right tilted a last grain in the balance.

"Is it any wonder," the poet asks, "when I thought / I would have second thoughts?" ("Terminus").

The Haw Lantern is a book of strict, even stiff, second thoughts. Such analytic poetry cannot permit itself a first careless rapture. No longer (at least, not often) do we follow the delightful slope of narrative: "And then, and then." Instead, we see the mind balancing debits and credits. "I balanced all, brought all to mind," said Yeats, using a scale to weigh years behind and years to come. A poet who began as luxuriously as Heaney could hardly have dreamed he would be called to such an audit. The need for adult reckoning must to some degree be attributed to his peculiar internal exile. Born among the Catholic minority in British Protestant Ulster, he came young to social awareness; now removed to the largely Catholic Republic of Ireland, he is part of an Ulster-bred minority substantially different in culture and upbringing from the majority.

The poetry of second thoughts has its own potential for literary elaboration. The Haw Lantern is full of parables and allegories, satires of Irish religious, social, and political life. The blank verse of these allegories is as far from the opulent rhymed stanzas of Heaney's sensual, Keatsian aspect as from the slender trimeters and dimeters of his "Irish" side. The strangest poem in The Haw Lantern, a blank-verse piece called "The Mud Vision," arises from Heaney's desire to respect amplitude, even in an analytic poem. I don't find the effort wholly successful, but I see in it the way Heaney is willing to flail at impossibility rather than divide his believing youth from his skeptical middle age.

This religious-political-social poem begins with a bitter satiric portrait of an unnamed country dithering between atavistic superstition and yuppie modernity. The landscape displays a thin layer of industrial modernization over a desolate rural emptiness; in a typical scene, terrorist casualties are carried, in a heliport, past the latest touring rock star:

> Statues with exposed hearts and barbed-wire crowns
> Still stood in alcoves, hares flitted beneath
> The dozing bellies of jets, our menu-writers
> And punks with aerosol sprays held their own
> With the best of them. Satellite link-ups

Wafted over us the blessings of popes, heliports
Maintained a charmed circle for idols on tour
And casualties on their stretchers. We sleepwalked
The line between panic and formulae, . . .
Watching ourselves at a distance, advantaged
And airy as a man on a springboard
Who keeps limbering up because the man cannot dive.

In that last image, Heaney catches the "advantaged and airy" compla-
cency of an impotent nation congratulating itself on political flexibility
as a way of concealing indecisiveness. The despair brilliantly hidden in
this sketch casts up a compensatory vision. What if a dispossessed coun-
try could believe not in its useless statues of the Sacred Heart nor in its
modern veneer of restaurants and heliports, but in its own solid earth?
In the "mud vision" of the title, a whirling rainbow-wheel of transparent
mud appears in the foggy midlands of this unnamed country, and a fine
silt of earth spreads from it to touch every cranny. Heaney tries to catch
the vision and its effect on those who see it:

And then in the foggy midlands it appeared,
Our mud vision, as if a rose window of mud
Had invented itself out of the glittery damp,
A gossamer wheel, concentric with its own hub
Of nebulous dirt, sullied yet lucent.
        . . . We were vouchsafed
Original clay, transfigured and spinning.

The poem runs out of steam trying to imagine how the "mud vision"
banishes traditional religion (bulrushes replace lilies on altars, invalids
line up for healing under the mud shower, and so on). Eventually, of
course, the vision disappears in the "*post factum* jabber" of experts. "We
had our chance," says the speaker, "to be mud-men, convinced and es-
tranged," but in hesitation, all opportunity was lost.

"Vision" is meant in the entirely human sense, as we might say Parnell
had a vision of a free Ireland, or Gandhi a vision of a free India; but "The
Mud Vision" puts perhaps a too religious cast on clay. Can a vision of

the earthy borrow its language from the conventional "vision" of the heavenly ("a rose window . . . lucent . . . original . . . transfigured")?

"The Mud Vision" puts many of Heaney's qualities on record—his territorial piety, his visual wit, his ambition for a better Ireland, his reflectiveness, and his anger—and attempts somehow to find a style that can absorb them all. However, "The Mud Vision" has none of the *sprezzatura* and firm elegance of other poems in *The Haw Lantern,* such as "Wolfe Tone." In this posthumous self-portrait, the speaker is the Irish Protestant revolutionary (1763–1798) who attempted a union of Catholics and Protestants against England, and was captured in 1798 after his invading fleet was defeated off Donegal. Tone committed suicide in prison before he could be executed for treason. He symbolizes the reformer estranged by his gifts, his style, and his daring from the very people he attempts to serve:

> Light as a skiff, manoeuvrable
> yet outmanoeuvred,
>
> I affected epaulettes and a cockade,
> wrote a style well-bred and impervious
>
> to the solidarity I angled for . . .
>
> I was the shouldered oar that ended up
> far from the brine and whiff of venture,
>
> like a scratching post or a crossroads flagpole,
> out of my element among small farmers.

Though the first two lines of "Wolfe Tone" owe something to Lowell's *Day by Day,* the poem has a dryness and reticence all its own. The force of the poem lies in the arid paradox—for reformers—that authentic style is often incompatible with political solidarity with the masses (a paradox on which Socialist Realism foundered). The desolate alienation of the artist/revolutionary is phrased here with the impersonality and obliqueness of Heaney's minimalist style (of which there was a foretaste in *Station Island*'s "Sweeney Redivivus").

I hope I have said enough to suggest where Heaney finds himself morally at this moment, poised between the "iron weight" of analysis and "the last grain" of fertile feeling, between cutting satire and a hopeful vision of possibility. Besides the blank-verse political parables I have mentioned, *The Haw Lantern* contains several notable elegies, among them a sequence of eight sonnets ("Clearances") in memory of Heaney's mother, who died in 1984. To make this hardest of genres new, Heaney moves away from both stateliness and skepticism. Borrowing from Miłosz's "The World," a poem in which a luminous past is evoked in the simplest, most childlike terms, Heaney writes a death-sonnet that imagines all Oedipal longings fulfilled:

> It is Number 5, New Row, Land of the Dead,
> Where grandfather is rising from his place
> With spectacles pushed back on a clean bald head
> To welcome a bewildered homing daughter
> Before she even knocks. 'What's this? What's this?'
> And they sit down in the shining room together.

Such felicity brings Miłosz's "naïve" effect fully into our idiom, and displays the son's self-denying capacity to write about his mother as ultimately her father's daughter.

But "Clearances" also touches on the irritability, the comedy, and the dailiness of the bond between sons and mothers. In one of its best sonnets, son and mother are folding sheets together; and here I recall Alfred Kazin's *An Apple for My Teacher*, his recent memoir of his youth in the thirties, when he wrote for a freshman English class at City College "an oedipal piece about helping my mother carry ice back to our kitchen, each of us holding one end of a towel": "This was such a familiar and happy experience for me in summer that I was astonished by the young instructor's disgust on reading my paper. He was a vaguely British type, a recent Oxford graduate . . . who openly disliked his predominantly Jewish students. My loving description of carrying ice in partnership with my mother seemed to him, as he tightly put it, 'impossible to comprehend.'" It is useful to be reminded how recently literature has been open to such experiences. Here is Heaney with his mother folding the sheets:

The cool that came off sheets just off the line
Made me think the damp must still be in them
But when I took my corners of the linen
And pulled against her, first straight down the hem
And then diagonally, then flapped and shook
The fabric like a sail in a cross-wind,
They made a dried-out undulating thwack.

Petrarch or Milton could hardly have imagined that this might be the octave of a sonnet. Yet the pretty "rhymes" echo tradition, as *line* stretches to *linen* (the clothesline and the sheets), and as *them* shrinks to *hem* (a folded sheet in itself). Frost, Heaney's precursor here, would have recognized the unobtrusive sentence-sounds; the line "Made me think the damp must still be in them" could slip into "Birches" without a hitch. (The "dried-out undulating thwack," though, is pure Heaney; Frost's eye was more on Roman moral epigram than on sensual fact.)

The seven-line "sestet" of the sonnet closes with a muted reference to the writing of the poem (the poet is now inscribing his family romance on a different set of folded sheets), but this literary marker is almost invisible in Heaney's intricately worked plainness:

So we'd stretch and fold and end up hand to hand
For a split second as if nothing had happened
For nothing had that had not always happened
Beforehand, day by day, just touch and go,
Coming close again by holding back
In moves where I was x and she was o
Inscribed in sheets she'd sewn from ripped-out flour sacks.

Taut lines and folded sheets connect mother and son, in art as in life.

Like "Clearances," the other elegies in this volume combine the density of living with the bleakness of loss, preserving the young, tender Heaney in the present stricken witness. "The Stone Verdict" is an anticipatory elegy for Heaney's father, who has since died; other poems commemorate his young niece Rachel, dead in an accident; his wife's mother ("The

Wishing Tree"); and his colleague at Harvard, Robert Fitzgerald. Heaney affirms that the space left in life by the absence of the dead takes on a shape so powerful that it becomes a presence in itself. In the elegy for his mother, Heaney's emblem for the shocking absence is a felled chestnut tree that was his "coeval"—planted in a jam jar the year he was born. Cut down, it becomes "utterly a source,"

> Its heft and hush become a bright nowhere,
> A soul ramifying and forever
> Silent, beyond silence listened for.

Heaney's sharply etched "nowhere" is a correction not only of Christian promises of heaven, but also of Yeats's exuberant purgatorial visions of esoteric afterlifes. It returns Irish elegy to truthfulness.

Heaney said, in a symposium on art and politics held at Northeastern University in 1986, that because people of any culture share standards and beliefs, the artist's "inner drama goes beyond the personal to become symptomatic and therefore political." To ascribe immense and unforgettable value to the missing human piece, simply because it is missing, is to put the power to ascribe value squarely in the human rather than in the religious sphere. Since institutional ideology everywhere reserves to itself alone the privilege of conferring value, it is all the more necessary for writers to remind us that control of value lies in individual, as well as in collective, hands.

Heaney directly addresses the question of value in "The Riddle," the poem placed last in this self-questioning book. His governing image here is the ancient one of the sieve that separates wheat from chaff. Such sieves are no longer in use, but the poet has seen one:

> You never saw it used but still can hear
> The sift and fall of stuff hopped on the mesh,
> Clods and buds in a little dust-up,
> The dribbled pile accruing under it.

Which would be better, what sticks or what falls through?
Or does the choice itself create the value?

This is the poem of a man who has discovered that much of what he has
been told was wheat is chaff, and a good deal that was dismissed as chaff
turns out to be what he might want to keep. Coleridge, remembering
classical myths of torment, wrote, "Work without hope draws nectar in
a sieve"; Heaney, rewriting Coleridge, thinks that the endless labors of
rejection and choice might yet be a way to salvation. He asks himself, at
the close of "The Riddle," to

> ... work out what was happening in that story
> Of the man who carried water in a riddle.
>
> Was it culpable ignorance, or was it rather
> A *via negativa* through drops and let-downs?

The great systems of dogma (patriotic, religious, ethical) must be aban-
doned, Heaney suggests, in favor of a ceaseless psychic sorting. Dis-
carding treasured pieties and traditional rules, the poet finds "drops and
let-downs," and he refuses to take much joy in the task of sifting, though
a middle couplet shows it to be undertaken with good will:

> Legs apart, deft-handed, start a mime
> To sift the sense of things from what's imagined.

In Heaney's earlier work, this couplet would have been the end of the
poem, breathing resolve and hope. Now he ends the poem asking
whether his sifting should be condemned as "culpable ignorance" (the
Roman Catholic phrase is taken from the penitentials) or allowed as a
via negativa. The latter phrase, which is also drawn from Catholicism, is
a theological term connected to mysticism, suggesting that we can know
God only as he is not.

The elegiac absences and riddles of *The Haw Lantern* are balanced by
powerful presences, none more striking than the emblematic winter

hawthorn of the title poem. This poem, by dwelling throughout on a single allegorical image, displays a relatively new manner in Heaney's work. In the past, Heaney's imagery has been almost indecently prolific; readers of *North* (1975) will remember, for instance, the Arcimboldo-like composite of the exhumed cadaver called the Grauballe Man:

> The grain of his wrists
> is like bog oak,
> the ball of his heel
>
> like a basalt egg.
> His instep has shrunk
> cold as a swan's foot
> or a wet swamp root.
>
> His hips are the ridge
> and purse of a mussel,
> his spine an eel arrested
> under a glisten of mud.

It is hard for a poet so fertile in sliding simile to stay put, to dwell on a single image until it becomes an emblem; it means going deeper rather than rippling on. "The Haw Lantern," doing just this, fixes on the one burning spot in the blank landscape of winter—the red berry, or haw, on the naked hawthorn branch. At first the poet sees the berry as an almost apologetic flame, indirectly suggesting his own quelled hopes as a spokesman for his fellow men. He goes deeper into self-questioning by transforming the haw into the lantern carried by Diogenes as he searches for one just man. The stoic haw, meditation reminds the poet, is both pith and pit, at once fleshy and stony. The birds peck at it, but it continues ripening. In this upside-down almost-sonnet, the stern haw lantern scrutinizes the poet scrutinizing it:

> The wintry haw is burning out of season,
> crab of the thorn, a small light for small people,
> wanting no more from them but that they keep
> the wick of self-respect from dying out,
> not having to blind them with illumination.

> But sometimes when your breath plumes in the frost
> it takes the roaming shape of Diogenes
> with his lantern, seeking one just man;
> so you end up scrutinized from behind the haw
> he holds up at eye-level on its twig,
> and you flinch before its bonded pith and stone,
> its blood-prick that you wish would test and clear you,
> its pecked-at ripeness that scans you, then moves on.

Like other poems in Heaney's new volume, "The Haw Lantern" reflects a near despair of country and of self.

Heaney's burning haw can bear comparison with Herbert's emblematic rose, "whose hue, angry and brave, / Bids the rash gazer wipe his eye." Forsaking topical reference, the artist writing in such genres as the emblem-poem ("The Haw Lantern") and allegory ("The Mud Vision") positions himself at a distance from daily events. Such analytic, generalized poetry hopes to gain in intelligence what it loses in immediacy of reference. (The greatest example of such an aesthetic choice is Milton's decision to write the epic of Puritan war, regicide, reform, and defeat by retelling Genesis.)

Heaney has several times quoted Mandelstam's "notion that poetry is addressed to . . . 'The reader in posterity.'" As he said at the Northeastern University symposium, "It is not directed exploitatively towards its immediate audience—although of course it does not set out to disdain the immediate audience either. It is directed towards the new perception which it is its function to create." The social, historical, and religious perceptions of *The Haw Lantern,* if they should become general in Ireland, would indeed create a new psychic reality there. Such a prospect has seemed so unlikely that it is only by believing in "the reader in posterity" that a writer can continue to address Irish issues at all.

I have saved the best of this collection for last: two excellent poems about the life of writing. The first, "Alphabets," written as the Phi Beta Kappa poem for Harvard, presents a series of joyous scenes that show the child becoming a writer. The alphabets of the title are those learned by the poet as he grew up: English, Latin, Irish, and Greek. They stand for the widening sense of place, time, and culture gained as the infant grows to be a youth, a teacher, and a poet. Against Wordsworth's myth of a childhood radiance lost, the poem sets a counter-myth of an imaginative power that becomes fuller and freer with the child's expanding linguistic and literary power.

With great charm, "Alphabets" shows us the child in school mastering his first alphabet:

> First it is 'copying out', and then 'English'
> Marked correct with a little leaning hoe.
> Smells of inkwells rise in the classroom hush.
> A globe in the window tilts like a coloured O.

Learning Irish, so different in prosody from English and Latin, awakens the boy's Muse:

> Here in her snooded garment and bare feet,
> All ringleted in assonance and woodnotes,
> The poet's dream stole over him like sunlight
> And passed into the tenebrous thickets.

The boy becomes a teacher, and the verse makes gentle fun of his self-conscious and forgivable vanity:

> The globe has spun. He stands in a wooden O.
> He alludes to Shakespeare. He alludes to Graves.

"Alphabets" closes with a hope for global vision, based on two exemplary human images. The first is that of a Renaissance humanist necromancer who hung from his ceiling "a figure of the world with colours in it," so that he could always carry it in his mind—

> So that the figure of the universe
> And 'not just single things' would meet his sight
>
> When he walked abroad.

The second figure is that of the scientist-astronaut, who also tries to comprehend the whole globe:

> . . . from his small window
> The astronaut sees all he has sprung from,
> The risen, aqueous, singular, lucent O
> Like a magnified and buoyant ovum.

Heaney implies that whatever infant alphabet we may start from, we will go on to others, by which we hope to encompass the world. Ours is the first generation to have a perceptual (rather than conceptual) grasp of the world as a single orbiting sphere—"the risen, aqueous, singular, lucent O"; and the almost inexpressible joy of sensuous possession lies in that line, a joy Heaney sees in the cultural and intellectual possession of the world, whether by humanist or scientist. "Alphabets" combines a humorous tenderness of self-mockery with an undiminished memory of the vigilant vows of youth, suggesting that middle age need not mark a discontinuity in life or writing.

The other brilliant poem here, "From the Frontier of Writing," offers a *vie de poète* altogether different from that of "Alphabets." Written in an adapted Dantesque terza rima, "The Frontier" retells a narrow escape from a modern hell. It takes as its emblem the paralyzing experience—familiar even to tourists—of being stopped and questioned at a military roadblock in Ireland. The writer, however, has not only to pass through real roadblocks but to confront as well the invisible roadblocks of consciousness and conscience. In either case, you can lose your nerve: in life, you can be cowed; in writing, you can be tempted to dishonesty or evasion. I quote this report from the frontier in full.

> The tightness and the nilness round that space
> when the car stops in the road, the troops inspect
> its make and number and, as one bends his face

towards your window, you catch sight of more
on a hill beyond, eyeing with intent
down cradled guns that hold you under cover

and everything is pure interrogation
until a rifle motions and you move
with guarded unconcerned acceleration—

a little emptier, a little spent
as always by that quiver in the self,
subjugated, yes, and obedient.

So you drive on to the frontier of writing
where it happens again. The guns on tripods;
the sergeant with his on-off mike repeating

data about you, waiting for the squawk
of clearance; the marksman training down
out of the sun upon you like a hawk.

And suddenly you're through, arraigned yet freed,
as if you'd passed from behind a waterfall
on the black current of a tarmac road

past armour-plated vehicles, out between
the posted soldiers flowing and receding
like tree shadows into the polished windscreen.

This poem is so expressive of the recent armed tension in Ireland that it is political simply by being. It produces in us an Irish weather—menacing, overcast, electric—so intense that for a while we live in it. It has the allegorical solidity of the *déjà vu,* and the formal solidity of its two twelve-line roadblocks.

But formal solidity is not the only manner in which Heaney composes good poems. He has always had a talent and an appetite for the organic (growing and decaying at once), for which he invented the "weeping" stanzas of the bog poems. The elusive short couplets in "Wolfe Tone" and "The Riddle" suggest a third temper in Heaney, one represented neither by commanding masonry nor by seeping earth but rather by rustling dust, leaves, and feathers. The epigraph to *The Haw Lantern* epitomizes this third manner as the poet waits for a sound beyond silence listened for:

> The riverbed, dried-up, half-full of leaves.
>
> Us, listening to a river in the trees.

In deprivation, the poet trusts the premonitory whisper from the stock of unfallen leaves. *The Haw Lantern* proves the trust is not misplaced.

17

A Wounded Man Falling Towards Me

Seamus Heaney's *The Government of the Tongue*

In 1970, a year after the intensification of hostilities in Northern Ireland, the Irish poet Seamus Heaney had a dream: "I was shaving at the mirror of the bathroom when I glimpsed in the mirror a wounded man falling towards me with his bloodied hands lifted to tear at me or to implore." Once the necessary narcissism of the youthful art-mirror was invaded by an ambiguous national—even familial—horror, Heaney's work began to exhibit an anxiety that has never left it, in spite of his move in 1972 from Ulster to the Republic. His new collection of essays, *The Government of the Tongue*, opens with an allegorical primer of this anxiety: "Both Art and Life have had a hand in the formation of any poet, and both are to be loved, honoured and obeyed. Yet both are often perceived to be in conflict."

The first half of this new book belongs chiefly to Life. Several of its essays praise modern poets who have been called upon to exhibit exceptional moral courage under totalitarian regimes (Mandelstam, Holub, Herbert). Other essays hold up for inspection postcolonial poets such as Kavanagh and Walcott. (There is also a brilliant essay on Larkin's visionary moments; it springs from Heaney's interest in the assertion of value in the absence of any proof of the existence of such value—a question not unrelated to resistance to state control.)

The second half of *The Government of the Tongue*—four essays delivered in 1986 as the T. S. Eliot Memorial Lectures at the University of Kent—belongs chiefly to Art. Writing on Auden, Lowell, and Plath, Heaney pays homage (not without criticism) to three contemporary poets of the English language who were, to his mind, exemplary in their aesthetic practice. Heaney does not pretend to solve the dilemma put to the poet in every era by the demands of life and of art, and at least two of the examples he cites (George Herbert and Sylvia Plath) seem to me less than adequately represented for the purposes of his argument. But to follow the darts and feints of Heaney's mind as he worries his own case through these surrogates is immensely instructive.

In his first collection of essays, *Preoccupations* (1980), Heaney was engaged in coming to terms with some of his early masters—Wordsworth, Hopkins, and Yeats. He went to school to them to learn ways, both conceptual and linguistic, of treating his original givens—rural life, Catholicism, Irish nationality. His essays on his predecessors—bravura pieces of characterization, the best in recent memory—ended up defending a Wordsworthian and Keatsian "wise passiveness" (absorptive, hidden, receptive, yielding) against the Hopkinsian and Yeatsian tendency to forcemarch language into compliance with an authorial will.

The Irish troubles, however, put pliability and privacy into question as literary values. When Heaney was subjected to considerable pressure at home to take a public stand, he responded by anthropologizing the Irish conflict. In his incomparable volume *North* (1975), he published poems referring to centuries of tribal warfare in a whole swath of northern countries, from Scandinavia to Ireland, and the long-preserved violence of historical memory took on symbolic form in poems about slaughtered bodies exhumed from the bogs of Jutland and Ireland alike. The long view was a counter-measure to those whose memories went back only to the plantation of Ulster.

Heaney may have been drawn to a poet like Zbigniew Herbert by Herbert's comparable historical allusions to totalitarianism in Roman times. All writers under political pressure find historical allusion and allegory congenial forms, since they are oblique and nonreferential in any legal sense. One solution to censorship—a solution that Herbert and Holub have adopted in eastern Europe—is to write in parable, and Heaney himself has written in parables in *The Haw Lantern*. Nonetheless, this solution—though interesting and fruitful stylistically—does not entirely satisfy Heaney as an answer to his central question: "What must the poet do in a politically troubled time?" The parable can smack too much of the political address.

Heaney's title—*The Government of the Tongue*—has, as he says, two meanings. In Heaney's first meaning, the writer's tongue takes governance over the world by the exercise of its transcriptive power and by its conferral of value. In Heaney's second meaning, the political world, perturbed by descriptions of itself not to its liking, attempts—by pressures ranging from censure to execution—to govern the tongue of the poet. And the poet's spirit, if it yields up its inner freedom, can engage in self-censorship and a disabling self-governing. In writing about these matters, Heaney explicitly disavows comparison of his own free position with that of poets writing under totalitarian regimes, but he makes it clear that open speech is rarely welcome in any divided community.

Heaney's critics in Ireland have come from many sides. He has been accused of cowardice (being insufficiently political) and of propaganda (being too political), of complicity in violence (by seeing sectarian murder as endemic in northern countries since the Vikings), and of complicity in the Ulster status quo (by refusing to lend his voice to sectarian politics). He has accused himself (in "Exposure") of evasion of responsibility and (in "Station Island") of prettifying assassination with the absolution of verse.

What attracts Heaney to poets like Holub and Herbert (and Miłosz) is their success in dealing with a relatively intractable subject matter. The poets of eastern Europe have proved that even the most volatile social concerns can, and must, be brought under the government of the poetic tongue if they are to be represented at all. At the same time, and at a deeper level, Heaney wonders whether, in order for the poet to act politically, it is indispensable for him to represent actual political history in poetry. Here, Heaney's mentor is Mandelstam, who, after five years during which he was unable to compose, discovered for himself that writing about anything at all—provided one writes as a free man uncoerced by political prudence—is itself a rebuke to the totalitarian attempt to govern the writer's tongue, to direct writing toward certain approved subjects. In writing on Mandelstam, Heaney speaks out for the unlimited freedom of lyric to take up private subjects as well as public ones, as long as it does so without respect to social pressure.

Human fearfulness under the threat of social disapproval—not to speak of the threat of punishment or death—assures the conformity of most writers to the will of the totalitarian state. Those who have resisted cooptation have been enrolled in what Heaney calls "a modern martyrology" of art. Though he equally admires, in a moral sense, nonpoets who resist immoral state pressure, what he values in the poets who resist is their preservation of "cultural memory" (so that authentic poetry does not cease to exist), their "indicative mood" of bold presentation, and the "fate and scope" of their wide social concern. Contemporary Western lyric poetry, by contrast, can seem confined within private walls and damned to the conditional mood of wish, yearning, and indeterminacy. It seems afraid to take on, in symbolic form, the question of the collective social fabric.

The central question, which Heaney does not sufficiently address with respect to collective ideology and art, is whether some artists at all times and all artists at some times can work happily within a civic or ecclesiastical ideological consensus. The numerous Madonnas and Masses of supreme aesthetic quality suggest that "living" ideologies, as long as they are believed in, are not so aesthetically oppressive as dead (totally codified, governmentally imposed) ones. The view of the artist as a living critique of ideological consensus is, of course, an attractive one to us, postromantics as we are, and can perhaps be applied retrospectively even to some Renaissance artists working within an ideology like Christianity, where Heaney sees only "acceptable themes . . . given variously resourceful treatments." To me it seems that a critique of received forms of religious expression is visible, for instance, in the work of George Herbert, whom Heaney prefers to regard as one who "surrendered himself to a framework of belief and an instituted religion; but in [Herbert's] case, it happened that his personality was structured in such a way that he could dwell in amity with doctrine." Amity and surrender are not the marks of any strenuous art; and Herbert deserves better praise than the "felicity or correctness of a work's execution," which is all that Heaney allows the Renaissance poet working within the Christian consensus. We need a better theory of what it means to an artist to struggle with an ideology from within, as a believer.

In treating the eastern European poets, Heaney necessarily works from translations. When he turns, in the second part of *The Government of the*

Tongue, to modern poets writing in English whom he admires, a palpable change of emphasis, from society to self, appears in his pages. Imaginative arts such as poetry, Heaney concedes, are "practically useless," but he adds, "They verify our singularity, they strike and stake out the ore of self which lies at the base of every individuated life." Here, it is the transcription not of the social fabric but of the private self—and a special sort of self, the "individuated life"—that is at stake. Knowingly or not, Heaney in this vocabulary breaks definitively with most of the literary theory that is interested in the social function of literature. Such theory refuses precedence to the "imaginative arts" (as Heaney calls them) of language, and puts writing that exhibits poesis on the same footing as all other "texts." This move, which is a political one, seeks to allocate equal cultural interest to all texts. Of course, this sociological view of writing allows no particular privilege to what Heaney calls "singularity" and to the "individuated life"—those qualities indispensable (but not sufficient) for identifiable literary style.

There have been singular and individuated selves who never wrote a word. But without a singular and individuated moral self, there has never been a singular and individuated literary style. The writing self does not have to be virtuous in the ordinary sense of the word; but it does have to be extraordinarily virtuous in its aesthetic moves. It must refuse— against the claims of fatigue, charm, popularity, money, and so on—the *idée reçue,* the imprecise word, the tired rhythm, the replication of past effects, the uninvestigated stanza. It is this heroic virtue in the realm of aesthetic endeavor that courses in great authors exist to teach (as courses in "texts" do not). And Heaney stands by this aesthetic arduousness, which he finds in each of his authors. Human testimony—from the poor, the uneducated, the prudishly conventional, the genteelly euphemistic, the propaganda hacks, the well-meaning sincere—is not uninteresting. It *is* interesting. But it does not convey the strict morality of the imaginative effort toward aesthetic embodiment. That morality is almost unimaginably exhausting.

In pointing out Lowell's deliberate breaking of his own style not once but twice, Plath's sedulous youthful work on poetic form, and Auden's pursuit of the Anglo-Saxon underpinnings of English, Heaney pays tribute to the sheer toil toward competence on the one hand, and toward freshness on the other, that is the indispensable preparatory work for poetry. The fact that Auden and Lowell and Plath all came from a privileged elite is not for Heaney an issue; it is axiomatic for him that privilege, somehow acquired, is necessary to becoming an accomplished artist. He does not confuse the political work of a just society (ensuring that talent has access to training) with aesthetic judgment (which can only say whether or not a writer has successfully deployed the moral, imaginative, and linguistic resources needed for the artwork in hand). Nor is Heaney diffident about the ranking of aesthetic efforts. He understands what his chosen writers are up to, can see where and how they succeed, and is entirely willing to demonstrate and defend what he sees. Practical criticism consists in just that evidential demonstration, but it is rarely had from one who knows the medium and its potential glories and pitfalls as well as Heaney.

In Heaney's Auden essay we catch a deflected glimpse of his own aims as a writer of prose. There he praises the critical "responses and formulations" of the poet Geoffrey Grigson as the sort that "count for most in the long poetic run, because they are the most intrinsically sensitive to the art of language." Some commentators on Auden, he remarks, have concentrated on the history of ideas, whether in noting Auden's "shifting allegiances to Marx and Freud" or, more recently, in finding Auden's texts metaphysically self-deconstructive. "It may be," Heaney continues, "that Grigson's way of talking about poems is not as strictly analytical as this, but the way it teases out the cultural implications and attachments which inhabit any poem's field of force is a critical activity not to be superseded, because it is so closely allied, as an act of reading, to what happens during the poet's act of writing." The art of Heaney's criticism is never to lose touch with the writing act, the texture of the lines on the page. And his next sentence is one that, revealingly enough, would never be uttered by a historian of ideas or a deconstructive critic: "A new rhythm, after all, is a new life given to the world, a resuscitation not just of the ear but of the springs of being." That sentence leads him into a splendid and energetic glance at the early Auden.

In canonizing an English Anglican, an American Brahmin, and a female expatriate American, Heaney stands aside from the depressing literary politics in which Marxists puff only Marxists, women puff only women, blacks puff only blacks, and so on, with a consequent loss of credibility for the whole enterprise of literary judgment. Of course, the fraternity of artists has its familial bonds, and Heaney has not hesitated to praise, with generational solidarity, admirable work by Irish artists and postcolonial writers. But he has reserved his extended and investigative critical writing for major writers, and in them he observes, with an insight impossible to anyone but a poet, their subtlest as well as their broadest powers. Space allows me only one brief example: Heaney's remarks about the way Lowell ends poems. He quotes a sample of last lines, and goes on:

> Closing lines like these would tremble in the centre of the ear like an arrow in a target and set the waves of suggestion rippling. A sense of something utterly completed vied with a sense of something startled into scope and freedom. The reader was permitted the sensation of a whole meaning simultaneously clicking shut and breaking open, a momentary illusion that the fulfilments which were being experienced in the ear spelled out meanings and fulfilments available in the world. So, no matter how much the poem insisted on breakdown or the evacuation of meaning from experience, its fall toward a valueless limbo was broken by the perfectly stretched safety net of poetic form itself.

Heaney's adverse criticism of his three poets—always courteous, but not the less incisive for that—suggests values that he is too sophisticated to prescribe but is nonetheless disappointed not to find in them. He regrets that Auden forsook his original wildness of language: in later Auden "the line is doctrinaire in its domesticity, wanting to comfort like a thread of wool rather than shock like a bare wire." Lowell in the late sonnet trilogy massed his shock troops too oppressively for a human scale: "To confront the whole triptych is to confront a phalanx. I feel driven off the field of my reader's freedom by the massive riveted façade, the armoured tread, the unconceding density of it all." Plath, instead of enlarging herself into myth, reduces powerful ancient myths to the confines of her own personal history: "In 'Lady Lazarus' . . . the cultural resonance of the original story is harnessed to a vehemently self-justifying purpose, so that the supra-personal dimensions of knowledge—to which myth typically gives access—are slighted in favour of the intense personal need of the poet." One may not always agree with Heaney, but one is moved to profitable thought by his metaphorically vivid judgments.

Heaney's volume tosses and turns between "the hedonism and jubilation" of the poetic act and the affront to human misery presented by that hedonism. In the most original moment of this very original book, Heaney finds a way into the space between creative hedonism and human suffering. He quotes the Gospel of John, in which the scribes and Pharisees bringing before Jesus a woman taken in adultery ask whether they should obey the Mosaic law and stone her:

> This they said, tempting him, that they might have to accuse him. But Jesus stooped down, and with his finger wrote on the ground, as though he heard them not.
>
> So when they continued asking him, he lifted up himself, and said unto them, He that is without sin among you, let him first cast a stone at her.
>
> And again he stooped down, and wrote on the ground.
>
> And they which heard it, being convicted by their own conscience, went out one by one, beginning at the eldest, even unto the last: and Jesus was left alone, and the woman standing in the midst.
>
> When Jesus had lifted up himself, and saw none but the woman, he said unto her, Woman, where are those thine accusers? hath no man condemned thee?
>
> She said, No man, Lord. And Jesus said unto her, Neither do I condemn thee: go, and sin no more.

Heaney finds in Jesus' silent writing an allegory for poetry:

> The drawing of those characters is like poetry, a break with the usual life but not an absconding from it. Poetry, like the writing, is arbitrary and marks time in every possible sense of that phrase. It does not say to the accusing crowd or to the helpless accused, "Now a solution will take place," it does not propose to be instrumental or effective. Instead, in the rift between what is going to happen and whatever we would wish to happen, poetry holds attention for a space, functions not as distraction but as pure concentration, a focus where our power to concentrate is concentrated back on ourselves.
>
> This is what gives poetry its governing power.

This remarkable exegesis of Jesus' mysterious and uninterpreted writing finds a way to place art where it must be situated in order to be correctly judged—within human action but at least partially disengaged from direct dispute with it. Propaganda and political action enter the dispute confrontationally. Poetry exists within it, marking (as one of the poet's many invoked senses would have it) the epoch, taking its measure. Heaney comments that when Osip and Nadezhda Mandelstam died, "nothing died with them." They still mark their time.

The writing about poetry done by a poet like Heaney is done out of need—the need to find ways to create a work and a life that are as yet only imagined. There is a later, colder writing concerning poets, done by others after their death, in which their moral choices and their relation to the politics of their age take on a historical interest rather than an existential urgency. At that moment, the values of the second half of this volume come into decisive dominance: Did the poet find an individuated language for a morally individuated self? During the poet's lifetime, however, the thousand daily choices of what is said and done in the moral life (actively and broadly conceived) exert a compulsion at least equal to that of language. The two halves of this volume—the first more responsible to the lived life, the second more responsible to the morality of style—declare that (as for Wallace Stevens) "It was not a choice / Between, but of." Heaney's recent powerful volumes of political verse, *Station Island* and *The Haw Lantern,* when they are read in the light of these essays, can be seen to exhibit in terse and symbolic form the poetic strategies Heaney has been finding to mark the time of his time.

18

Earth and Ethereality

Seamus Heaney's
Selected Poems, 1966–1987

Seamus Heaney's *Selected Poems, 1966–1987* represents an unsparingly severe winnowing of twenty-one years (eight volumes) of work. Heaney has been much reviewed, and there are already several acute book-length studies of his work. His early themes—a rural childhood as an Ulster Catholic; the awareness of death (his four-year-old brother killed in a road accident); the consciousness of minority status; the acknowledging of sexual fear and joy—as well as his later ones (Irish politics, self-exile in the Republic, the archaeology of tribal hatred, domestic life, cultural taboos, the death of parents) have been often described, argued over, condemned, and defended. Predictably enough, a younger set of Irish poets, over whom the shadow of Heaney necessarily lies, have both imitated him and, in greater or lesser resistance, moved away from his styles (both realistic and allegorical) to compose either neo-surrealist verse or verse defiantly populist. Writing now about Heaney (who is my colleague at Harvard), I would like to move away from his themes (which preoccupied me when I reviewed several of the volumes represented in the *Selected Poems*) and think in more literary terms about Heaney's journey from his twenties to his fifties, which represents an unusually alert and self-taxing artistic evolution. Of course, all of us want a *Collected Poems* (as David Perkins said with impatience in his review of the *Selected*), but there is something to be said for a volume like this one, stringently self-chosen: it defines Heaney's own developing poetic, and suggests by its deletions paths that the poet found less profitable or instances in which he has silently criticized his own productions.

Much in Heaney has not changed over the years. He has never repudiated his early thematic masters, Wordsworth, Keats, and Kavanagh; he has simply found different parts of them useful at different times. The same is true of his early stylistic masters, Yeats and Auden, with their slant rhymes and stanzaic ingenuity. What was odd in Heaney from the beginning was his individual degradation (so to speak) of Keatsian organic richness into intimations of leaching, deliquescence, and rot; his enhancing of Wordsworthian natural fear (which in Wordsworth arises from the eerie or the sublime) into fear of the surreptitious (a rat), of natural evil (drowned extra kittens), of moral dubiety (an illegitimate child drowned by its mother). Heaney, unlike Wordsworth or Keats, grew up on a farm, and his view of nature is both more down-to-earth than theirs and more wary. Though Patrick Kavanagh's poetry of rural Irish life *(The Great Hunger)* helped Heaney find his way, Heaney's verse was always more symbolic than Kavanagh's. The youthful Heaney was beset, always, by moral riddles that suggested symbols in everything, even—as the title poem of his first book, *Death of a Naturalist,* shows—the ooze of frog spawn. The frog spawn is a delightful object to the young child:

> But best of all was the warm thick slobber
> Of frogspawn that grew like clotted water
> In the shade of the banks.

But when the child grows old enough to connect the frog spawn (and its coarse producers) to his own emerging sexuality, he is terrified:

> Right down the dam gross-bellied frogs were cocked
> On sods; their loose necks pulsed like sails. Some hopped:
> The slap and plop were obscene threats. . . .
> I sickened, turned, and ran. The great slime kings
> Were gathered there for vengeance and I knew
> That if I dipped my hand the spawn would clutch it.

Heaney's enviable descriptive powers pointed his morals with insidious images. After picking blackberries:

> We hoarded the fresh berries in the byre.
> But when the bath was filled we found a fur,
> A rat-grey fungus, glutting on our cache.

The young poet could not resist adding a moral:

> It wasn't fair
> That all the lovely canfuls smelt of rot.
> Each year I hoped they'd keep, knew they would not.

When we leave the Heaney of 1966 and pass to the Heaney of twenty years later, we can still find poems ending with a conclusion, though the conclusions tend to be far more equivocal. Here is the first section of "Terminus" (1987), almost a riddle-poem about Heaney's origins in a rural part of the industrialized world:

> When I hoked there, I would find
> An acorn and a rusted bolt.
>
> If I lifted my eyes, a factory chimney
> And a dormant mountain.
>
> If I listened, an engine shunting
> And a trotting horse.
>
> Is it any wonder when I thought
> I would have second thoughts?

The rich Keatsian vocabulary, the "English" pentameters, and the neat rhymes of the blackberries have been abjured here in favor of bare statement, short lines, and an absence of rhyme as such.

Heaney now moves freely among several such sets of poetic resources. The main challenge to his English inheritance came from his deliberate work of translating a medieval Irish poem, "Sweeney Astray": the "thinner music" of the Irish language was a second training for his pen, which had already, in his great volume *North* (1975), begun to use terse lines to enormous effect—for example, the description in "Funeral Rites" of an imagined burial cortège for those killed in the political "troubles," a cortège working its way back to the prehistoric chamber-tombs in the Boyne valley:

> Now as news comes in
> of each neighbourly murder
> we pine for ceremony,
> customary rhythms:
>
> the temperate footsteps
> of a cortège, winding past
> each blinded home.
> I would restore
>
> the great chambers of Boyne,
> prepare a sepulchre
> under the cupmarked stones. . . .
>
> Quiet as a serpent
> in its grassy boulevard,
>
> the procession drags its tail
> out of the Gap of the North
> as its head already enters
> the megalithic doorway.

This is unquestionably splendid writing, deriving its strength as much from its savage irony ("each neighbourly murder") as from its metaphor (the serpent-cortège dragging its tail).

Such a poem is unmistakably political, and allusively Catholic in its use of religious words like "ceremony" and "sepulchre" to sanctify the cortège. The poet is the aloof Yeatsian master of ceremonies: "I would restore / the great chambers of Boyne." There were aesthetic dangers for Heaney in the role of spokesman for one side of the Northern Irish conflict; and in his unwillingness to be purely partisan (a position no intelligence can assume toward such complex questions) he delved deeper, behind twentieth-century history, into the ancient customs of tribal violence in a geographic belt including not only Ireland but other north-ern countries—Iceland, Scandinavia. In a move indicting both sides, Heaney wrote of murders centuries ago, of bodies of victims exhumed in both Ireland and Scandinavia—bodies that bore mute witness to the ineradicability of violence from human relations.

In describing these bodies, Heaney touched a vein that lies between his earliest luxuriance and his later austerity. The bog bodies are both inestimably rich and leached of all pulp, so to speak: they have almost become statuary, and they take on the mute aesthetic authority of monu-ments whose reason for being has been entirely forgotten. Unlike wholly abstract art, however, Heaney's mummified bodies, though they are no longer of living substance, still exhibit human contours. This is Heaney's response to Yeats's insistence on marble or bronze as the aesthetic equiva-lents of flesh. Not marble, Heaney says of the exhumed corpse of the Grauballe Man, but tar, petrified oak, basalt, roots:

> As if he had been poured
> in tar, he lies
> on a pillow of turf
> and seems to weep
>
> the black river of himself.
> The grain of his wrists
> is like bog oak,
> the ball of his heel
>
> like a basalt egg.
> His instep has shrunk
> cold as a swan's foot
> or a wet swamp root. . . .
>
> Who will say 'corpse'
> to his vivid cast?
> Who will say 'body'
> to his opaque repose?

Who would not want such majestic writing to continue forever? Its severe two-beat and three-beat rhythms (elegiac drum taps); its alternation of "living" words ("weep," "shrunk") and petrified ones ("basalt," "cast"); its pitiless observation ("as if," "seems," "like," "cold as") restricting itself to similes (a more factual trope than metaphor)—these are marks of mastery, justifying the closing questions: Can we call this sublime figure a "corpse," a "body"? Such writing is another version of the writer's boast of perpetuity: "So long as men can breathe or eyes can see, / So long lives this." It is Heaney's organic, underground substitute for Horatian bronze or Yeatsian marble.

I believe that Heaney took his greatest aesthetic risk in departing from this triumphantly perfected classicism of the petrified organic to write, at the same moment, poems that depart from the oracular and the monumental to speak in an ordinary voice about the messy present:

> I'm writing this just after an encounter
> With an English journalist in search of 'views
> On the Irish thing.' I'm back in winter
> Quarters where bad news is no longer news,
>
> Where media-men and stringers sniff and point,
> Where zoom lenses, recorders and coiled leads
> Litter the hotels.

The "Irish thing" is written about in swinging, Drydenesque heroic quatrains, marking Heaney's decision to be satiric, and not solely reverential, about "the troubles."

Heaney's satiric bent was unleashed again in the long Dantesque poem "Station Island," which is included in its entirety in the *Selected Poems*. "Station Island," under the guise of a pilgrimage during which Heaney meets a series of vanished people from his cultural and personal past, attacks almost all the sacred cows of Irish writing, from nationalist piety to religious sentimentality, from elegiac decorativeness to colonial protest. "Stay clear of all processions!" shouts the first of Heaney's revenants; and the closing speech of the last of them, James Joyce, embodies Heaney's decision to find his own path:

> "That subject people stuff is a cod's game,
> infantile, like your peasant pilgrimage. . . .

> It's time to swim
>
> out on your own and fill the element
> with signatures on your own frequency,
> echo-soundings, searches, probes, allurements,
>
> elver-gleams in the dark of the whole sea."

Since "Station Island," the poet's radar and sonar have operated on various frequencies. "The whole sea" is an element different from both Heaney's early agricultural earth and his middle archeological bog, but there had been anticipations of the sea earlier in Heaney—notably in "A Lough Neagh Sequence," from his second collection, *Door Into the Dark*. (I miss in this *Selected* both that sequence and the poem from which that volume takes its title.) "The whole sea" is matched in later Heaney by what one could call "the whole air," especially as Heaney takes on, in a brilliant series of poems ("Sweeney Redivivus"), the persona of the Irish poet Sweeney, who was punished by Saint Ronan by being changed into a bird. Living in the sea, living in the air: both are perhaps ways of not living in social terrain, on earth, but they equally avoid living in what Yeats called "God's holy fire." One way of being in the air is to climb a tree, to be "In the Beech":

> My hidebound boundary tree. My tree of knowledge.
> My thick-tapped, soft-fledged, airy listening post.

What would a poetics of "airy listening" be like? It would have to forgo the grateful reciprocity with the fruitful earth which characterizes an agricultural poetics, rooted in the seasons, growth, and decay; it would have to do without the soaked immersion in history which characterizes a poetics of exhumed and petrified ancient bodies; and it would have to forswear the activist choices for or against present cultural pressures which characterize the poetics of "Station Island."

When the revived Sweeney asks himself in "The Cleric" what the result has been of his being driven into the kingdom of the air by Saint Ronan, executor of the (clerical) politics of the day, he says:

> Give him his due, in the end
>
> he opened my path to a kingdom
> of such scope and neuter allegiance
> my emptiness reigns at its whim.

This "neuter allegiance" is a position of great psychological danger for a passionate poet, and yet it is the only recourse in the face of solicitations from all sides to betray the accuracy of art in favor of the tendentiousness of argument. Dangerous as it is, it is less dangerous than following the path of incipient grandiosity in "I would restore / the great chambers of Boyne."

Heaney had in his youth an ineradicable Hopkinsian sense of the pleasure principle, of a sensual richness manifest in objects, feelings, and words. It buttressed him against fears of weakness and the abrasions of politics; it generated, in "Bone Dreams," some of his most untroubled and beautiful lines:

> I push back
> through dictions,
> Elizabethan canopies,
> Norman devices,
>
> the erotic mayflowers
> of Provence
> and the ivied Latins
> of churchmen
>
> to the scop's
> twang, the iron
> flash of consonants
> cleaving the line.

But when earth stopped being a habitable element, the pleasure principle seemed to dry up with it. Heaney imagined himself, in "On the Road," as a bird exhaustedly looking for water and a resting place and finding them only in a prehistoric cave without real water but with a wall-carving of a drinking deer:

For my book of changes
I would meditate
that stone-faced vigil

until the long dumbfounded
spirit broke cover
to raise a dust
in the font of exhaustion.

In the last volume excerpted in the *Selected*, Heaney's airy listening has remade the entire earth-world in an airy dimension. The dedicatory poem, "For Bernard and Jane McCabe," is a simple couplet broken into two one-line "stanzas" of a sentence apiece, containing the resolve to re-create the forsaken and exhausted earth-and-water world in a virtual air-world:

The riverbed, dried-up, half-full of leaves.

Us, listening to a river in the trees.

This "aftermath," as Heaney calls it in the poem "Hailstones," is made "out of the melt of the real thing / smarting into its absence." Touching on a comparable instance in Yeats, Heaney wrote, "We are at that thrilling moment when the place of writing shifts its locus into psychic space." At that moment, absence takes on the full freight of what it has replaced.

The fullest expression of "aftermath" can be found in the last of Heaney's sonnets commemorating his mother's death, Number 8 of "Clearances": in it Heaney remembers the felling of a chestnut tree that was planted in the year of his birth. Its virtual existence in his mind, now that its "real" existence is over, is "a space / Utterly empty, utterly a source":

I thought of walking round and round a space
Utterly empty, utterly a source
Where the decked chestnut tree had lost its place
In our front hedge above the wallflowers.
The white chips jumped and jumped and skited high.

> I heard the hatchet's differentiated
> Accurate cut, the crack, the sigh
> And collapse of what luxuriated
> Through the shocked tips and wreckage of it all.
> Deep-planted and long gone, my coeval
> Chestnut from a jam jar in a hole.
> Its heft and hush become a bright nowhere,
> A soul ramifying and forever
> Silent, beyond silence listened for.

The "bright nowhere" of the virtual world is composed of memories of the dead, the visions of natural faith and hope, and the forms of art which stabilize such losses and unrealized visions. In Heaney, the "space / Utterly empty" has always originally been filled, often audaciously: one of the sonnets in "Clearances" begins, "When all the others were away at Mass / I was all hers as we peeled potatoes"—a far cry from either the sonnet tradition or the tradition of elegies for one's mother. Yet even this strong original grounding in earth is persistently sieved upward into the sphere of value, away from fact and history. Mud becomes "The Mud Vision."

Heaney said recently on Radio 3, Ireland, "I felt that my first poems were trying to write like stained glass but that I would like to write a poetry of window glass." Heaney's metaphor may recall Herbert's "The Elixir":

> A man that looks on glasse,
>   On it may stay his eye;
> Or if he pleaseth, through it passe,
>   And then the heav'n espie.

The "poetry of window glass" has deep connections to the tension Heaney remarks in Wordsworth's poetry: the "contradictory allegiances . . . to the numinous and to the matter-of-fact." Heaney understands the "conflicting awarenesses of a necessity to attend to 'the calm that nature breathes' and a responsibility to confront the grievous facts of 'what man has made of man,' his double bind between politics and transcendence."

That double bind remains Heaney's own, but he has redefined its terms. In his recent, "airy" phase, he has written about politics via allegory (a strategy absorbed from poets of eastern Europe like Zbigniew Herbert, Miroslav Holub, and Czesław Miłosz). Religious and philosophical certainty have been left behind, and transcendence has been reimagined as that which can occur in "psychic space" so as to create a virtual world of both memory and value. Heaney fully recognizes the elements of hallucination and self-delusion in the realms of memory and value. On the other hand, he accepts the realm of imaginative force as one of indubitable emotional and historical power (as some who share his epistemological and religious skepticism do not).

Heaney is not entirely at home in allegory, I suspect; and that suspicion is borne out by the nonallegorical pieces he has been publishing subsequent to this *Selected Poems*. They are, many of them, exquisitely reticent and unassuming poems, often recalling moments almost too evanescent to be described. They are "allurements, elver-gleams," expressing phases of sensation neglected by the poetry of sturdy fact or political contention. They retain air and water as their habitat, and have as their poetics the representation of "equilibrium; brim."

In a recent poem, "Fosterling," Heaney reviews his earlier attachment to silt, lowlands, "heaviness of being." The result was a "poetry / Sluggish in the doldrums of what happens." Now there is a change upward:

> Me waiting until I was nearly fifty
> To credit marvels. Like the tree clock of tin cans
> The tinkers made. So long for air to brighten,
> Time to be dazzled and the heart to lighten.

If, as both Auden and Stevens have suggested, every poet is part Caliban (earthiness, nature, gravity) and part Ariel (ethereality, invisibility, velocity), Heaney is now giving his Ariel voice its moment. Never pure air entirely, the latest Heaney poems bear traces of earth and water in their lightest and most vaporous forms: dust, silt, mist, clouds. Dispersion, aeration, reflection, and susurrus are the modes of the poetry following this *Selected Poems,* ensuring that the Heaney represented in these pages has not closed off his lines of aesthetic and moral inquiry.

Mapping the Air

Adrienne Rich and Jorie Graham

The titles of these volumes by two distinguished poets remind us of literary predecessors. Jorie Graham's title, *Region of Unlikeness,* comes from Saint Augustine, who said he found himself far from God, in "a region of unlikeness." (The phrase—in the form *Land of Unlikeness*—was used by Robert Lowell, too.) Rich's geographic title, *An Atlas of the Difficult World,* may recall titles by Elizabeth Bishop, who called her last book *Geography III,* and thought of herself as a mapper of those regions named, in the title of another book, *North and South.* Both Graham and Rich, in their titles, are emphasizing that the description of the contemporary world is a primary commitment of the artist. If for the reader the description is convincing—formally as well as thematically—the poems have a chance; if not, not.

Many of the poems in both these books are several pages long (we are far from the origins of lyric in the short song, the charm, the riddle, the quip, the carol, the epigram). Here are some of their "real-life" subjects. Among Graham's twenty-four poems we find the following:

1. "Fission": Being an adolescent in 1963, sitting in a movie theater and watching Stanley Kubrick's *Lolita;* a man suddenly runs in shouting "The President's been shot";
2. "From the New World": A splicing-together of three vignettes—

    a. A historical scene: a young girl in a concentration camp "who didn't die in the gas chamber" comes back out asking for her mother and is raped before being sent back in;

    b. A contemporary (1987) scene: the trial in Israel of a former Nazi concentration camp guard, the one who ordered the rape;

    c. A personal anecdote: the author's senile grandmother, confined in a nursing home, is no longer able to recognize her granddaughter;

3. "The Hiding Place": The "disturbances" in Paris of 1968 (*"les événements,"* as the French called the student strikes and closing of universities);

4. "The Region of Unlikeness": A thirteen-year-old girl wakes up disoriented and frightened from a first sexual experience and runs home through the dawn;

5. "The Phase after History": The attempted suicide of a young man; his commitment to a hospital; his subsequent successful suicide. These episodes are spliced between the phases of an incident in which two birds are trapped in the speaker's house.

Among Rich's thirteen poems, we find the following:

1. "An Atlas of the Difficult World," the title poem, a sequence, of which these are some parts:

    —Migrant workers ill from the effects of picking strawberries dusted with malathion;

    —A trailer; the man in it beating his wife, tearing up her writing, throwing the kerosene lantern at her, backing the truck into her as she tries to run away;

    —Memories of Rich's young married life in Barton, Vermont, with her husband, before he died;

    —The 1968 shotgun attack by a man on two women camping on the Appalachian Trail; the attack was made (according to Rich's note) because the women were lesbians. One was killed, the other wounded by five bullets;

    —The life of the father of Annie Sullivan (Helen Keller's

teacher); his emigration to America as a result of the Irish po-
tato famine;
—George Jackson in prison, with quotations from *Soledad
Brother,* his prison letters;
2. "Eastern War Time": Splicings of the anti-Semitic lynching of Leo
Frank in 1915 in Baltimore; the concentration camps; the "Final
Solution."

The two lists should suggest the thematic ambitions of both poets, who
range far into public life and into the predicaments of history, as well as
into ethical (Rich) and metaphysical (Graham) questions. Though both
poets swing their poems into large orbits, they retrench with brief closing
poems, as though to come back to the almost forgotten lyric norm. Nei-
ther of these books is easy to read; each is in its way fiercely uncompro-
mising. But the aesthetics they embody could not be more different.

To the casual eye, Rich's poetry appears representational; she writes
about events and ethical issues in the "real world," and usually takes a
polemical or sorrowing position with respect to them. The chief imagi-
native act in Rich's work would appear to be the choice, from all the
difficulties of this difficult world, of a set of difficulties to map. I believe,
as I will go on to say, that she is not primarily a representational poet,
nor is she very free in the apparent choice of terrain in her atlas.

Rich is inclined to represent certain distinct kinds of social evil. A
natural "evil" like the Irish potato famine would not interest her were its
results not compounded by British indifference and mismanagement.
Such things as slavery, marital brutality, racist persecution, social dis-
crimination, industrial crimes against health, and the conditions of im-
prisonment are her natural territory (rather than, for instance, the kinds
of sophisticated individual moral evil that interested Henry James or
Proust). She thinks it is the duty of the poet to bear witness to, and
protest against, these social evils. She appears to manifest the reformer's
faith that there is something that can be done against evil, and her poems
invoke heroes and heroines (more often the latter) who fought for so-
cial welfare.

Her poems also commemorate people from marginal groups who
have been victims of (usually violent or socially codified) oppression. In
this volume, they include the imprisoned George Jackson, the lynched

Leo Frank, a murdered lesbian, a beaten trailer-camp wife, Annie Sulli-van's father (the victim of forced emigration from the Irish famine), the Jews in the camps, and Hispanic migrant workers in California. A so-cially oppressed group from an "elite" class or a "dominant" sex does not much interest her (for example, well-off Jews in a Christian society, impoverished white males), even though the suffering of such people may be considerable and prolonged and damaging. Nor is she much in-terested in those who have been oppressed by women (notably children, but also some husbands, parents, and siblings). This is my chief difficulty with the moral position of her poems; there seems no obvious reason to sympathize more with one set of victims than with the others.

The positive values Rich has embraced thematically in her books in-clude female friendship and love, outspokenness, working for reform, truth telling, sympathy, conversation, moral outrage, persistence in work, introspection, and memory. These have as their aesthetic counter-parts a devotion to plainness of style and to unremitting earnestness of tone. As Randall Jarrell once wittily said (in *Kipling, Auden & Co.*), "Her poetry so thoroughly escapes all of the vices of modernist poetry that it has escaped many of its virtues too."

Rich's most visible American predecessor in social sympathy is Walt Whitman, but her work goes back in English poetry at least to Langland's *Piers Plowman,* with its sociological personifications and stratified social analysis. For Langland, moral theology is the norm by which sinners are judged, each individually, as Christian souls. But in modern life, sociol-ogy, with its treatment of people in groups rather than as individuals, has replaced theology as the analytic mode for attacking evil. According to Christian theology, *all* people are sinners, the socially victimized and oppressed as well as the victimizers and oppressors, the social reformer as well as the governing class he reproaches. All persons—victims *and* victimizers *and* reformers—share some sins (adultery, theft, blasphemy, slander, anger, intemperance, envy, and so on); the oppressors, no doubt, do have more opportunity for a special set of sins—more leisure for sloth, more money for gluttony, more economic wherewithal for pride; and the reformers might have more temptations to intellectual pride, anger, and pharisaical complacency.

Sociological analysis tends to ascribe sinlessness to the oppressed—or at least to excuse their sins as the deplorable consequences of their being oppressed (without extending a similar charity to the oppressors). Therefore we do not, in Rich, see the malathion-sickened migrant worker beating his wife, or the murdered lesbian being indifferent to her sick mother, or the black prisoner victimizing another prisoner. No: Rich's victims are all morally innocent. The poor wife in the trailer offended her husband only by her writing; the Jewish camp prisoner is not an oppressive Kapo but "a young girl." And the victimizers are all unredeemed: the husband who backs the truck into his wife is not shown to have been an abused child; the Nazi doctor is not (like, say, Gottfried Benn) a man of divided sentiments serving as an army surgeon; no, he is the experimenter in human flesh "who plays string quartets with his staff in the laboratory."

For all her stylistic appearance of realism, then, Rich is actually a moral allegorist. We might as well have the Spenserian Una and Archimago (Truth and Evil) as the innocent girl and the doctor/aesthete/sadist. Rich has a powerful Manichaean conviction that the world exhibits a struggle to the death between structural Good and structural Evil, and she picks (from history, from the news, from sociological analysis) allegorical illustrations of her Manichaean world. Personal good and evil, one-on-one (the possessive mother dominating the victimized son, the cruel brother tormenting the naïve brother, the attractive sister stealing the boyfriend of the plodding sister) don't interest her because such relations don't stand for anything in her allegorical scheme of Oppression and Victimage. For another writer, such examples of personal evil might stand for that other powerful allegory, Original Sin, anathema to reformers because it means nothing can be done.

The Protestant allegorical tradition from which Rich descends is a rich one, complicated by its best practitioners in a variety of ways. In Spenser it is "contaminated" by fairy tale, Greek romance, and neo-Platonic idealization, all of which keep *The Faerie Queene* from a fatal mimetic earnestness. In Bunyan, it is enlivened by considerable satiric energy (Mr. Facing-Both-Ways, for example) and by an exalted religious faith. Rich has stripped this tradition to its basic conflict—of Christian and Apollyon, of good and evil—but she lacks the radiant confidence of Bunyan and other religious allegorists (from the author of Job on) in the eventual triumph of the good. The good in Rich are the weak, the social under-dogs—women, blacks, lesbians, the poor, prisoners, Jews, mothers of the disappeared. And though at first glance it would appear that Rich has a reformer's faith in social improvement, one hears, for all her condemna-tory energy and active sympathy, an air of lament rather than of certainty pervading her work. "Join me in condemning the reprobates and griev-ing for the victims," she seems to say, and we can, because there are, as we recognize, real reprobates and real victims. But because (unlike, say, Miłosz) she never places herself among the reprobates (even in imagina-tion), and never tarnishes the victims with evil qualities of their own, we may feel she imperfectly understands social phenomena. The capacity to be a reprobate is as alive in victims as in the victimized, as the young Joyce (no allegorist) showed in his story "Counterparts," where the vic-timized becomes in his turn a victimizer. Victimization in *Dubliners,* as in lived life, is a chain reaction.

As an allegorist stopping this chain reaction, letting her victims be "good people," Rich has to see her victimizers as not themselves victims. If we give her her way, and agree to see the world through her eyes as a morality play, we find that her work, like other stylizations employing simplification, can have a powerful effect. That effect is chiefly one of pathos, of the innocent wronged. Perhaps this is an especially maternal feeling. Good mothers spend so much of their energy trying to protect children, who are by definition weak in all respects, that the impulse to close ranks and lament is about all that mothers can fall back on as a means of defending their children, who are physically and mentally un-developed, economically impotent, legally dependent, and institutionally in subjection.

Rich's "children," whose fate she laments, whose unjust treatment she protests against, seem mostly versions of her present or past self. Like charity, pity (as Elizabeth Bishop said in "Crusoe in England") begins at home. This suggests that Rich still imagines herself in the position of the helpless child rather than that of the adult. She presents herself less as a champion or a leader than as a co-sufferer, pitying herself (indirectly) in others. There is nothing so confident in this book as Shelley's Prometh-ean determination "To hope, till Hope creates / From its own wreck the thing it contemplates."

* * *

The title of Rich's book is revealing: *An Atlas of the Difficult World*.
"Difficult" is an adjective of bafflement and struggle rather than of revolt
and revolution; this is a marked change from her previous titles, such as
Leaflets and *The Will to Change*. The word "atlas" implies a steady-state
world that has always been, and always will be, difficult. The difficulty
that Rich recurs to in this book is the standoff between discouragement
at social evil and attachment to natural life. For all the ills she sees, Rich
also has a poet's deep attachment to the beautiful—the beautiful as she
has found it in the material universe, in sexual connection, in ethical
action. She has been too much of an activist perhaps, in recent years, to
say much about beauty, but she salutes it in this book in unashamed love.
Here she is on her attachment to the California landscape:

> . . . I am stuck to earth. What I love here
> is old ranches, leaning seaward, lowroofed spreads between
>   rocks
> small canyons running through pitched hillsides
> liveoaks twisted on steepness, the eucalyptus avenue leading
> to the wrecked homestead, the fog-wreathed heavy-chested
>   cattle
> on their blond hills.

And here she is describing the combined beauty and usefulness of the
universally found black-eyed Susan:

> Late summers, early autumns, you can see something that binds
> the map of this country together: the girasol, orange
>   gold-petalled
> with her black eye, laces the roadsides from Vermont to
>   California . . .
> . . . her tubers the jerusalem artichoke
> that has fed the Indians, fed the hobos, could feed us all.

These hymns to beauty are addressed to natural beauty, not the beauty
created in art. Rich seems mistrustful of art, and contradicts outright the
conviction of both Keats and Dickinson that truth and beauty are insepa-
rable:

... What homage will be paid to beauty
that insists on speaking truth, knows the two are not always the
    same,
beauty that won't deny . . .?

This seems Rich's question about her own fate; she implies that her own lines insist on speaking truth and are willing to forgo the sort of beauty that denies the truth or conceals it. She doesn't explain what sort of beauty this concealing or denying beauty is, or what we find beautiful in it. Reproving art for leaving out the unbeautiful is an old accusation. It is perhaps a just reproach to sentimental versifying, in valentines, say, but it is not a reproach that is sustainable (so far as I know) against any verse we would want to call art. (In fact, the presence of undeniable truth is one of the usual criteria for separating true art from kitsch. True art, even of the most "beautiful" Spenserian or Keatsian sort, doesn't shrink from the difficult, the ungraceful, the ugly, and the evil, whereas kitsch chooses to represent only the pliant, the pathetic, the lissome, the acceptable, and the inoffensive.) What can Rich mean, then, by opposing her "beauty that won't deny" to some (uncharacterized) "beauty" that does, or will, deny truth? Does she mean the idealization, say, of the body in Greek statuary versus the realism, say, of Roman sculpture? Is it correct to call the former a beauty that denies the truth? If her sort of beauty "knows [that truth and beauty] are not always the same," are we to deduce that truth is always beautiful but beauty is not always truthful?

These are important questions, and old ones. But an artist who distinguishes beauty that denies truth from beauty that does not deny truth, and seems to choose the latter, needs to explain what she means by the former.

However, Rich does predicate Truth, Goodness, and Beauty of life, so that what she separates metaphysically (when she argues that truth and beauty may not coincide) she unites in her accounts of experience. She says about the murdered lesbian:

... I don't want to know
but this is not a bad dream of mine   these are the materials

and so are the smell of wild mint and coursing water
remembered
and the sweet salt darkred tissue I lay my face
upon, my tongue within.

Sex, notoriously hard to write about, comes off less well here than the wild mint in the brook, but the poem makes the point that sensuous and sexual satisfaction are earthly counterweights to human violence and victimage.

If I understand Rich correctly in this book, she even brings into question her own fundamental Manichaean myth, as she offers her readers, in the eleventh section of her "Atlas," the figure of an androgynous patriot attempting to know what America (this "difficult world") really is. A patriot, she says, is a citizen trying to wake from the burnt-out dream of American innocence:

A patriot is not a weapon. A patriot is one who wrestles for the
    soul of her country
as she wrestles for her own being, for the soul of his country
(gazing through the great circle at Window Rock into the sheen
    of the Viet Nam Wall)
as he wrestles for his own being. A patriot is a citizen trying to
    wake
from the burnt-out dream of innocence, the nightmare
of the white general and the Black general posed in their
    camouflage,
to remember her true country, remember his suffering land:
    remember
that blessing and cursing are born as twins and separated at
    birth to meet again in mourning
that the internal emigrant is the most homesick of all women
    and of all men
that every flag that flies today is a cry of pain.
    Where are we moored?
    What are the bindings?
    What behooves us?

The three closing questions ask, in turn, what our history is, what our culture or religion is ("bindings" glances at *re-ligare*), and what our ethics should be. The final question is an ethical one, as we would expect from Rich, but it uses as its verb an archaic word both ethical and aesthetic: What is needful to us, what befits us?

Rich has two characteristic methods of transforming her sociological generalizations into lyrical meditations, both of them methods that Whitman also found useful. They are the enumeration or catalog, and the vignette or anecdote. Both confer a deceptive particularity on what is essentially a single-class group. Whereas Whitman's catalogs tend to summon together quite diverse species within the group (see "The Sleepers"), Rich's tend to offer successive members of the same species. She will list, for instance, a variety of readers to show how (to use Keats's metaphor) a poet can be physician to ills of the spirit. Here is part of her catalog poem "Dedications," with its address to all readers from any poet:

> I know you are reading this poem
> late, before leaving your office . . .
>
> . . . I know you are reading this poem
> standing up in a bookstore far from the ocean. . . .
> I know you are reading this poem
> in a room where too much has happened for you to bear
> where the bedclothes lie in stagnant coils on the bed
> and the open valise speaks of flight
> but you cannot leave yet. . . .
> I know you are reading this poem by fluorescent light
> in the boredom and fatigue of the young who are counted out,
> count themselves out, at too early an age. . . .
> I know you are reading this poem which is not in your language
> guessing at some words while others keep you reading. . . .
> I know you are reading this poem listening for something, torn
>   between bitterness and hope
> turning back once again to the task you cannot refuse.
> I know you are reading this poem because there is nothing else

> left to read
> there where you have landed, stripped as you are.

Rich's second Whitmanesque method of conferring particularity on what are at bottom group observations is the use of anecdote. She succeeds less well at this than at the catalog, too often falling into stereotype. Before she can write an anecdote, she has to have classified under some allegorical rubric the person it concerns. (Whitman was more interested in specific occurrences in life and history—for example, his mother's meeting with an Indian girl or Washington's farewell to his troops.) Sometimes, Rich's crispness of expression will save the allegory. So, for instance, in "Through Corralitos under Rolls of Cloud," she proclaims the eternal twinning of the survivor-self and the victim-self, seeing the survivor as ultimately heartsick and bereft without the victim-self that went under. "You" died, says Rich to the victim-self, and the survivor is "uncertain who she is or will be without you." And then the poet addresses the survivor:

> If you know who died in that bed, do you know
> who has survived?   If you say, *she was weaker*
> *held life less dear, expected others*
> *to fight for her*   if pride lets you name her
> *victim*   and the one who got up and threw
> the windows open, stripped the bed, *survivor*
> —what have you said, what do you know
> of the survivor when you know her
> only in opposition to the lost?
> What does it mean to say *I have survived*
> until you take the mirrors and turn them outward
> and read your own face in their outraged light?

This has a fierceness and wit that justify Rich's habit of stripping her poems until they consist almost solely of nouns and verbs, eschewing those adjectives and adverbs which have normally been the stuff of lyric description. It remains, I think, for Rich to extend this twinning of the-self-that-went-under with the self-that-survived to the relation of victimizer and victim: Can't those positions be structurally interchangeable, too? If Rich can see herself as in part the weaker dying sister, in part the immunized survivor, can't she see herself too as potentially Judas, or Macbeth, or Iago? "What shocks the virtuous philosopher," says Keats, "delights the chameleon poet." For Rich, blessing and cursing are twins separated at birth, to be joined again in mourning; perhaps outrage and criminality are also such twins.

The value of Rich's poems, ethically speaking, is that they have continued to press against insoluble questions of suffering, evil, love, justice, and patriotism. For all their epic wish to generalize to the social whole, they are both limited by, and enhanced by, their essentially first-person lyric status. They hate what the person Adrienne Rich hates, love what she loves. Their sympathies are her self-sympathies, their victims the victims closest to her own heart. They are not dispassionately epic, and broadly socially curious, as Whitman's poems strove to be. Perhaps Whitman was more heterogeneously moved, emotionally speaking, than Rich; whereas his poems tend to arise from observations from without (his letters bearing witness to his delightful and insatiable curiosity about the whole comic and tragic spectacle of America), her poems are exfoliations from within. Her present work shows a version of lyric almost reluctant to confess its own inwardness and privacy, resolved to find a match in the larger world for its own deprivations. But the real and complex Rich remains more convincing than her allegorical surrogate victims.

Like Rich, Jorie Graham, a younger poet now teaching at the University of Iowa, uses vignettes and anecdotes, but to raise metaphysical, more than ethical, questions. Graham's grand metaphysical theme is the tension between existence and death. These are its ultimate terms; but the tension is also expressed as that between other polarities, such as continuity and closure, indeterminacy and outline, being and temporality, or experience and art. Graham sees human beings as creatures capable both of "intentionality"—directedness of aim—and of suspension in moments of pure being without aim.

These two inherent, inescapable capacities are fatal to each other. Nothing goes nowhere, however much we might want it to. Courtship presses toward commitment, idea toward its enactment, sensation to-

ward exhaustion. For the artist especially, the passion to impose a deter-
minate shape on experience is at war with the passion to live suspended
within experience. The Graham muse sings two siren songs: one says,
"Hurry: *name* it"; the other says, "Delay: *be* it."

In her earlier work (*Hybrids of Plants and of Ghosts*, 1980; *Erosion*, 1983;
and *The End of Beauty*, 1987) Graham was already sketching the crucial
intersection of the passional and the philosophical from which the
poems radiate. The metamorphoses of the theme, even in her early work,
were numerous and inventive—yet this is the wrong way to put it.
Rather, experience kept leading Graham back, by way of formal discover-
ies, to her central theme: to what one could call openness versus shape.
At first, each moment of experience tended to have its own single poem,
in which the tension between being and interpretation was named rather
than shown, as in "Strangers," from *Hybrids of Plants and of Ghosts*:

> . . . Dusk,

> when objects lose their way, you
> throw a small
> red ball at me
> and I return it.
> The miracle is this:
> the perfect arc

> of red we intercept
> over and over
> until it is too dark
> to see, reaches beyond us
> to contemplate
> only itself.

Later, the moment of suspension—imagined in the poem "Updraft"
as an upward motion bearing us temporarily away from gravity—begins
to be shown in action rather than described, and Graham's use of long
present-tense unfolding sentences keeps us afloat in the updraft for a
long time. The actual moment of suspension itself becomes the center
of the poem, as in "San Sepolcro" from her second volume, *Erosion*,
where we see the Madonna unbuttoning her dress before labor:

. . . It is this girl
    by Piero
della Francesca, unbuttoning
    her blue dress,
her mantle of weather,
    to go into

labor. Come, we can go in.
    It is before
the birth of god. . . .

    . . . This is
what the living do: go in.
    It's a long way.
And the dress keeps opening
    from eternity

to privacy, quickening.
    Inside, at the heart,
is tragedy, the present moment
    forever stillborn,
but going in, each breath
    is a button

coming undone, something terribly
    nimble-fingered
finding all of the stops.

These poems often end in a standoff between suspension and finality: "Wanting a Child" (from *Erosion*) ends with the force of the ocean pushing up into the tidal estuary,, meeting the force of the river draining into the ocean.

The ecstasy of the state of suspension itself, however, had finally to be analytically examined as well as sensually rendered; and this became the (partly chilling) achievement of Graham's third book, *The End of Beauty* (with its intended pun: the aim of beauty and the termination of beauty are one). Graham's technique in *The End of Beauty* was to anatomize the moment of suspension in being by isolating each of its successive seconds in its own numbered freeze-frame. Here, for instance, is Eve, tired of the stasis of Paradise, deciding to eat of the apple and give it to Adam.

15
so that she had to turn and touch him to give it away
16
to have him pick it from her as the answer takes the question
17
that he should read in her the rigid inscription
18
in a scintillant fold the fabric of the daylight bending
19
where the form is complete where the thing must be torn off
20
momentarily angelic, the instant writhing into a shape,
21
the two wedded, the readyness and the instant,
22
the extra bit that shifts the scales the other way now in his hand,
the gift that changes the balance,
23
the balance that cannot be broken owned by the air until he
touches,
24
the balance like an apple held up into the sunlight
25
then taken down, the air changing by its passage . . .

Here motion is no longer absorbed in a swirl of impulse, but is broken down and minutely studied, its progress almost halted in the slow-motion inching forward of the film, frame by frame.

But we are still concerned here with a single action, a moment of fateful impulse given a mythological shape. Poems on subjects like this are the defining poems of *The End of Beauty,* where archetypal moments of relation (Apollo and Daphne, Orpheus and Eurydice, Demeter and

Persephone) are isolated, unsparingly (even cruelly) investigated, magnified, slowed down, and understood.

In *Region of Unlikeness* (1991), Graham took what seems, with hindsight, an inevitable step. She made the demanding leap to a practice of connecting together moments widely separated in time and space and occurring on disparate mental levels (usually the autobiographical, the historical, and the mythical). Each of these moments is important; each has its own unintelligiblity; each demands to be both recorded and comprehended. But even more, the hidden connections among them in the writer's sensibility (and perhaps in the culture at large) have to be exhumed. The mode of comprehension derives from the connection of separate stories in the writer's mind—a connection that is at first unintelligible. As she comes to understand why she has intuitively connected them, she can compose a poem juxtaposing and interlacing them.

For instance, Graham's maternal grandmother appeared in *Erosion* (1983) in an unremarkable poem ("At the Long Island Jewish Geriatric Home") showing her consigned to a nursing home. The image then occurring to the poet as corresponding to her grandmother's confinement was the myth of Daphne enclosed in bark. The link between the autobiographical and the mythical is the speaker recalling a tree in her grandmother's "tiny orchard." "She looks," says the poet (fusing grandmother and Daphne), "like she could / outrun / anything,"

> . . . although of course
>   she's stuck
>
> for good here in this
>   memory,
> and in the myth it calls
>   to mind,
> and in this late interpretation
>   stolen from
> a half-remembered tree
>   which stands

> there still like some god's
>> narrow throat
>
> or mind nothing can slit her
>> free of.

The rather heavy-handed transition here ("in the myth it calls / to mind, / and in this late interpretation") gives the story of the grandmother temporal priority, makes the myth secondary and decorative, and puts interpretation in the place of honor, closing the poem.

The grandmother appears in *Region of Unlikeness* in two far more complex poems (one called "From the New World" and the other called "Chaos"), both containing a visit from the granddaughter to the nursing home. To see one of the later poems against the earlier one is to see a writer returning to troubling material to do it over, do it better, do it— if such a thing is possible—right. No longer are the autobiographical, the mythical, and the intellectual on three different planes.

"From the New World" splices together three stories, two of them historical, one autobiographical (as I have earlier noted). The first is a 1940s story of a young girl "who didn't die / in the gas chamber, who came back out asking / for her mother." The second is the story of the 1987 trial, in Israel, of a man identified as the concentration camp worker who ordered the rape of the young girl before she was sent back into the gas chamber. The third story is Graham's personal one—the last chapter of the life of her grandparents:

> We put her in a Home, mother paid.
> We put him in a Home, mother paid.
>> There wasn't one that would take both of them we
> could afford.
>> We were right we put him down the road it's all
> there was,
>> there was a marriage of fifty years, you know this
>
> already don't you fill in the blanks,
>> they never saw each other again . . .

> we put her in X, she'd fallen out we put her back in,
> there in her diaper sitting with her purse in her hands all day
>   every
>   day, asking can I go now
> meaning him, meaning the
> apartment by then long since let go you know this

The moral of this story is not explicitly drawn, but we are intended to see the parallel between the helpless "Please" of the girl in the camp and the equally helpless "can I go now" of the grandmother. The granddaughter's place in the story is revealed at the crucial moment of the grandmother's shocking amnesia:

> The one time I knew something about us
> though I couldn't say what
>
> my grandmother then already ill
>   took me by the hand asking to be introduced.
> And then *no, you are not Jorie—but thank you for*
>   *saying you are. No, I'm sure. I know her you*
> *see.*

The granddaughter flees into the nursing-home bathroom and acknowledges, for the first time, the certain extinction of everyone in the world. Yet she realizes at the same time how nature's infinite desire for life presses more and more beings into existence, though all of them are headed for death. The bathroom becomes a surreal gas chamber:

> they were all in there, I didn't look up,
> they were all in there, the coiling and uncoiling
>   billions,
>
> the about-to-be-seized,
>   the about to be held down,
>
> the about to be held down, bit clean, shaped,
>   and the others, too, the ones gone back out, the ending
> wrapped round them,
>   hands up to their faces why I don't know,

and the about-to-be stepping in. . . .

Without existence and then with existence.
    Then into the clearing as it clamps down.
all round.
    Then into the fable as it clamps down.

Even in this abbreviated quotation, we can see the two cruelties—
the intentional cruelty of the camp and the "necessary" cruelty of the
confinement of the senile, both ending in extinction. But the poem can-
not stay "in existence" ("the clearing") or in history ("the fable"); it must
examine itself as consciously shifting between the close perspective of
living and the detached focus of telling. There is a rapid montage of the
familial (the grandfather talking to his wife, nursing home to nursing
home, on the telephone), the historical (the guard in the dock), and the
personal (the horrified granddaughter watching her grandmother ner-
vously and pleadingly clasping her pocketbook with its "forties sunburst
silver clasp")—all of this bequeathed by time to the grownup grand-
daughter, now the poet, who has in her keeping these fragments of
history:

> and Ivan (you saw this) offering his hand, click, whoever
> he is, and the old man getting a dial-tone, friend,
>   and old whoever clicking and unclicking the clasp the
> silver knobs,
>   shall we end on them? a tracking shot? a
>
> close-up on the clasp a two-headed beast it turns out
>   made of silvery
> leaves?

The montage and the self-conscious, formal questions are steps toward
the overwhelming metaphysical question: Why, if these are the condi-
tions of existence, do we want life? What is Being *like?* In what words, in
what symbols, can it be made intelligible?

> *Like* what, I wonder, to make the bodies come on, to make
>   room,

like what, I whisper,

like which is the last new world, *like, like,* which is the thin

young body (before it's made to go back in) whispering *please.*

The story can finally end only if satisfactory words can be found to en-compass the facts—the facts of man's inhumanity to man, of senility, and of death, but equally the fact of the subversive, persistent, and ran-dom energies of life. I have here flattened out and made logical the tissue of language which, in the poem itself, comes to us in a zigzag of half-articulated suspicions, invocations, silences, hints, glimpses, stumblings, and contradictions—the very picture of the mind making meaning.

Graham now uses the lyric to connect things widely disparate in time and space by means of metaphor and simile. The dramatic, even theatri-cal sweeping of the searchlight of the artist asking, "What is like this?" or "Why do I feel that these things or stories are alike?" provides the tension of the poem, as it leaps from past to present to past again, from passively absorbed personal history to intellectual self-consciousness, from confusion to mythological or metaphysical clarification. Under-neath the parallel layers of autobiography, history, myth, and philosophi-cal interpretation lies the faith that "the storyline" (as Graham has often called it) is not linear but a "coil" (the name she gives it in "From the New World"). This means that resemblances spiral over resemblances with each turn of the coil of time. Deciphering the coiled sequencing of memory on different planes is the artist's task—finding (or inventing) likenesses in a region of unlikeness.

Insofar as the artist's materials lie in the half-forgotten events of her childhood and youth, she has to describe those events, reclaim them from partial amnesia, in order to explain why certain later impressions (from history, literature, experience) seem obscurely urgent, meant, re-velatory, demanding. To catch, accurately, the impressions undergone by a child twenty years ago is a strange endeavor, brought most vividly into literary representation by Wordsworth in *The Prelude.* Like Wordsworth, Graham "sees by glimpses" and must capture a past almost uncapturable. The title poem, "The Region of Unlikeness," shows us a thirteen-year-old girl fleeing home, in the dawn, from the bed in a man's apartment where she has had her first sexual experience. The poet makes herself maintain a trance-state between sleep and waking, staying in the long-past memory:

> Don't wake up. Keep this in black and white. It's
>
> Rome. The man's name . . .? The speaker
>   thirteen. Walls bare. Light like a dirty towel.
> It's *Claudio.* He will overdose before the age of
>   thirty. . . .
>
> A black dog barks. Was it more than
>
> one night? Was it all right? Where are
>   the parents? Dress and get to the door.

Each sense impression of the girl's flight roots itself in her flesh, "the field where it will grow." Each impression is "a new planting—different from all the others— / each planted fast, there, into that soil." Later, the poet will have to find an exact word for each memory-planting, or she will not reach the essential psychic assuagement for her adolescent violation:

> Later she will walk along, a word in
>   each moment, to slap them down onto the plantings,
> to keep them still.

For twenty years the poet has been in bondage to the memory, twenty years in which the thirteen-year-old has not stopped running, twenty years in which the right words have not been found to "slap down" on the plantings and lay the ghost. Life lies "entombed in being," as Graham says in her poem "Immobilism." But the mind's search for the adequate expression of the past is arduous and tormenting—

> It darts, it stretches out along the dry hard ground,
>   it cannot find the end, it darts, it stretches out—

When Augustine awoke after a vision of God's "unchangeable light" to say he found himself "far from You in a region of unlikeness," he suggested that the region of likeness would be a place where no meta-phors would be needed, where thing, thought, memory, imagination, and language would all coalesce in the oneness of eternity. But in tempo-rality, as we yearn forward and the object of desire or the object of mem-ory perpetually recedes, we are shaped by the absence of the object of our longing. Graham quotes Augustine and Heidegger *(What Is Called Thinking)* among her epigraphs, but she could as well have quoted Cole-ridge's "Constancy to an Ideal Object," where "the enamoured rustic" does not realize that it is his own shadow, cast before him on the morning mists, that he worships as a divine presence: "Nor knows he makes him-self the shadow he pursues." The concept of desire fulfilled is always de-duced from desire unfulfilled, yet we give it ontological priority in our imaginings of original perfection.

Graham is a poet of strong polarities, playing in the space between male and female, being and ceasing to be, sense and thought, ritual and eschatology, veiling and apocalypse, matter and interpretation, immobil-ism and shape-making, nesting and flying free. Her music is that of the traditional lyric in its highs and lows, its accelerations and ritardandos, but the new poems are so long in themselves and so stretched-out in their elastic and "illogical" lines that it is difficult to master, measure, or enclose them, especially at first reading. Eventually one can map them, connect the dots, see the "coil"—but by their arabesques of language on different planes they frustrate this desire both at first and in the long run, however much one grasps the underlying map. The reader must, to remain "in" the poem, stay with the poet, going deeper and deeper down, not knowing whether or not the labyrinth has an exit.

The expansion of the poetic line visible in both Rich and Graham (and in other contemporary poets, from Ginsberg to Wright and Ashbery) means that many poems are coming to resemble cloud chambers full of colliding protons rather than well-wrought urns. Many particles of experience and history are put into play; they are bombarded by more particles of thought and feeling as both imagination and analysis are ex-erted on the materials at hand; the excited states resulting from the colli-sions are registered by the poem as a new field of energy, rather than as a linear "result" or "conclusion." Rich argues that we have to compile an atlas of the whole "difficult world"; Graham wants us to find words for the whole "region of unlikeness." Rich said years ago, in the person of a woman astronomer, "I am bombarded   yet I stand." This could be the motto of both of these new volumes, which ask lyric poetry to take on epic dimensions. As if to temper their breadth and earnestness, however, both poets, as I have said, end their volumes with a short poem. Graham closes, in "Soul Says," with cosmic laughter enveloping human mortality:

> Now then, I said, I go to meet that which I liken to
> (even though the wave break and drown me in laughter)
> the wave breaking, the wave drowning me in laughter—

And Rich ends, in "Final Notations," with a prophecy about the poem of the future:

> it will not be simple, it will not be long
> it will take little time, it will take all your thought
> it will take all your heart, it will take all your breath
> it will be short, it will not be simple

Even the new poetry of the force field, it seems, cannot forget its origins in simple song.

Married to Hurry
and Grim Song

Jorie Graham's
The End of Beauty

In calling her volume *The End of Beauty,* Jorie Graham situates the book, and herself, at that watershed in creative life when "beauty" can no longer be seen, in any simple sense, as the aim of art. Young artists usually seek the beautiful and also try to create it; older artists learn to incorporate into their work irony, tragedy, violence, and death. We imagine that Michelangelo finally thought his rough and anguished Rondanini Pietà more beautiful than his younger, smooth, exquisite, "lyrical" version of the theme. The fraught moment of youthful struggle into the tragic is the moment of Graham's book.

American writing has never had an easy conscience about being "merely" beautiful. There is a marked moral strenuousness in American poetry, from Anne Bradstreet through Robert Lowell. But American poetry has usually passed from the beautiful to the tragic through the strait gate of the ethical. Whitman's ideal brotherhood, Dickinson's select society, Stevens' major man, Eliot's Hindu commands ("Give, sympathize, control"), Berryman's end-man Conscience all represent controls put on aesthetic delectation by the moral sense. I think Graham has found a different way—the way of thought—to pass from the beautiful to the tragic, and *The End of Beauty* offers, in consequence, a new sort of poetry.

When poets shift ground, they shift form, too, and Graham's book turns visibly away from her earlier, self-contained, short, "beautiful" lyrics in *Hybrids of Plants and of Ghosts* (1980) and *Erosion* (1983). *The End of Beauty* investigates not a "new control" (Wordsworth's phrase about his turn from pleasure to duty) but, rather, a new speculative abundance. Though Graham's long meditations have something in common with John Ashbery's, Ashbery's deliberate geniality even in suffering (on the theory of nothing in excess) is very far from Graham's exultant or sardonic or ecstatic cascades of language. For her, once the end of beauty has been glimpsed everything is up for reexamination. If not beauty, what? And Graham's answer is not morality but free and far-ranging thought.

Graham's new manner goes to visible extremes. She aims at what Keats called "solitary thinkings; such as dodge / Conception to the very bourne of heaven," and when she comes to a concept not yet conceivable she leaves a gap in the middle of a sentence:

> Like a _____ this look between us . . .
> this long thin angel whose body is a stalk, rootfree, blossomfree,
> whose body we are making, whose body is a _____.

Thought is revealed to be a progress that sometimes goes haltingly, perception by perception. For each perception, a number imposes the halt:

6

It was then she remembered and looked the other way

7

Why this sky why this air why these mountains why this sky

8

And what does he ask of you, only to fear Him

The extended orbits of thought cannot be mimed in the short sensory takes of William Carlos Williams, whose lines move down the page on little cat feet. Thought plays in long arabesques, long lines made to encompass what Graham calls (in a poem about Penelope) "the story and its undoing, the days the kings and the soil they're groundcover for."

This manner—its spill and hurry and, equally, its halts and breaks—
simulates the psyche as Graham understands it. What the end of beauty
provides is the beginning of wonder. If the ideals of shape and closure
(provided as much by moral control as by aesthetic finality) are not to
be the guide of life and art, then what can be the guide but contemplative
thought? Graham trusts, if anything, the roaming cinematography of the
mind, which pictures and replays the necessary decisions of life and
keeps them perpetually in question.

This poetics leads to poems—the best in recent memory—on human
self-division. Marriage is one of Graham's recurrent topics: as a type of
self-limiting action (this person and no other; this life and no other) it
gives a nameable shape to existence, but as circumscription it is struggled
against even though it has been chosen. Similarly, human intelligence
reaches not only toward investigation (pure science) but also toward con-
solidation of that hypothesis into material form (technology, the em-
bodiment of inquiry). The wish of the speculative mind to halt its drift
and take visible shape leads not only to marriage but to atomic piles and
B-52's, which are as much at home in Graham's poetry as are the
other decisive shapes (paintings, myths) that human culture has taken.
The intrapsychic conflict between drift and shape is, in this book,
insoluble and therefore tragic. As in any true tragedy, both sides are
in the right.

The sheer freedom invoked by Graham's poetry is liberating. The
downtrodden Benthamism of most ethical poetry—wedded either to the
pragmatic claims of the oppressed or to the totalitarian claims of some
ethical system—has no poetics by which to rise to the full-winged reach
of untrammeled meditation. Graham's lines mimic the fertile ruses of the
mind—exploratory rush and decisive interruption, interrogatory speech
and intermittent silence. The lines ripple and pause, utter and subside.
The poems are often long, like sonatas, carrying the musical moment of
process through its hurry, its delay, its fears and repentings, its tragedies
of fixity, its restlessness and rebellion. Graham, if we compare her with
her Romantic predecessors, is nearest to Shelley in her creation of clouds
of thought, accumulating and breaking open in a shower of conse-
quences.

It is no wonder, given her attention to suspended thought, that one of
the privileged iconographic scenes for Graham is the moment between

Christ's burial and his public reappearance. This moment is a type of spiritual intermittence:

> You see the angels have come to sit on the delay
>   for a while,
> they have come to harrow the fixities, the sharp edges
>   of this open
> sepulcher.

Jesus will not permit Mary Magdalen, at their encounter in the garden, to touch him: *"Noli me tangere."* The distance between them represents the repudiation, by the spiritual, of the embodied; the Magdalen's duty is to become the vehicle (in painting, in story) of the longing of the embodied for the discarnate. Graham interrogates her own medium as she asks why embodiment can never be other than delimited, why the radiant vision that is the occasion of art can leave behind only a darkened terrestrial trace:

> But you see it is not clear to me why she
>
> must be driven back,
>   why it is the whole darkness that belongs to her
> and its days,
>   why it is these hillsides she must become,
> supporting even now the whole weight of the weightless,
>   letting the plotlines wander all over her,
>
> crumbling into every digressive beauty,
>   her longings all stitchwork towards his immaculate rent.

The gap between Jesus and Mary Magdalen becomes, in another poem, the gap between Demeter (the form of established culture) and Persephone (the daughter who strays into experience):

> O but you have to learn to let her go you said
> out into the open field through the waiting the waving grasses
> way out to the edge of that drastic field of distinctions

each new possibility molting off the back of the one motion,
    creation,
until there are so many truths each one its own color
it's a flower the picking of which would open the world
the mouth over the unsaid whispering loves me not loves me . . .

This oscillation between the indefinite invisible and the defined visible
propels all thought, and Graham has taken it as the propulsive system of
her poetics. Unlike Moore and Bishop, who were also drawn to indefi-
niteness (the profusion of glacial flora and fauna, the ocean) as one pole
of their poetry, Graham declines to conclude at one pole or the other.
She wants to conclude evenhandedly, trusting invisibility and embodi-
ment alike. In her verse, things and thoughts form and dissolve in a mys-
terious but purposive instinct for comprehensiveness, making a poetry
full of "arabesques of foraging . . . / married to hurry / and grim song."

In an essay called "Some Notes on Silence," explaining why she writes
poems of inconclusive, ongoing presentness, Graham contrasts such
poems with narratives, reminiscences, and prophecies—poetic forms
that are strung on the temporal axis of past, present, and future: "Narra-
tive sequences . . . believe in the changes of history and experience . . .
while [poems that engage silence] often view the flesh itself . . . as the
obstacle, and crave stillness, form, law, over the formulation of hope
which is *cause and effect.*" She adds that poems in the past tense are told
by a survivor of the experience recounted. Such poems are containers for
understood experience rather than a precarious enacting of experience as
it is being undergone. "A poem which is an *act* could be the very last act,
couldn't it, every time?" she says. Rushing into temporality, Graham's
new verse is the verbal equivalent of Action painting in words.

Graham used to think that poetry could not have a double protago-
nist. In *Hybrids of Plants and of Ghosts* she wrote:

We are able to listen to someone else's story, believe in
another protagonist, but within,
his presence would kill us.

But now, in tragic verse, the inner second protagonist is remembered
with a vengeance, and many of the new poems are written by a single

self playing two opposed mythological parts (Demeter and Persephone, Apollo and Daphne, Orpheus and Eurydice). What is the self, these poems ask, but the gap between two inner personae bound in a single drama? At the beginning of *The End of Beauty,* the figure for that gap is the gesture with which Eve offers the apple to Adam; in a moment, he will take it, bringing paradisal reverie to an end by introducing into life the principle of choice, definition, closure. Though this poem is about a long hesitation before marriage, it can also be read as a poem of self-knowledge by Eve, who decides, like Persephone, for "a new direction, an offshoot, the limb going on elsewhere":

31

. . . loving that error, loving that filial form, that break from
    perfection

32

where the complex mechanism fails, where the stranger appears
    in the clearing,

33

out of nowhere and uncalled for, out of nowhere to share the
    day.

It is, of course, not sufficient for a poet merely to announce that she is both parties; the double consciousness has to convince. Poems on myth have tended to adopt one side of the story as their own. But Eurydice in Graham's version both does and does not want to resume her body and be loved; Orpheus both wants her back as she is and wants her back on his terms. Eurydice's double wish (to rise up to Orpheus and to sink back to Hades) and Orpheus' double wish (to raise her as she was and to redefine both her and himself) are voiced in an intricate portrait of the self at many cross-purposes, freeing lyric from its perennial labyrinth of the single voice.

In "Self-Portrait as Both Parties," Orpheus is the sun, Hades the river bottom, and Eurydice, after thinking she might rise and be reincarnated among the weeds at the surface, decides against embodiment and begins a shadowy return to darkness:

the weeds cannot hold her
who is all rancor, all valves now, all destination,
dizzy with wanting to sink back in,
thinning terribly in the holy separateness.
And though he would hold her up, this light all open hands,
seeking her edges, seeking to make her palpable again,
curling around her to find crevices by which to carry her up,
flaws by which to be himself arrested and made,
made whole, made sharp and limbed, a shape,
she cannot, the drowning is too kind,
the silks of the bottom rubbing their vague hands
over her forehead.

The rhythms of cinematography—this moment, then this moment—
direct such incremental writing, and the inevitable present tense of film
is assumed as a natural formal principle in this poetry, marking it with
the signature of a postmodernist generation.

Like some of her predecessors, Graham is determined to track ongoing
mental action even at the risk of diffuseness. Blake's dialectics of mental
fight, Whitman's songs of the open road, Stevens' "endlessly proliferating
poem," Eliot's Quartets, Ashbery's prose poems have all taken some of
the same chances. Graham keeps creative energy alive and unpredictable
in these poems by sudden changes of focus; her psychic elations and
hesitations are Romantic in their volatility but post-Romantic in their
skepticism, their self-interruptions, their own stage directions—tech-
niques used for comic purposes by Byron, of course, but uncommon till
now in serious lyric.

Graham unexpectedly mixes stage-set instructions and demotic
American phrases with mythic plot and lyrical description. Her retellings
of myth would be reverent (in their inquiry into the psychic reality of
such traditional stories) were they not so irreverent. (On Apollo and
Daphne: "The truth is this had been going on for a long time during
which / they both wanted it to last.") Such moments are like brusque
interruptions in music, a deliberate going against the grain, where irrita-
bility and discord reflect the difficulty of proceeding. One follows these
poems as one follows music—not a music like Ashbery's, which eddies
back to its beginning, but a music onwardly purposive, obliterating its

past. It is the music of will—a hoping or thinking or exploratory will, sometimes jeering, more often frightened, fatally seeing the other side of its own intentions. It follows some invisible line of possibility (curiosity, love) into actuality (suffering, fixity, disappearance). It imagines, in short, what is happening in the restless contemporary flux of thought untethered by a stable culture.

Graham, the daughter of American parents living in Italy, grew up trilingual (through French schooling) and has an unembarrassed range of cultural and linguistic reference, which she does not censor out of her poems. In contrast, for instance, to Adrienne Rich's language (deliberately impoverished in the service of egalitarian availability), Graham's is opulent. However, it does not assert high culture as an unquestioned value. Graham is one of a generation to whom the whole past appears in an anthropological light: classical and Christian motifs, conventional psychology and Freudian orthodoxy, divorce and marriage are all equally familiar, all equally questionable. To this skeptical generation the iron laws of physics and biology seem the only believable truths, and Graham is drawn to rewrite Shelley's necessitarian "Ode to the West Wind" in her own hymn to Necessity, a memorable poem entitled (from Wyatt) "Of Forced Sightes and Trusty Ferefulness." With a reminiscence of Dickinson's description of chaos ("Stopless—cool"), she addresses the impersonal wind of physical law:

> Stopless
> and unessential, half-hiss, half-
> lullaby, if I fell in among your laws,
> if I fell down into your mind your snow, into the miles
>
> of spirit-drafts you drive, frenetic multitudes,
> out from timber to the open ground and back to no
> avail, if I fell down, warmblooded, ill, into your endless
> evenness . . .
>
> If I fell in?
> What is your law to my law, unhurried hurrying?

In enlarging her scope to include the metaphysical questions of necessity, intentionality, human self-definition, and cultural inscription, Graham, like other philosophical poets, reminds us that human beings have, in addition to an erotic, domestic, and ethical life, a life of speculative thought. But Graham's thinking is not cool and speculative alone; it has a strong component of the ecstatic (and of its dark counterpart, the despairing). The European contemplative saints (Saint Francis, Saint Clare, Saint Teresa) figure in Graham's poems as models not only of spiritual concentration but also of psychic rapture. The rapture of the contemplating mind is not a new topic in poetry, but it tends to be forgotten in our pragmatic America. In the classic narrative of contemplation, early ecstasy is followed by tragic desiccation, after which the contemplative, rescued by joy, rests again among the lilies of fulfilled desire. It is strange to find this European story beginning to unfold once more in a young and mesmerizing American voice; one wants to hear its continuation.

21

Fin-de-Siècle Poetry

Jorie Graham

In spite of the arbitrariness of century marking, the approach of the end of a century casts a shadow over our consciousness. This shadow appears in the media in the form of somewhat trumped-up retrospects and forecasts, but manifests itself in poets as an intensified reflection on history as event and on historiography as a problematic science. Our Western culture has proposed two basic models of history: the circular classical one, in which, after the decline from the Golden Age to the Age of Iron, Astraea returns and "the world's great age begins anew" (Shelley); and the linear Christian one, centrally marked by the Incarnation and progressing from Creation through Fall and Redemption to the Second Coming. These have generated two models of the fin-de-siècle: one is tragic, as it witnesses decadence, decay, and despair; the other is comic, as it envisages a glorious restoration.

What interests me in Jorie Graham's recent work on models of history is that she avoids not only the classical and Christian models invoked by Yeats and others, but also the utopian models popular with socialist and feminist poets. Instead, like Ashbery, whose favorite image of life is a ride on a circling carousel with no destination, Graham attempts to be in the flow before demarcating it, though she also ponders demarcation. The continuum of history—rather than the events that demarcate and thereby organize time—is her subject. The continuum resists being called the *fin* of anything. Yet in Graham's poems, ends—or at least significant events—keep happening; this is not usually the case in Ashbery, who tends, with his theoretical commitment to irony, to will "events" as such into one single level of pleasant insignificance.

Jorie Graham is now in her forties, not far from Yeats's age as the last century turned; the absence in her work of the world-weariness of his in the 1890s suggests that what we are accustomed to call a fin-de-siècle tone—blanched, pale, sighing—is a limited phenomenon derived from certain poems of Swinburne, the Rossettis, and Yeats, themselves reacting against strenuous and even bombastic Romantic and Victorian tonalities of revolution and moral endeavor. This reaction against revolutionary bombast and utopian conviction (with their concurrent preachiness) may have only coincidentally arrived at the end of the last century, and our fin-de-siècle, as the twentieth century draws to a close, promises to have, whether in novels like Don DeLillo's *Mao II* or in poetry like Graham's, a tone of its own—confused rather than weary, screen-mobile rather than painting-static, jump-cut rather than continuous, interrogative rather than declarative, and ambiguous rather than conclusive. The conviction that one can speak authentically only of "lyric" personal experience (in *Mao II,* that of the writer and photographer, for instance) and an equal conviction that one must speak also of incomprehensible mass events (in *Mao II,* the Moonie mass marriage) struggle for dominance at this historical moment. Mass synecdoche, if one may call it that, is our substitute for the nineties synecdoche of the detail. Yet the falsification of anything in representing it as a group phenomenon results in a compensatory insistence on the private. The formal incoherence caused in a novel like *Mao II* by authorial insistence—without nineteenth-century ligatures of plot coherence—on a simultaneity of mass and private phenomena offers textual evidence of the imaginative strain involved in such witnessing.

Graham's preoccupation with history and the end of history appears in marked form in several poems found in her book *Region of Unlikeness* (1991). The poems I have in mind reveal, even in their titles, Graham's intent to reflect on aspects of history—the significant event, the temporal continuum, the forms of narrative, and the competitive roles of participant and watcher. The poems in question have as titles "History" (two poems are given that title), "Act III, Sc. 2," "Who Watches from the Dark Porch," and "The Phase after History."

Graham's foreword to *Region of Unlikeness* quotes Augustine in the

Confessions (as did Yeats's epigraph to his 1893 volume *The Rose,* as though one could not enter Western time except through the thought of Augustine). In a citation from the *Confessions,* Graham's Augustine, addressing God, broods on language as successivity and the human wish to spatialize that successivity: "You hear what we speak . . . and you do not want the syllables to stand where they are; rather you want them to fly away so that others may come and you may hear a whole sentence. So it is with all things that make up a whole by the succession of parts; such a whole would please us much more if all the parts could be perceived at once rather than in succession." Graham spatializes her own life into textual form in the poem "Act III, Sc. 2," significantly not choosing, as Yeats would have done, the decisive moment of inception or conclusion, but rather borrowing from Stevens an intermediate moment in the epic drama. The poem of Stevens from which she borrows is one called "Chaos in Motion and Not in Motion," where Stevens first names the moment in actual time ("Chaos in Motion") and then in textual space ("and not in Motion"). In it, he announces that at this late moment "Scene 10 becomes 11, / In Series X, Act IV, et cetera." Graham's theme in "Act III, Sc. 2" is the problem of representing accurately one's emotional position as participator once one has begun, in middle life, to be a watcher of one's own history even as one enacts it:

> Look she said this is not the distance
> we wanted to stay at—We wanted to get
> close, very close. But what
> is the way in again? And is it
>
> too late? She could hear the actions
> rushing past—but they are on
> another track.

Many of Graham's poems act out a rapid zooming, in alternately long and short lines, between getting close and gaining distance; this poses a problem of historical representation at all times. But a preoccupation with the degree to which the events of history, including the fin-de-siècle, are mentally and textually constructed into acts and scenes rather than "objectively" recorded is what differentiates contemporary historiographers and poets of the fin-de-siècle from those who, like Spengler and Yeats, tended to accept schemes of history already invented, even if such schemes—linear, circular, spiral-shaped—were inconsistent with one another. As Stevens said of the mind in "Of Modern Poetry":

> It has not always had
> To find: the scene was set; it repeated what
> Was in the script. Then the theatre was changed
> To something else. Its past was a souvenir.

In Graham's recent poetry, Time itself and the recorder of Time cannot be conceptually separated, in that it is only the recorder who demarcates Time, points out moments worth remembrance. All the other moments in the continuum will sink unnoticed. How do we explain what gets recorded? Perhaps attention is random: people might record what they happened to witness or happened to come across. But Graham will not entertain that possibility: it is, for her, the sacred obligation of the Recorder to pay attention at the precisely fated moment:

> the only
> right time, the intended time,
> punctual,
> the millisecond I was bred to look up into, click, no
> half-tone, no orchard of
> possibilities,
>
> up into the eyes of my own
> fate not the world's.

Graham's formulation here reflects the biblical idea of *kairos,* the time intended by God—usually a brief time—for some aspect of his will to become fulfilled: see, for example, Romans 13:11, "Knowing the time . . . now it is high time to awake out of sleep"; or I Corinthians 4:5, "Therefore judge nothing before the time, until the Lord come, who both will bring to light the hidden things of darkness, and will make manifest the counsels of the hearts."

As this passage asserts, Graham believes, in opposition to many historical poets, that it is only by chronicling accurately and punctually one's individual fate that one can, in lyric, "do" history; Graham records the world's fate through her own. She can write about the Holocaust only by filtering it through the memory of a childhood visit to her Jewish grandmother confined to a nursing home. In this way, Graham sets herself against the purely spectatorial perspective of, say, Yeats's Chinamen or Himalayan hermits, and against the conventionally generalized prophetic position of contemporary poets like Rich, who often write about broad social conditions without explicit autobiographical reference to their own inner motivation, or their own limits with respect to the social problem at hand.

Attention, says Graham in the second poem she entitles "History," is always processing time; but Attention, gnawing the minutes like Ovid's *tempus edax* (Shakespeare's "Devouring Time"), is not, she argues, as we might think, free-ranging, but fettered. Historical attention, which Graham in the following passage calls x, is always chained, at least for the poet, to the private vocation of the artist:

> Listen:
> the x gnaws, making stories like small smacking
>
> sounds,
>   whole long stories which are its gentle gnawing. . . .
>   If the x is on a chain, licking its bone,
>
> making the sounds now of monks
>   copying the texts out,
> muttering to themselves,
>   if it is on a chain
>
> that hisses as it moves with the moving x,
>   link by link with the turning x
> (the gnawing now Europe burning)
>   (the delicate chewing where the atom splits),
>   if it is on a chain—
>   even this beast—even this the favorite beast—
>   then this is the chain, the gleaming

chain: that what I wanted was to have looked up at the right
time,
    to see what I was meant to see,
to be pried up out of my immortal soul,
    up, into the sizzling quick—

That what I wanted was to have looked up at the only
    right time, the intended time,
punctual,
    the millisecond I was bred to look up into.

Reflection on history is peculiarly intensified by the arrival of the fin de siècle ("she's deep into the lateness now," says the first "History") because of the arbitrary and relatively recent nature of century demarcation. One wants to characterize the departing century and to anticipate the new one, while conscious of the fictional and ultimately textual nature of such characterizations. The worst—or best—fin-de-siècle speculation is the apocalyptic one: that this is the absolute end of time, that there will be no more history. If the Christian apocalypse—where all shall be revealed, and justice shall be made manifest—is the sublimely comic version of the end of history, for Graham, Shakespearean tragedy—with its fifth-act obliteration of the central dramatis personae—is the atheist and materialist version of the end of history.

In her extraordinary poem "The Phase after History," Graham brings together, in her characteristic way of coping with simultaneity, three linked narratives—one a physical event, one an emotional experience, and one a literary archetype. In the first narrative, a bird has become lost in Graham's house and is about to batter itself to death against a windowpane unless she can find it and release it. The second narrative retells the suicide attempt (subsequently followed by a successful suicide) of one of Graham's young students, who attempted with a knife to carve his face away from his body. The third narrative, representing the archetype behind both anterior narratives, is drawn from *Macbeth*, in which an old order, represented by Duncan, is brought to an end by Lady Macbeth, who hopes to begin a new phase of history, the dynastic reign of the

Macbeths over Scotland. Taking on the person of Lady Macbeth, Graham represents the fin-de-siècle as an active moment of assassination, in which the poet must kill the old century and the future it envisioned—Duncan and Duncan's sons—in order to begin a new era. The guilt and self-murder entailed are fully acted out in Graham's horrifying "phase after history."

For Graham, the human face symbolizes the forward-pointing, future-envisioning part of the self. The story of the suicidal student shows that one's normal tenderness toward one's own envisaged future can be sharply checked by a self-hatred which causes either self-murder or drastic self-revision. One is convinced that for oneself there must come a moment of decisive change, a fin-de-siècle—that whatever follows must be different. An attempt to hear in one's inner being the rustle of a hitherto unenvisaged future—the bird's attempt to find a way out of the present trap of the house—produces whatever meaning can be extracted from the fin-de-siècle. Meaning is never merely personal, in Graham: it is also situated in one's larger identifications, which widen one's responsibility. As Graham huddles on her staircase hoping that the bird will once again come into view so she can free it, she generalizes to the condition of America:

> Which America is it in?
> Which America are we in here?
>   Is there an America comprised wholly
> of its waiting and my waiting and all forms of the thing
>   . . . . .
>
> a place of *attention?*

Poets who try to peer into a destiny which is no longer manifest must discard the shallower answers to present questions. Most of the notions of the future that first occur to the mind are false, trivial, wrong, incomplete, exhausted, inadequate. The Muse, rejecting these, tells the poet to wait until the right sentence of art, Keats's unheard melody, Graham's "inaudible . . . utterance" formulates itself:

> The voice says wait. Taking a lot of words.
> The voice always says wait.

The sentence like a tongue
in a higher mouth

to make the other utterance, the inaudible one,
possible,
the sentence in its hole, its cavity
of listening,
flapping, half dead on the wing, through the
hollow indoors,
the house like a head
with nothing inside
except this breeze—
shall we keep going?
Where is it, in the century clicking by?
Where, in the America that *exists?*

It is at this point in "The Phase after History" that Shakespeare enters:
we hear a version of the voice of Duncan in *Macbeth,* wholly wrong about
the future, as he says, arriving at the castle where he will be murdered,
"This castle hath a pleasant seat, / . . . / the air nimbly recommends it-
self." The play makes it clear that Duncan's subsequent use of the word
"guest" refers to "the temple-haunting martlet," but Graham, trusting us
to remember the baffled bird flying crazily through her house, continues
in an ironic misquotation, thinking of both the deceived Duncan and
the endangered bird, "the guest approves" / by his beloved mansionry
[for "loved masionry"] / that heaven's breath smells wooingly here."

Thus ends Part 1 of "The Phase after History." Part 2 begins, "The
police came and got Stuart, brought him to / Psych Hospital. / The face
on him the face he'd tried to cut off." The voice of Shakespeare, now as
Lady Macbeth, reenters, saying in altered words, of the student, not of
Duncan, "Who would have imagined a face / could be so full of blood."
Stuart's future suicide is seen as a flashforward in the past tense: "Later
he had to take the whole body off // to get the face." Stuart in the hospital,
between attempted suicide and subsequent successful suicide, becomes
the terrified bird unable to imagine its own future, as the poet waits

to hear something rustle
and get to it

> before it rammed its lights out
>   aiming for the brightest spot, the only clue.

The end of this fin-de-siècle poem comes in a flutter of inability to kill the old order, or, if the old is killed, to bring to birth the new. We cannot truly see "the phase after history." The poet becomes Lady Macbeth, not knowing whether the bird / sentence / face / old order / is alive or dead, and, if dead, how she can cleanse her hands of the deed of murder:

> (make my keen knife see not the
> wound it makes)—
>
> . . . . .
>
>   Is the house empty?
> Is the emptiness housed?
>   Where is America here from the landing, my face on
>
> my knees, eyes closed to hear
>   further?
> Lady M. is the intermediary phase.
>   God help us.
> Unsexed unmanned.
>   Her open hand like a verb slowly descending onto
>   the free,
> her open hand fluttering all round her face now,
>   trying to still her gaze, to snag it on
>
> those white hands waving and diving
>   in the water that is not there.

It is the most hopeless ending in Graham, in effect ending the tragedy with the suicidal Lady Macbeth. It refuses the Shakespearean closing pseudo-consolation, the restoration of the anterior old order in the crowning of Duncan's son Malcolm. In this way, Graham remains faithful to the imaginative truth of Shakespeare's play, which is interested in the fate of the Macbeths rather than of the Duncan dynasty. For Graham here, the fin-de-siècle lies suspended in Lady Macbeth's fluttering hand, unable to still her dreaming gaze, helpless to find the absolving water. If history is a construction, then nothing guarantees its future except the restless and unstillable flux of the human gaze, suicidal in its metaphysical uncertainty and in its constant determination to annihilate its own past.

We can deduce, from this poem, that Graham thinks any account of "the phase after history" incomplete without some reference to her three simultaneities—natural event, personal complicity, and archetypal literary patterning. Her jump-cuts among these, and especially her concern with middleness rather than with inception, conclusion, or repetition, suggest that the fin-de-siècle, as we now imagine it, is something we actively will—as Graham's student willed his suicide—in an attempt to shake off an irredeemable past; or that it is something we hesitate over—as Lady Macbeth hesitates in her dream-reprise of the murder. We seek to find something to justify our murder of the past, as we try to coordinate our executive hand and our intentional gaze; or we decide that the future is something that we head blindly into, like the bird crashing into the invisible windowpane. The indeterminacy of these possibilities, and the poet's inability to decide among them, leaves Graham as watcher, but also, in the end (in the person of Lady Macbeth) as participant in a history she does not understand.

The poem of Graham's that most explicitly inquires into the construction of historical event, "Who Watches from the Dark Porch," offers the watcher an ambiguous child-cry (is it laughter? is it pain?) to interpret. Is Nature—or, as Graham calls it in this poem, "Matter"—inherently comic or tragic? Interpretation, which appears here allegorically personified as the male consort of female Matter, is necessarily tragic because mortal. Here is the beginning of "Who Watches," which asks why we feel sure that our previous attempts to codify our history were lies:

> Is it because of history or is it because of matter,
>   mother Matter—the opposite of In-
>   terpretation: his consort: (his purple body lies
>   shattered against terrible
>   reefs)—matter, (is it
>   a shriek or is it

    laughter)
(a mist or is it an angel they strangle)—
    that we feel so sure we lied?

The "instant replay" of interpretation arouses a nostalgia for presence:

    Said Moses show me Your face.
        Not the voice-over, not
    the sound track (thou shalt not thou
        shalt not), not the interpretation—buzz—
    the face.
        But what can we do?

Graham ends this typical flurry of injunctions, questions, and parenthetical interjections—so different from Yeats's agitated but dominating declarativeness in apocalypse—with the injunction to sit still, a command borrowed from Eliot, but lacking Eliot's Christian aspiration. Both the writer's desire for revelation (which can lead to a false willed meaning) and the nostalgia for presence (which can lead to religious sentimentality) threaten the artist of the fin-de-siècle. Yielding to the first will create another abstract utopia of the sort too prevalent in the twentieth century; yielding to the second will offer a premature ontology and a premature sentimental ethics.

    . . . sit still sit still the lively understandable
    spirit said,
    still, still,
    so that it can be completely the

    now.

If this sitting—"don't wait, just sit, sit"—reveals only that one is at *"the scene of the accident"* and that one can only face the "pileup of erasures— play, reverse play" in the scene of writing, then this will have to be the poetics exacted by Graham's disbelief, in this "lateness," in predetermined schemes of history—those schemes which have given us, in fact, the very model of the fin-de-siècle that Graham must, aware of the approaching fin-de-siècle, refuse. The Yeatsian curtain of "The Second Coming" is not lifted, but then the Yeatsian darkness does not drop. Play, reverse play, instant replay, erase, play again—this model makes every moment both a beginning and an end. The tape runs both ways, and is always provisional, always expressed (formally speaking) in the cresting and troughing irregularities of Graham's prosody. Or, in another of Graham's Yeatsian metaphors, the dice are "being incessantly retossed."

Where, then, does the poet obtain confidence in representation? According to the last poem in *Region of Unlikeness,* her confidence lies finally in the idiom of presentness itself, in the simplicity with which we say, without thinking, "The river *glints,*" or "The mother *opens the table-cloth up into the wind.*" These sentences make a text, or fabric, which descends over the earth for a moment in an "alphabet of ripenesses, / what is, what could have been." As Wordsworth concluded long ago, the verbal object, insofar as it persists, becomes a natural part of the material world: "(This is a form of matter of matter she sang)," Graham writes. As history becomes text, it is spatialized into fabric, a tarpaulin (as Ashbery has called it) spread to cover the perceptual field. This is, in the end, a comic resolution, by which the temporal wave of presentness causes the hilarity of articulated expression in song.

The last words in *Region of Unlikeness* close the lyric called "Soul Says," spoken (according to Graham's endnote) by Prospero, who utters it as he lays down his art:

> Now then, I said, I go to meet that which I liken to
> (even though the wave break and drown me in laughter)
> the wave breaking, the wave drowning me in laughter—

Matters of such gravity as how to demarcate time are not solved, of course, in lyric; they are merely reimagined. Graham's drowning wave (tragedy) cannot be demarcated into inception, event, conclusion, or even into repetition; it can only be redescribed as comedy—an annihilating cosmic laughter. *The Tempest,* the single Shakespearean play that observes the unities of time, space, and action, chooses to describe the coextension of space, time, and human will as, finally, a comic form. Each ends only when all are ended, and the end of textuality and the end of history become, in *The Tempest* and "Soul Says," the comic ending of the dramatized world. While present event and textuality—the forms of lyric—persist, there can be, Graham's work suggests, no conclusive fin-de-siècle; but the strain of remaining in the now of the song cannot be entirely obliterated. The song is the place, Graham writes in "Soul Says," "(Where the hurry [of Time] is stopped) (and held) (but not extinguished) (no)." Each of these parentheses inserted in the soul's lyric claim is a small fin-de-siècle in itself.

Credits

1. Introduction to Allen Ginsberg, *"Kaddish," "Black Shroud," and "White Shroud"* (San Francisco: Arion Press, 1992).
2. *The New Republic,* May 24, 1993, pp. 35–38.
3. *The New Yorker,* February 15, 1988, pp. 100–104.
4. *The New Republic,* April 3, 1989, pp. 35–38.
5. *The New Yorker,* April 2, 1990, pp. 113–116.
6. *The New Yorker,* December 26, 1988, pp. 91–95.
7. *The New York Review of Books,* September 29, 1988, pp. 11–12.
8. *The New Yorker,* June 10, 1991, pp. 103–111.
9. *The New Yorker,* January 18, 1993, pp. 107–110.
10. *Parnassus,* vol. 18, no. 2, 1993, pp. 86–99.
11. Published for the first time in this volume.
12. *The New Yorker,* August 3, 1992, pp. 73–76.
13. *Parnassus,* vol. 16, no. 2, 1991, pp. 391–404.
14. Published for the first time in this volume.
15. *The New Yorker,* August 7, 1989, pp. 93–96.
16. *The New York Review of Books,* April 28, 1988, pp. 41–45.
17. *The New Yorker,* March 13, 1989, pp. 102–107.
18. *The New Yorker,* April 15, 1991, pp. 99–103.
19. *The New York Review of Books,* November 21, 1991, pp. 50–56.
20. *The New Yorker,* July 27, 1987, pp. 74–77.
21. Elaine Scarry, ed., *Fins-de-Siècle: English Poetry in 1590, 1690, 1790, 1890, 1990* (Baltimore: Johns Hopkins University Press, 1994), pp. 123–140. Copyright © 1994 by The Johns Hopkins University Press.

Index